take a hint from the heavens ...

1986 is packed with promise. Make the most of it with the predictions, insights, clues and suggestions America's most popular astrologer, Sydney Omarr, has prepared for you!

Learn about the "geometry" of relationships—who you get along with, and why ... pore over celebrity sun signs and personality profiles ... discover how and why the movements of the zodiac affect men and women so differently ... and much, much more. Whatever your desire, whatever your dilemma, let Sydney Omarr's time-tested wisdom guide you through 1986, and watch your dreams become exciting realities!

For Expanding Your Personal Knowledge of Astrology, SIGNET Brings to You

SYDNEY OMARR'S ASTROLOGICAL GUIDES FOR YOU IN 1986

- [ ] **ARIES** .... (136764—$2.75)*
- [ ] **TAURUS** .... (136772—$2.75)*
- [ ] **GEMINI** .... (136780—$2.75)*
- [ ] **CANCER** .... (136799—$2.75)*
- [ ] **LEO** .... (136802—$2.75)*
- [ ] **VIRGO** .... (136810—$2.75)*
- [ ] **LIBRA** .... (136829—$2.75)*
- [ ] **SCORPIO** .... (136837—$2.75)*
- [ ] **SAGITTARIUS** .... (136845—$2.75)*
- [ ] **CAPRICORN** .... (136853—$2.75)*
- [ ] **AQUARIUS** .... (136861—$2.75)*
- [ ] **PISCES** .... (136888—$2.75)*

*Price is $3.25 in Canada

Buy them at your local bookstore or use this convenient coupon for ordering.

NEW AMERICAN LIBRARY
P.O. Box 999, Bergenfield, New Jersey 07621

Please send me the books I have checked above. I am enclosing $_____
(please add $1.00 to this order to cover postage and handling). Send check or money order—no cash or C.O.D.'s. Prices and numbers are subject to change without notice.

Name_____

Address_____

City _____ State _____ Zip Code _____

Allow 4-6 weeks for delivery.
This offer is subject to withdrawal without notice.

SYDNEY OMARR'S
DAY-BY-DAY ASTROLOGICAL GUIDE FOR
Leo
(JULY 23–AUGUST 22)
1986

A SIGNET BOOK
NEW AMERICAN LIBRARY

NAL BOOKS ARE AVAILABLE AT QUANTITY DISCOUNTS
WHEN USED TO PROMOTE PRODUCTS OR SERVICES.
FOR INFORMATION PLEASE WRITE TO PREMIUM MARKETING DIVISION,
NEW AMERICAN LIBRARY, 1633 BROADWAY,
NEW YORK, NEW YORK 10019.

Copyright © 1985 by Sydney Omarr

All rights reserved

Sydney Omarr is syndicated worldwide by Los Angeles Times Syndicate.

SIGNET TRADEMARK REG. U.S. PAT. OFF. AND FOREIGN COUNTRIES
REGISTERED TRADEMARK—MARCA REGISTRADA
HECHO EN CHICAGO, U.S.A.

SIGNET, SIGNET CLASSIC, MENTOR, PLUME, MERIDIAN and NAL BOOKS
are published by New American Library,
1633 Broadway, New York, New York 10019

First Printing, July 1985

1 2 3 4 5 6 7 8 9

PRINTED IN THE UNITED STATES OF AMERICA

CONTENTS

1. **Defining Terms** — 7
   - *Astrology* — 7
   - *The Zodiac* — 8
   - *Sun Sign* — 9
   - *Element* — 9
   - *Quality* — 11
   - *Element and Quality Together* — 12
   - *Planet* — 13
   - *House* — 15
   - *Rising Sign* — 16
   - *Horoscope* — 17
   - *Aspect* — 18
   - *Transiting Planet* — 19

2. **Your House of the Sun** — 21
   Your "Piece of the Pie"

3. **The Geometry of Relationships** — 32
   What Signs You Get Along with—and Why

4. **Twelve Places at the Table** — 35
   Personality Profiles of the Signs

5. **Moods of the Moon** — 44
   Day-by-Day Changes

6. **Venus and Mars** — 55
   Love and Sex . . . Peace and War . . .
   Cooperating and Competing

7	**Venus Sign Position Chart 1910–1975**	*70*
8	**Mars Sign Position Chart 1910–1975**	*76*
9	**The Planets As "Stars"** Astrological Cast of Characters	*80*
10	**Astrotrivia—Rating Yourself in the Best Game in Town**	*95*
	I Sun Signs of the Rich and Famous	*95*
	II More Celebrity Sun Sign Lore	*97*
	III Fascinating Facts About the Signs	*99*
	IV Where Do You Belong?	*100*
	V Which Animal Best Suits You?	*102*
11	**Sun Sign Changes 1920–1975**	*105*
12	**LEO: The Big Picture**	*113*
13	**LEO: Objectives and Obstacles** A Game Plan for Being the Most Successful LEO Under the Sun	*116*
14	**Pairing Off with LEO** Your Compatability with Other Signs of the Zodiac	*121*
15	**The LEO Sex Role Dilemma**	*125*
16	**The LEO Female** Child . . . Young Woman . . . Mate . . . Mother	*128*
17	**The LEO Male** Child . . . Young Man . . . Mate . . . Father	*132*
18	**LEO Help Wanted** Selecting a Career/Your On-the-Job Style	*136*
19	**How "Pure" a LEO Are You?** Your Moon Sign . . . Your Rising Sign	*139*
20	**Find Your Rising Sign**	*145*
21	**LEO Astro-Outlook for 1986**	*148*
22	**Fifteen Months of Day-by-Day Predictions**	*150*

1

Defining Terms

What Are Those Astrologers Talking About?

Everyone knows it is more fun to visit another country if you know a bit of the language, and it's a lot easier to find your way around, too. The same idea applies to astrology, which is still foreign territory to many people. Astrology has its very own language, but it really isn't difficult to get a handle on it as long as you understand a few important terms. What follows is a kind of "Astrological Phrase Book," a brief compendium of the most basic words and concepts in the astrological language. Once you've learned them, you'll find you know a lot more about the why of your sun sign as well as information that will help you understand other astrological factors that make you what you are. Best of all, your new language can help you enjoy and explore one of the most exciting, underdeveloped territories under the sun—modern astrology!

Astrology Is an Ancient and Practical "Science"

The first definition of astrology in the standard dictionary is "astronomy," and at one time in history the two studies were synonymous. The word astrology derives from Greek and literally means "the science (or study) of the stars." However, even in earliest times astrology has had much less to do with the "fixed" stars, which appear to remain in one place, than the planets, which move. (The word "planet" means wanderer.) Early man noticed that, as these heavenly bodies moved, their movements coincided with certain earthly events—mainly the changing of the seasons. Gradually, the movement of the planets was observed to coincide with other important worldly events, such as wars, and the science of "divination" (prediction) by the planets was born. Astronomy and astrology lived happily together until the Christian church banned the latter in about 1550, condemning it as mere superstition. Astrology bounced back in the 1700s, when it came into use as an indicator of human personality, as well as a way to foretell future events. However, this so-called modern astrology is based on the same premise the ancients set down thousands of years ago: "As above, so below." Simply put, what it means is that the positions of the planets, which represent the cosmic order, are related in a significant and observable way to both human behavior and events in human life.

The Zodiac Is a "Circle of Signs"
The zodiac ("circle of animals") is an invisible band in the sky which corresponds to the apparent yearly path of the sun, moon, and the major planets around the earth. It is the "apparent" path in the sense that it is what we *observe* from here on earth. Obviously we know that the earth and other planets revolve around the sun, but the study of astrology (and astronomy) takes earth as the reference point.

The 360-degree circle of the zodiac around the earth is divided into twelve thirty-degree segments—the twelve astrological signs. Throughout the year, as the sun appears to move, it passes through each of these segments in about thirty days. Zero degrees Aries, the vernal equinox or beginning of spring, is the beginning of the zodiac and the start of the seasonal year. It is at that point, on or about March 22, that the sun crosses or intersects with the *ecliptic*—another imaginary band that is (in the mind's eye) the extension of the earth's equator. Another major intersection of the sun's path and the ecliptic takes place at the fall equinox about September 22, the beginning of the seventh sign of the zodiac, Libra. (Equinox means equal days and nights, which is what we experience briefly in the early spring and early fall.) The zodiac "finishes" with the end of the twelfth sign Pisces, about March 21, then begins again with Aries.

Though the segments of the zodiac (the astrological signs) are *named* for the constellations of stars in the sky, they do not correspond with them. The constellations served as convenient visual markers for the ancient astrologer/priests, but the zodiac—and astrology—has always been based on the seasonal year, which never changes. The position of the constellations have changed with reference to our point of view here on earth, however, due to the slipping of the earth's axis. The constellations return a couple of degrees every year and have been doing so for centuries. That's why when the modern *astronomer* says "Aries," he is referring to a group of stars that is in a different position in the sky than the segment of the zodiac the *astrologer* calls "Aries."

Your Sun Sign is Determined by the Month and Day You Were Born

The twelve segments of the zodiac are the twelve astrological signs, from Aries through Pisces, and it takes the sun exactly one year to pass through all twelve signs. A person born when the sun is passing through a particular segment of the zodiac is said to be born under that sign, and it is his/her sun sign. For example, a person born October 14 is said to be born under the sign of Libra. Your sun sign is the most important component of your astrological personality, it is the "real you." However, there are nine other planets besides the sun, and at the moment of a person's birth, those planets are passing through certain segments of the zodiac, or signs, as well. You will learn about some of these lesser influences on your personality in this book later on.

An Element Is Part of a Sign

Obviously your sun sign is a lot more than simply a piece of the sky, or it wouldn't have any meaning. The meaning it has is based on two ancient astrological concepts, the *four elements* and the *three modes*. When these two factors are combined they form the basis of all astrological descriptions of human personality. You can't *see* an element or a quality; they are only to be understood in terms of analogy, but they are fundamental to everything else in astrology, so it is important to understand them.

The four elements, defined by ancient philosophers as the basic components of everything and everybody, are *fire, earth, air,* and *water.* It is doubtful that even in earliest times this breakdown was to be taken as a physical reality: The elements are really four different ways we experience both things and people. For instance, if a thing or a person was experienced as hot rather than cold, sharp rather than dull, active rather than passive, it was said to partake of the *fire* element. And it's easy to see the connection.

Later on, during the Renaissance, the four elements were called "humors," starting a whole new way of typing people. *Fire was the humor choler*, and people who were said to have too much of it were those angry, impatient types who are subject to modern-day diseases like high blood pressure and heart attacks. *The earth element was called black bile* and could cause extreme melancholia (depression) in a person who had too much of it. *Air was the sanguine or rosy humor* and meant a lighter personality. *The water element was the humor phlegm*, and people with too much of it had rather "soggy" personalities and tended to be fat, as well. If the relationship between the elements (or humors) and the signs of the zodiac is beginning to ring a bell, it should. Here's the way the twelve signs break down into elements:

Fire signs: Aries, Leo, Sagittarius
Earth signs: Taurus, Virgo, Capricorn
Air signs: Gemini, Libra, Aquarius
Water signs: Cancer, Scorpio, Pisces

The four elements as four primal types of being exist today in the way many psychologists categorize people's thought processes. Once again, the relationship to the ways in which the twelve astrological signs really do perceive and react to the world is uncannily correct:

The fire signs are instant reactors who put it all together very quickly; things rarely have to be spelled out for a fire sign. These types of people also see the future possibilities inherent in the present and want to bring them about *now*. Obviously, fire signs tend to be impatient, but they have strong wills. Fire is the principle of *action*.

The earth signs are more pragmatic and slower to react. If they can't literally see something or touch it, they have difficulty visualizing it. They operate out of *sense perceptions* and are the realists of the zodiac—the builders who provide stability and continuity. Earth is the principle of *sustenance*.

The air signs see everything as connected to everything else. They are sequential thinkers for whom there must be a beginning, a middle, and an end to everything. For the most part these people operate on *logic* and act only when they can see the sense of their actions. The air signs are endlessly curious and represent the principle of *connecting and reasoning*.

The water signs tend to feel their way through life. What is most real to them is what their emotions tell them; they do what their emotions tell them to do as well. They are imaginative thinkers, the poets and artists of the zodiac. The water principle is that of *caring, nurturing, and protecting*.

A Quality Is Part of a Sign

There are only four elements, but there are twelve signs. In astrological arithmetic, the *three qualities* which divide the *four elements* make up the difference. It isn't easy to grasp the concept of the elements, but the qualities (or "modes" as they are sometimes called) help a lot, because they make the elements a lot more tangible. Called *cardinal*, *fixed*, and *mutable*, the three modes can best be understood as *kinds of motion*.

Cardinal motion is start-up movement. It is the principle of bringing into being. Cardinal goes forward, so, the cardinal signs are *initiators*.

The four cardinal signs are those that start the four seasons:
  Aries (*spring*)
  Cancer (*summer*)

Libra (*fall*)
Capricorn (*Winter*)

Fixed motion means staying in place. Fixed things have come into being, and now simply are. The fixed signs represent stability, and are difficult to move. The four fixed signs represent the middle of each season:
Tarus (*spring*)
Leo (*summer*)
Scorpio (*fall*)
Aquarius (*winter*)

Mutable motion means flexible motion. Things that are mutable are changing, able to turn into something else. The mutable signs represent the *ability to adjust, and to accept change.* The four mutable signs are those that end the seasons:
Gemini (*spring*)
Virgo (*summer*)
Sagittarius (*fall*)
Pisces (*winter*)

Elements and Qualities Together Add Up to Signs
When you put elements and qualities together you begin to get a picture of what they add up to—the twelve astrological signs. Here is how each quality modifies each element.

Fire element/Cardinal quality = Aries
This get-up-and-go sign has all the flash and dash of fire plus an added dose of a pioneering spirit by virtue of its cardinal quality.

Fire element/Fixed quality = Leo
Leo burns with the ardor and enthusiasms of fire, but gives off very steady heat due to its fixed quality.

Fire element/Mutable quality = Sagittarius
Sagittarius represents the kind of fire that spreads, igniting everything and everybody in its path—which is rather erratic because of Sagittarius's mutable quality.

Earth element /Cardinal quality = Capricorn
Capricorn is the most active builder of the earth signs because of its cardinal quality. Capricorn's brand

of reality demands that something be brought into being.

Earth element/Fixed quality = **Taurus**
This strong sign stands and waits, holding things and people together. Taurus is the warmest and most nurturing of the earth signs, and is always "there."

Earth element/Mutable quality = **Virgo**
Virgo's practical sense knows that all things must change. This mutable sign represents the principle of stability with flux; that is, permanence in the face of change.

Air element/Cardinal quality = **Libra**
Libra's air nature moves forward, actively connecting people and things into partnerships via its cardinal quality of initiation.

Air element/Fixed quality = **Aquarius**
Aquarius is the most immovable of the air signs, representing the permanance of ideas and their practical application.

Air element/Mutable quality = **Gemini**
This very movable sign represents changing thoughts and opinions, the breaking up of static ideas so that new ones can come about.

Water element/Cardinal quality = **Cancer**
Cancer is the most initiating of the water signs because of the cardinal quality. Though shy, Cancer generally moves quietly but effectively to the forefront.

Water element/Fixed quality = **Scorpio**
Scorpio's powerful self-control comes from the emotional water element that is contained and compressed because of this sign's fixed quality.

Water element/Mutable quality = **Pisces**
Pisces extreme emotionalism—as well as this sign's creativity—comes from feelings that constantly change and move into new areas, creating new outlets.

Planets Are the Most Important Factor in Astrology
"Planet" is probably an even more important word in the astrological language than "sign." How can that be?

Because it is the placement of the planets in various signs which indicates personality and it is the movement of the planets through the zodiac that indicates events. In other words, without the planets the signs would have no application to people and what happens to them.

As early man noticed that the planets moved in fairly regular patterns, he began to associate certain characteristics with each of the planets, and each planet gradually took on a "personality." In a number of different cultures, certain planets were hooked up with certain gods, because it was the gods who really controlled life on earth. The moon was virtually always a female god—like Diana or Artemis. Jupiter, always a "good guy" planet, was known as Vishnu, the preserver, to the Hindus. Before he got his Roman name of Jupiter, the Greeks knew him as Zeus, a lusty fellow who had a heart of gold. (You'll get a complete rundown on each of the planets in Chapter p, "The Planets As Stars.")

From these planetary "personalities" came the idea that each planet caused a certain kind of behavior or event by virtue of its own nature. For instance, Mars, always the war god, is still regarded by modern astrologers as an indicator of strife and conflict. When predicting events, the astrologer looks at what sign and what house Mars will be passing through at a certain point in time to see what kind of influence it is most likely to bring into a person's life.

When looking at personality, the astrologer determines which sign a person's Mars is in at the time of the person's birth to see how that individual is most likely to assert him-/herself. The sun, the most important planet makes us what we are in totality according to which sign the sun is placed in at our birth; i.e., our sun sign's Venus is the planet of relationships, and its placement in a specific sign shows how a person is likely to relate to others.

In short, planets indicate *action*, and the signs in which the planets are placed indicate *the kind of action*.

Since ancient times, astrologers have recognized seven planets. The sun (which is really a star), the moon (which is really a satellite of our own planet, earth) Mercury, Venus, Mars, Jupiter, and Saturn.

With the development of the telescope, three more planets were discovered (although there is some evidence that early astrologer/priests divined their existence). Uranus was first spotted in 1781, Neptune in 1846, and Pluto as late as 1930. Some astrologers/astronomers anticipate that there are two more to be found, so that there would be twelve planets instead of the current ten.

A House Is an Area of Life—and a Planet's "Home"

Just as there is a great circle in the sky called the zodiac, and it is divided into twelve equal units of *space*, there is another circle which is based on units of *time*. As we all know, the earth makes one complete rotation on its own axis every twenty-four hours. Imagine yourself standing in one place during a twenty-four-hour period and making a mark on the sky every two hours while that sky appears to pass by you as the earth turns. At the end of twenty-four hours, you will have marked off twelve different units of sky. A "house" is simply one of those pieces of sky that has passed by during your day-long vigil. Toward the end of your day of skywatching, twelve houses will have gone by, and "house one" will be coming up again.

When an astrologer draws up a natal horoscope—which is simply a map of the sky when you were born—he/she does it by drawing a picture of the sky as it appeared from the exact place of birth, at the exact time of your birth. What happens is that the twelve houses are lined up in a very specific way—a very different way than if you had been born *in another place at the same time* or *at the same time in another place*.

What is most important about the particular lineup of the houses is that each house represents a different area of human life, and how those areas are positioned *for you* has a tremendous effect on your astrological makeup. For instance, the second house is the house of income and personal possessions and has a lot to do with attitude toward money and how easy or how difficult it will be to come by in your lifetime. The seventh house is the house of partnership and offers clues about who you are likely to marry. If you know the time of your birth within one hour or so, you can add a very important dimension to your astrological self-knowledge by reading the chapter "Your House of the Sun—Your 'Piece of the Pie,'" because the house of the horoscope into which the sun falls in your horoscope usually indicates what area of life will absorb you during your lifetime.

Your Rising Sign Is the One that Starts the First House

Your rising sign is sometimes called the ascendant, because it is the sign of the zodiac that was "ascending" on the eastern horizon at the time of your birth, no matter what time your birth occured. It is the "sunrise sign," corresponding to the nine o'clock position on the face of an ordinary clock. The astrologer's "clock" starts at this position and is read counter-clockwise around the circle of the face. If you were born around sundown, your rising sign will be the one 180 degrees *opposite* the sign you were born under. For instance, if you are an Aries born at sundown, your rising sign will be Libra. If you are an Aries born at sunrise, your rising sign is probably Aries as well.

Why is your rising sign so important? Because it starts the first house of personality, or your very individual way of presenting yourself to the world. No matter what your sun sign is, your rising sign will cover it to a greater or lesser degree (which is why it is so difficult to guess someone's Sun Sign when you first meet them). The rising sign has to do with appearances and can actually influence your physical looks.

If you don't know the time of day you were born, you can't determine your rising sign (although some astrologers can by doing what is called a "rectification," based on the events in your life so far). However, even those who do not know their rising sign can have their horoscopes read; what the astrologer does is put your sun sign on the first house, and do an analysis of what is called a solar horoscope. If you *do* know your birthtime within an hour or so, you can use the rising sign chart in this book to determine yours.

Planets in Signs in Houses Make Up a Horoscope

The whole basis of astrology is that anyone born in a particular moment in time partakes of the qualities of that moment in time. Actually, the same applies for things; for instance, a business that has its beginnings at a precise astrological moment also has a horoscope which can be read, and tells a lot about its potential for success or failure.

An astrologer looks at the particular moment in drawing up a horoscope—or "picture of the hour." A horoscope is basically a map of the sky, showing exactly where the planets were in relation to the signs and the houses, to each other, and from the particular reference point of your birthplace. It is also called a "natal chart" or "natal map."

Everyone's horoscope has ten planets and twelve houses. Those ten planets can be in a variety of signs, and in a variety of houses. Each planet means something different according to its own nature, how that nature operates in a particular sign, and what area of life the planet is most likely to affect by virtue of which house of the horoscope it falls into. Sound complicated? It is, and only a highly trained astrologer can interpret the many factors and put them together for you in a meaningful way. The most exciting part of astrology is the fact that *no two individuals are ever exactly alike*—not even twins, who are born a few minutes apart.

Although you can find out a lot about your astrological personality right in this book, many people like to take the next step and have a personalized horoscope drawn up for them and interpreted by a professional astrologer. There are a number of ways to find a good person to do this for you; in astrology, as in every other profession, there are variations in the level of competence. Two places you can start your search are:

National Astrological Society
62 West 39th St.
New York, NY 10018

American Federation of Astrologers
Tempe, AZ 85282

An Aspect Is the Distance Between Planets

Among the more sophisticated factors an astrologer looks for in your horoscope are the *aspects*. Within the 360-degree circle of the horoscope (and the zodiac), planets form certain aspects to each other by virtue of the distance between them. Some distances are considered harmonious, and some are inharmonious, in terms of how those two (or more) planets work together. It's all a matter of mathematics. The soft or harmonious aspects are the sextile (60 degrees apart) and the trine (120 degrees apart). The hard or inharmonious aspects are formed when planets are in square to each other (90 degrees apart) or in opposition, 180 degrees or exactly half a circle apart. These are only the major aspects, and there are lots and lots of minor ones between, but you can get a good picture of interplanetary relationships with only these few.

For example, if your sun sign is Aries, and at the time of your birth the planet Saturn was in the sign of Libra, or 180 degrees away from Aries, you are likely to have a more serious (Saturnine) disposition than the typical "happy" Aries. Depending on your point of view, this can be a positive note in your horoscope, because you will have greater powers of concentration than many an Aries—or a negative note, because you will be less happy-go-lucky. In another example, a person with a Capricorn sun sign may have a horoscope in which Jupiter, the planet of expansiveness, is 120 degrees away from the sun—either in the sign of Virgo or Taurus— and therefore in "trine" aspect to his/her sun. The result: a much more outgoing, giving Capricorn than the run-of-the-mill type. On the other hand, such an easy aspect could expand Capricorn's acquisitive nature too much, and make for a megalomanic (someone who craves worldly goods and power).

The ancients separated aspects into "favorable" and "unfavorable," but psychologically-thinking modern astrologers know that it is not that simple; it all depends on the total horoscope, plus the individual's reactions to the particular vibrations of the planets in that horoscope.

A Transiting Planet Affects Your Life Now

When someone goes to an astrologer for the first time, he/she usually has *two* readings—separate, but interrelated. The first will be an interpretation of your natal chart or birth horoscope. This tells you about your given personality—the traits, problems, abilities, and advantages you are most likely to have by virtue of the placement of the planets in the sky at the time of your birth. The second reading will have to do with what you can expect in your life at the present time and the near future. Your birth horoscope always remains the same, but the planets in the sky keep changing their relationships to your birth horoscope throughout your lifetime. The astrologer will acquaint you with the current "transit"—or movements—of the planets and how you, the individual, can expect them to affect you. For instance, if an astrologer notes that Uranus, the "earthquake planet," is approaching your fourth house (the house of emotional security, the place where we really live), the astrologer might alert you to the fact that big changes are in the offing: even a total shaking of the foundations, or a pulling up of roots. This is a major transit, and many people change their residence, partners, or jobs when it occurs. Similarly, but on a less critical note, the astrologer may notice that the planet Venus is going to make a transit over the place in the zodiac occupied by Mars in your birthchart. This could indicate a firey romantic interlude or the rekindling of an old flame.

There are two important things to keep in mind about astrological predictions. The first is that your natal horoscope—your "birth imprint"—really determines how you will react to life's events. To put it even more strongly, your innate personality will really *create* the events of your life, because "character is destiny." There is no doubt that the planets create conditions, but we must take responsibility for how we cooperate with those conditions. The second thing is that *there are very few hard and fast rules*. There are guidelines, to be sure, and most of them have ancient roots; a lot of astrological prediction is based on the case history technique. However, since no two sets of conditions—

the one in the sky and the one in an individual birthchart—are ever *exactly* the same, it is virtually impossible for any astrologer to tell you specifically what is going to happen.

2

Your House of the Sun

Your "Piece of the Pie"

The prime symbol in the very symbolic language of astrology is the perfect circle; it represents the sky around us, the cosmic atmosphere into which we are all born. All astro-math is based on division of the 360-degree figure, which since ancient times has been regarded as having mystical qualities. When thinking about the houses of the horoscope, however, it helps to use a very down-to-earth analogy. Look at that circle as a great "pie in the sky," which is divided into twelve cosmic slices—each slice representing one house and a different facet of human experience.

Just as there are ten planets in everyone's horoscope, there are twelve houses. However, not all those houses may be occupied by a planet; it all depends on where the planets were in the sky at the moment of your birth. The placement of any planet in a specific house is a *very* important factor in your individual horoscope, but the most important is the placement of the sun. No matter what your sun sign, your House of the Sun has a lot to tell you about the life you've been "given" to live on this earth. As your sun sign is the prime indicator of *character and personality,* your house of the sun points to the *area of human affairs* that you are most likely to find yourself concentrating on in your lifetime.

In the sense that it helps define the boundaries of your life, your house of the sun is your "piece of the pie"—that slice of life within which you will live. Does your house of the sun totally box you in? In a way it does, but it is more productive to think of the dimensions of your house of the sun as *guidelines* about where you can most profitably focus your energies.

Here's the way it works:

- The *sun* is the most important planet in your horoscope. It is the planets that do the "acting," and the sun plays the leading role.
- Your sun sign determines *how* your sun (the real you) acts, i.e., the characteristics of the character you play.
- Your house of the sun is the "stage" on which you will play out your role.

For instance, if your sun sign is Scorpio (the great investigator) and your house of the sun is the twelfth (hidden things), you find yourself drawn to some kind of career in which you must "dig" to do your investigating. Ergo, you might make a good psychoanalyst, archeologist, or genetic researcher. Or, your greatest pleasure in life might be reading mystery novels or spy thrillers—or writing or editing them.

In order to figure out which piece of the pie you've been served, you have to know your birth-time within an hour or so. If you were born during Daylight Savings Time or War Time, you have to subtract one hour from your birth time to determine the "real sun time."

Each house is described here from three different angles:

- The matters or principles connected with it
- The people/places/things related to it
- The problems and the possibilities of having your sun in that house.

Birth time, 4 to 6 a.m.: **Sun in First House**

- *First house matters:* Exploration . . . use of the physical body . . . being on the scene . . . breaking new ground . . . independent action . . . emergencies . . . conquest . . . controversy . . . strategy . . . competition . . . being in the vanguard.

- *First house people/places/things:* Entrepreneurs ... acrobats ... cutting instruments ... rock music ... metals ... satire ... hardware ... the head and face ... opticians ... adrenalin ... new products ... commodities ... salesmen ... fighters ... firemen.
- *Problems and possibilities:* With your sun in the first house, your sun sign personality is quite strong. Regardless of what your sun sign is, you should be able to make clear-cut decisions and have a good sense of your own identity. If you are to gain control over your life, you are going to have to banish fear from it and develop both the moral and the physical courage that is available to you. Though your will should be strong, you will have to keep yourself from a tendency to tyrannize others. When you feel most defeated is the time your first house sun will come to your rescue. The one thing that could keep you from living out the very vivid life this house placement gives you is inflexibility and intolerance. Be willing to listen.

Birth time, 2 to 4 a.m.: **Sun in Second House**

- *Second house matters:* Calmness ... conservation ... ability to make grow ... eroticism ... collecting ... comforting ... administrating ... luxury ... stabilizing ... building up ... perpetuating ... patience ... using ... making stronger ... indulging.
- *Second house people/places/things:* Possessions ... money ... the voice ... landscape gardeners ... brokers and bankers ... love/passion ... personal adornment ... life-sustaining skills ... buying and selling ... security needs ... nurses ... food and shelter ... good music ... creature comforts.
- *Problems and possibilities:* You should be able to establish yourself firmly and securely in whatever you choose to do; self-adjustment should come easily to you. Your economic life could be relatively worry-free but you must resist valuing money and

possessions for their own sake and becoming overly materialistic. You must develop the will that is given you and turn it into willpower, or you could lose self-respect. You are a good manager, but if you allow yourself to become too settled, you will fear to take the necessary risks to make your life less limited. Though things come to you fairly easily, do not let yourself over-indulge in any of them, including rich food.

Birth time midnight to 2 a.m.: **Sun in Third House**

- *Third house matters:* Connecting ... associating ... verbalizing ... dexterity ... inquisitiveness ... distribution ... novelty ... thinking and reasoning ... cause and effect ... exchanging ... bringing the news ... being responsive ... "here today, gone tomorrow."
- *Third house people/places/things:* Short journeys ... realatives (especially siblings) ... speech/languages ... high school teachers ... role-playing/entertaining ... computers ... graphic arts ... handwork ... transportation ... the nervous system ... handwriting .. repair men ... gossip ... comedy ... ventriloquists.
- *Problems and possibilities:* You should be an excellent communicator who reports things clearly and accurately. In your desire for information, however, you could become rather superficial and a bit of a talebearer. If you don't focus your mental energies carefully, you may waste the gift of curiosity your third house sun gives you. You must also learn to live with uncertainty, and to keep your opinions flexible. If life scares you, you are likely to become very defensive and locked in to your ideas. Develop your capacity for listening as well as your talent for talking.

Birth time 10 p.m. to 12 a.m.: **Sun in Fourth House**

- *Fourth house matters:* Adaptability ... change ... instinctiveness ... fluctuation ... protecting ...

imagination . . . softness . . . the subconscious . . . survival . . . enveloping . . . integrating . . . fertility . . . mothering.
- *Fourth house people/places/things:* Dreams . . . the past . . . roots . . . home and family . . . physical sensation . . . museums . . . caterers . . . water and other liquid . . . introverts . . . obstetrics . . . boats . . . domestics . . . imagination.
- *Problems and possibilities:* Via your fourth house sun, you are given the possibility of understanding yourself and your motivations quite thoroughly. If you handle your life in a mature way, you will establish a warm and comfortable home for you and your family. However, you must strive for real self-knowledge if you are not to become simply self-absorbed and self-centered. Your imagination is considerable, and you could be highly creative; the down side is that you could develop irrational fears that verge on paranoia. Work to see the world clearly at all times and try to conquer your tendency to play the introvert. No mater what your sun sign, the placement of that sun in the fourth house will make you instinctively avoid the limelight. Get out there and shine!

Birth time 8 to 10 p.m.: **Sun in Fifth House**

- *Fifth house matters:* Being at the heart of things . . . pleasures . . . power . . . ambition . . . generosity/giving . . . "gilding the lily" . . . showmanship . . . stability . . . management . . . territorial rights . . . self-expression . . . autocracy . . . organization.
- *Fifth house people/places/things:* Philanthropy . . . corporations . . . impresarios . . . holidays and vacations . . . romantic love . . . children . . . gamblers . . . gold . . . circuses . . . nursery teachers . . . fashion and fashion designers . . . public life.
- *Problems and possibilities:* Even if you have a "shy" sun sign, your fifth house placement of the sun will force you into some form of self-expression that is possibly very creative. You also have a capability

for approaching life with a joyful, expectant manner; however, your pursuit of pleasure and play could become extreme. Consciously avoid any pleasure that threatens to get out of control. Your affairs of the heart could be many, but it is important to keep alert for anything that smacks of an abusive partner; it's possible you could enjoy the drama of an unhappy situation. Develop your capacity for warmly accepting others.

Birth time 6 to 8 p.m.: **Sun in Sixth House**

- *Sixth house matters:* Competence/skill ... specialization ... refining ... categorizing ... analyzing ... obedience ... realism ... responsibility ... purifying ... invention ... making things work ... ministering ... discriminating.
- *Sixth house people/places/things:* Service ... critics ... crafts ... libraries ... closets ... public health ... the harvest ... small animals ... dependents ... dental hygienists ... research ... diagnosing ... numbers work ... chemists.
- *Problems and possibilities:* With your sun in the sixth house you have the potential of becoming a true master at something; however, if you allow yourself to get bogged down in life's details, you could possibly end up being a wage slave. No matter what your sun sign, your instincts tell you to be of service to others. While you are capable of great self-sacrifice, you must avoid the temptation to be overly humble and to assume the servant role. You are mentally very keen, and can break things and jobs down into smaller parts in order to accomplish them. Do not let the state of your own health become an obsession. With the sun is the sixth house, your basic constitution should be quite strong. Don't worry!

Birth time 4 to 6 p.m.: **Sun in Seventh House**

- *Seventh house matters:* Sharing ... comparing ... give-and-take ... peacemaking ... negotiation ...

making things beautiful ... creating balance ... fairness ... sociability ... gratification ... advocacy ... diplomacy ... aestheticism.
- *Seventh house people/places/things:* Divorce lawyers ... love poetry ... marriage brokers ... the kidneys and lower back ... illustration ... resort managers ... public relations ... fine arts ... receptionists ... boutiques ... jugglers ... tailors ... pianos.
- Possibilities and problems: You have a great need to identify with others, and can create a wonderful rapport with them easily. However, your need for a life partner could make you overly dependent. If you have an independent sun sign, this could create a serious life conflict. With this placement, you are able to adjust to new people and new situations easily, but you must avoid a tendency not to stick with a position when you really believe in it. You have the potential of forming very warm, balanced and intimate relationships; however, if you do not handle this gift in a mature manner, you could develop a fear of intimacy, and shy away from it or become an outrageous and insincere flirt.

Birth time 2 to 4 p.m.: **Sun in Eighth House**

- *Eighth house matters:* Release of blockages ... probing ... anonymity ... procreation ... rejuvenation ... willpower ... endurance ... controlling ... investigation ... aloneness ... demolishing and rebuilding ... crisis ... elimination.
- *Eighth house people/places/things:* Puzzles ... generals ... political parties ... labor lawyers ... the healing arts ... death and dying ... taxes ... spies ... superathletes ... crime detection ... statesmen ... sex symbols ... geologists ... explorers ... mating instinct ... sanitation engineers.
- *Problems and possibilities:* A light sun sign (like Gemini or Libra), the placement of the sun in this house will add depth to your character. You will feel compelled to investigate things that are hidden or

even dangerous. While it is good to probe, you must beware of a tendency to concentrate on what is morbid. All things being equal, you will be highly sexed; however, with insufficient self-knowledge, your healthy sexual instincts could turn into obsession with the subject—or a total advoidance of it. Learn to live with your dynamic physical body and you will live with others quite happily. Also, encourage your religious or mystical feelings, which are quite real. You have the potential of totally transforming your life at one point or another.

Birth time noon to 2 p.m.: **Sun in Ninth House**

- *Ninth house matters:* Anticipating ... aspiring ... moving around ... expanding things ... speculating ... idealism ... advising ... unpredictability ... search for truth ... search for opportunity ... taking aim ... magnanimity ... excess.
- *Ninth house people/places/things* Casinos ... ambassadors ... passport offices ... luck ... international transportation ... trading/high finance ... dancers ... aristocrats ... large animals ... higher studies ... lawmaking ... profiteers ... veterinarians.
- *Problems and possibilities:* Even if you have a routine-loving sun sign (like Virgo), this placement of the sun will give you the desire and the ability to constantly renew your life, and to adapt to new patterns of behavior. You will feel strongly about one religious or ethical system or another, or at least have a very strong personal philosophy. However, you could become rather dogmatic and rigid in your opinions. Your adaptability is admirable, but a desire for the new and novel could be the "downside" of your openness to new experience. Exercise control. With certain sun signs, there may be a tendency toward inner battles between opportunity-seeking and a firm set of principles. You are a spender—of both your money and your physical resources.

Birth time 10 a.m. to 12 a.m.: **Sun in Tenth House**

- *Tenth house matters:* Realism ... structure ... ambition ... rigidity ... integrating ... limitation ... disciplining ... reputation ... social position ... creating the useful ... contraction ... coolness ... convention.
- *Tenth house people/places/things:* Figures ... fame ... common sense ... property ... correctional systems and facilities ... ceramics ... money lenders ... efficiency experts ... the bones ... the elderly ... sculptors ... watches and clocks.
- *Problems and possibilities:* You have the capacity of becoming a respected member of whatever group you move in, because your public image is very important to you. If you play your cards right, you can arrive at a sense that you are fulfilling your destiny. However, if you become obsessed with power and appearances, you could end up living a shallow, meaningless life behind your strong facade. It is most important with this placement of the sun to find the right outlet for you to express yourself and get positive feedback from others. You won't be happy starving in a garret, because both money and recognition are too important to you. This position of the sun often brings fame.

Birth time 8 to 10 a.m.: **Sun in Eleventh House**

- *Eleventh house matters:* Helping ... experimentation ... humanitarianism ... association ... liberalism .. freedom ... suddenness ... awakenings ... combining ... freethinking ... rationality ... caring ... breaking through ... observing coolly ... predicting.
- *Eleventh house people/places/things:* Paradoxes ... stunt men ... electricity ... zealots ... divorce ... fireworks ... the social sciences ... reform ... geniuses ... aviation ... weathermen ... brotherly love ... magnetism ... groups ... friends ... causes.
- *Problems and possibilities:* If you are a very personal

sun sign (like Cancer), you will gain a lot of objectivity with the placement of the sun in this house. You should have very high aims and goals, and some of them will undoubtedly involve helping the less fortunate in some way or another. Though this is admirable, if you don't set yourself on a definite path in life and stick to a definite plan, you could simply drift along, with only vague ideas about where you can shine. It is important to be quite realistic with the sun in this house. Your own crowd is important to you, but you must avoid becoming such a part of the group that you lose a sense of your own individuality—which is potentially very great. Some people with the sun in the 11th house are downright wacky, but often very achieving people.

Birth Time 6 to 8 a.m.: **Sun in Twelfth House**

- *Twelfth house matters:* Dissolving ... ambiguity ... disguising ... retreating ... sensualism ... enchantment ... paying dues ... healing spiritually ... insubstantiality ... confinement ... persuading ... comprehending the incomprehensible ... merging ... pretending.
- *Twelfth house people/places/things:* Makeup ... escapism ... alcohol and drugs ... drama and dramatic actors ... films ... advertising ... pastoral work ... fishing ... astrophysics ... con men ... magicians ... hospitals ... alibis ... myths ... prisons.
- *Problems and possibilities:* Yours is not an easy house of the sun to have—especially if you are a very self-expressive sun sign type like Leo. You may feel that life is confining you in some way or another; what you are really sensing is your gift of the ability to transcend self to a much higher spiritual level. You should be an expert at coping with intangibles and sensing the nuances of any situation. In a sense, you have a kind of ESP which can be developed for life success. However, the real down side of the twelfth house sun is that it

can lead to a very confused, unfocussed attitude toward life. It is essential that you give yourself a definite structure to work within if you are to free yourself from the worries and cares of life. By all means avoid any form of escapism that is dangerous.

3

The Geometry of Relationships

What Signs You Get Along with—and Why

The first thing most people want to know about their sun sign is what other signs they are compatible with. It's a natural question, and a good one to ask an astrologer, because one aspect of astrology, called "synastry" (literally, "stars together") concentrates on the subject of relationships. When practising synastry, the astrologer compares the two birth charts of the two people involved to find what connections there are between them. It is a complicated process, but it provides excellent clues about how two people will relate to each other. What chart comparison does is *describe the nature of the relationship*. Actually, to an astrologer there are no "bad" or "good" relationships; there are just a lot of different kinds and each has a special character. Of course it is true that some relationships end up on the rocks, sometimes devastating one or both parties involved. But, even in such cases, the astrologer looks at it as a "karmic" relationship—one in which people *had* to come together in order to learn some life lessons.

While comparing two complete horoscopes is the ideal way to look at a relationship, there is a very simple method of looking at two sun signs, and coming up with an overall prediction of how two people will relate to each other. This method goes back to the great circle of the zodiac and to the division of the twelve signs into four elements: fire, earth, air, and water.

Here's the lineup of signs in each element:

Fire: Aries, Leo, Sagittarius

Earth: Taurus, Virgo, Capricorn
Air: Gemini, Libra, Aquarius
Water: Cancer, Scorpio, Pisces

The general rules of thumb for element-mixing are as follows:

Great	Good	Semi-tough or Difficult
Fire and air	Fire and fire	Fire and water
Water and earth	Earth and earth	Earth and air
	Air and air	Fire and earth
	Water and water	Air and water

Here's the way it looks mathmatically:
If you divide the 360-degree circle of the zodiac by the twelve signs, you find that each sign is 30 degrees away from the next.
- Signs that are 30 degrees apart—or next to each other—are semi-tough.
- Signs that are 60 degrees (two signs) or 180 degrees (six signs) away from each other are the best combinations. (The latter, 180 degrees away from each other, makes these signs polar opposites, and in astrology polar opposites attract.)
- Signs that are 120 degrees apart—four signs away from each other—are in the same element, and their relationship is good, but far from perfect.
- Signs that are 90 degrees or three signs away from each other have the most difficult relationships of all. They are said to be in "square aspect" to each other.

When you look at the four elements in terms of what they signify in the physical world, you get a good idea why some elements get along more easily.

Fire turns water into steam (hot air).
Water puts fire out.
Fire scorches earth.

Earth smothers fire.
Air fans fire and makes it brighter.
Fire warms up cool air.
Water softens up hard earth.
Earth makes water keep its shape.
Water and air do nothing (unless you add heat).
Air blows earth around.

What about combinations of the same element, such as fire with fire? In effect, they tend to neutralize or cancel each other out. Or, they can simply be too much of one element for comfort.

- Two fire signs together could experience "burn out" fairly quickly.
- Two air signs might analyze each other to the death of the relationship.
- Two earth signs could depress each other a lot.
- Two water signs could make for an overly "heavy" relationship.

4

Twelve Places at the Table

A Mini Astrodrama in Which the Twelve Signs Play Themselves

No matter how accurate or colorful any description of a zodiac sign may be, it is still a description—not the real thing. A sign is simply an abstract concept until it takes form in a living, breathing human being. There are obviously as many different types of people as there are individual horoscopes, and no two are exactly alike. However, the twelve signs of the zodiac are still the best guidelines we have for sorting out human behavior into broad but meaningful categories. There are even fiction writers who use the zodiac signs as prototypes for characters they create because it makes them more realistic, i.e., more like people you are likely to meet.

What follows is fiction, but it gets closer to the truth about each zodiacal sign than a general description ever can. The twelve characters in this docudrama are obviously caricatures, because their behavior is highly exaggerated. But it is exaggeration for emphasis, and for the purpose of bringing to life the twelve signs of the zodiac, which don't really exist except as real people. Like real people, these twelve characters have foibles; but they have fine points too. As you read this drama, you may find yourself drawn to some signs and put off by others. Make mental notes of which signs you find yourself most sympathetic with and check out your findings in the parts of this book about astrological compatibility. It could prove very interesting—

and very revealing. As each sign of the zodiac has a sex or gender, they are portrayed here as male or female accordingly. But the basic behavior pattern is applicable to both sexes.

The twelve signs of the zodiac are invited to dinner at that great dining room in the sky. When they arrive, they find that their host (who shall remain signless) has slipped up, and there are only eleven places set at the table. Since it is a fancy affair, each sign is trying to be on his/her best behavior. However, the situation is a bit unsettling, so in the course of trying to resolve it, they all relapse into their natural zodiacal characteristics.

Aries An energetic young man, he comes bounding into the room, almost tripping on an untied shoelace. He is dressed rather casually for the occasion, and looks as if he got dressed rather quickly. When he realizes what the situation is, there's no doubt in his mind how to handle it.

"Only eleven places? Don't worry; Pisces will probably never show anyway. But, I got here before anybody else (the doorman will prove it) so I should definitely get a seat. In fact, I should sit down *first*. No, I don't need to wash my hands or anything. I'm *starved*, so I hope you aren't having anything like the gooey mess with the French name you had before. A hamburger will do just fine. And don't serve it cold like you did the last time. Hey, there's a great-looking dish over there, ha ha! Seat me next to her, will you Cancer? Well, she looks like a nice warm type, so I think I'll go let her warm me up. By the way, I'm organizing a sky-diving club. Want to join? Seriously, if you can't afford the membership fee, I'll put it up for you, because I'd love to have you join. Oh, you're doing okay now? Glad to hear you're off the rack. Got any pretzels?"

Taurus An attractive young woman with faint dimples in her roundish cheeks and a slightly unruly but pretty mass of curly hair comes sauntering into the room. She is dressed in a soft and pretty outfit that looks expensive, and has her handbag clutched tightly under her arm. She looks around the room with moderate curiosity. As the host walks up to her, she gives him a warm smile; when she speaks, her voice is low and melodious—but firm.

"Only eleven places? You mean, only eleven *chairs*. All you have to do is set another place and give me a pillow to sit on. I don't mind, as long as I'm comfortable. And I smell something wonderful, so I know the food is going to be delicious. To be honest with you, that's really why I came. I don't like to go out much, you know. What I really like is curling up in my warm and comfy bed—with someone warm and comfy, of course. (Are you busy later on?) But, now that I'm *here*, there's no way I'm not going to eat. What's for dessert? Who's that nervous-looking lady over there? Virgo? I'll go try to make her feel comfortable."

Gemini It's hard to tell just how old this fellow is as he springs in the door; he could be any age, though he looks about eighteen. He is dressed in the very latest style, though nothing he has on is really extreme. His eyes dart all over the room, and he is carrying a notebook under his arm. When the host tells him about the eleven places, he is so busy listening to another conversation, he almost misses it. When he reacts, it is in a typically casual way.

"Don't worry about me; I don't need a place. I'll just float around the room, because what I really came here for is the conversation. I'm writing a book, you know—it's called *1001 Opening Conversational Gambits* and tonight I'm researching. I see you've got some really fascinating types here. How did you make up the guest list? Are they all married? Why did they come alone? What's the menu? Who's the chef? Can I see the wine list? Who's that blowsy-looking type over there? Taurus? I'll bet *she's* got a story. Where's the telephone? I've got to make a call."

Cancer A sexy, voluptuous woman of indeterminate age pauses at the door; she seems shy, but conscious of the impression she is making. Her clothes are a bit unusual, and some things are from the thrift shop. However, her antique jewelry is genuine, and the whole effect is glamorous. When she discovers there are only eleven places, she is visibly upset, and there is a touch of a whine in her voice as she speaks.

"I wish I'd known; I could have stayed home with the children. They have colds, you know. If you want, I'll simply leave; but I really don't want to go home by myself; I'll get scared and have bad dreams. Upset? Yes, I am upset, and when I get upset I can't eat. Unless it's really soothing and nourishing. Did you know that a touch of heavy cream in mashed potatoes is simply heavenly? Chicken soup? I make it by the gallon. Say, you look as if you could stand a little fattening up. Well, all right. I *guess* I'll stay—unless I change my mind, of course."

Leo This is a fine figure of a man—fairly tall, rather muscular, and with a thick crop of curly hair that is somewhere between blond and red. He is elegantly dressed and his gold cufflinks probably put a real drain on Fort Knox. His grand entrance is smooth and practised, and his handshake is hearty and warm. When his host tells him the news, he takes it very personally.

"Well, let me tell you, this is embarrassing! I mean, all these people here to see me, and I may have to stand? I've given bigger parties than this, and they've always gone off without a hitch. Let me handle things for you the next time. For now, just get that chair over there and squeeze someone in—Virgo won't mind. No, *here*; not *there!* While we're all waiting I guess I can entertain everyone with my tantrum act. What? No, I'm only kidding—though I am mad. I'll do my Hamlet number instead. Like my cufflinks? They match my Gold Card. I've ordered another pair with sapphires, too."

Virgo A rather prim woman stands quietly at the door looking as if she would like to blend into the woodwork. She is dressed very neatly, but conservatively, with flat-heeled sensible shoes. In her handbag she carries a surgical mask to wear in case any of the other guests has a cold. Her reaction to the news that there are only eleven places is swift and shrill.

"Well, it certainly isn't *my* fault. I answered the invitation the minute I got it. I *always* do! Why didn't you check on things more carefully? If you had, this wouldn't have happened, and you wouldn't have all these people standing around thinking terrible things about you. I don't mind for myself, you understand, I don't eat much anyway; you never know what you're going to get. I'll stay in the kitchen and help the cook clean up. You can't be too careful about these things, you know. You wouldn't believe the sanitary conditions I've found in *some* kitchens. Not mentioning any names, of course. Oh, *why* did you mess things up this way; you are simply impossible. . . ."

Intermission: Our host walks away as Virgo continues to complain. As he checks on the guests, he discovers that Libra has just arrived. Sagittarius and Pisces are nowhere to be found, but Scorpio, Capricorn, and Aquarius are waiting to greet him. Because he looks like he's a bit uncomfortable, the host talks to Libra first.

Libra   A very attractive male, wearing all the right things, walks tentatively into the room, looking as if he is searching for someone. He is visibly uncomfortable alone. His gaze scans the room, quietly appraising everything and everybody in it. He seems to approve, but in his nervousness, he approaches the table, and starts rearranging one of the settings, then rearranging it again. All this is done very tactfully and gracefully. In fact, he looks as if he couldn't make an awkward gesture if he tried. His host approaches him and breaks the news. Libra's reaction is smooth and unruffled.

"Oh, how *clever* of you to arrange this little puzzle for us. It will make things so much more fun. Of course, we've got to make things absolutely fair; we wouldn't want to hurt anyone's feelings. I could leave if it would help, but . . . Oh, how nice of you to tell me I'll definitely have a place; it makes me feel a lot less awkward. I rarely go places alone, you know. Who would I like to sit next to? Well, the Capricorn lady looks like a sturdy and sensible type. But on the other hand, Scorpio is a *knockout*. Is she attached? Hmmm, Taurus looks like she'd like to chat, but oh, that Cancer! Decisions, decisions; I'll make up my mind later on. Where did you get that *great* painting?

Scorpio A slim and sexy woman dressed totally in black comes slinking into the room. Her style and movement are absolutely magnetic, and every eye turns to look at her. But she gives no visible response that she is aware of it. She doesn't seem to be feeling anything at all, but when her host approaches and tells her what is going on, she is seething with quiet rage.

"Do you really think you are going to get away with this? I suspected something when I got that weird invitation. Who in the world would ever come as they are and let everybody else know what they're really like? No matter how many times you tell me it was an innocent mistake to set only eleven places, I'll never believe it. Nothing in this world is innocent. And when it comes to drawing straws, just remember you owe me one from the last time. You know, the *last* time! Who's that wimpy looking guy over there? Gemini? Maybe I'll amuse myself with him for a while. I need a new conquest; I'm getting out of practice."

Sagittarius While Scorpio has been talking with the host, a tall rather rangy male has come loping into the room carrying a suitcase. He is a bit disheveled because his flight was late. He throws the suitcase in a corner and starts putting himself back together—a bit absentmindedly because he is looking around the room with a big smile and a lot of anticipation. He moves toward the host and gives a slap on his back that is almost *too* hearty.

"Only eleven places? Why worry? We'll work it out somehow. Life's too short to get uptight anyway. Had the greatest trip, and I'm turning right around tomorrow and going to the Orient so I can practice my Chinese. Say, are you serving Chinese food? I love Chinese food—and a good beer to go with it. At least I hope you're serving better wine than you did last time. You're looking a little pale . . . been partying too much lately? Ha ha, only kidding. Who's that guy over there with the flashy cufflinks? And the mouse with the sensible shoes? Think I'll see if I can loosen her up a bit. Did you hear I'm going to win the lottery again? What do you mean, how do I know? I just *know*. And I've got a great idea for an international fast food chain I'm going to bankroll with my winnings. I'm gonna call it 'The Great Gobler' and serve only turkey sandwiches. Hey, I'm thirsty. Where's the bar?"

Aquarius An intellectual-looking gentleman—sort of an absentminded professor type—has been standing in the doorway quietly puffing his pipe and scrutinizing the crowd. His jacket and pants don't match, but he isn't aware of it. An even stranger—but typical—sartorial note is his electric blue tie with orange stripes. He's got his earphones with him; if things get too dull, he'll listen to some hard rock or electronic music and be in seventh heaven. When he finds out about the missing place, he gives a thoughtful answer and makes an impractical suggestion.

"Oh, well, rather than make anyone feel left out, we could cancel the whole dinner and bring the food to the local shelter for the homeless. Ah, you don't care for that idea. Too bad; I'm becoming more and more concerned about poverty in our own backyard. Of course, I'm no bleeding heart like Pisces, but fair's fair. Want to hear about a new invention I'm working on? It's an electronic stamp sorter that will revolutionize the whole philatelic world. Huh? Oh, that's stamp collecting. Glad you asked me to come alone, since I'm free as a bird now. My last attachment got so *sticky!* I've sworn off. At least off those emotional types who want you to get so involved. No, I never get lonely—I've got too many friends for that. By the way, I can just sit on the floor in the lotus position, and get some meditating in at the same time."

Capricorn A rather handsome, perfectly put together woman has been quietly observing the crowd and the room, mentally putting a price tag on everything. What she has on is very expensive, but understated and in excellent taste. In her handbag she carries a petition with her name on it. She wants to run for local office, and is hoping to pick up some supporters tonight. If they are "her kind of people," that is. Her reaction to the host's situation is sober but logical.

"Well, it's obvious someone will have to go, but I

trust your judgment to decide who is most important—if you know what I mean. Your appointments are in excellent taste; I see you like Tiffany as much as I do. Who's that rather tacky looking type over there? Cancer? Where *does* she get her clothes? I have little sympathy for people who can't get their act together and run their lives successfully. She's probably a poet. Ah, well, different strokes for different folks; fantasy has no place in *my* life, you know. By the way, I have some excellent ideas about how to shape things up in the community; will you sign my petition? At dinner, are we going to discuss great books? I just bought a whole series . . . all leather-bound, of course. They look smashing in my living room."

Pisces Meanwhile, a rather wispy but very pretty woman has been wandering in and out of the doorway, looking as if she isn't quite sure she is in the right place. She is dressed in a misty fabric of very pale colors; there doesn't seem to be a clear-cut edge anywhere. In fact, if you don't rub your eyes, you might think you are seeing an apparition. The host knows it's Pisces and catches her just as she's about to drift out the door again. He doesn't bother telling her about the missing place, because he knows she wouldn't understand why that was important.

"Late? Am I late? I lost my watch two weeks ago. Or was it three? Oh well, what's time anyway in the larger scheme of things? Hungry? Not really, though I can't remember the last time I ate. *Love*—it's *love* that's food for the soul, and that's what I care about nourishing. I wonder if any of these people have had any *real* soul food lately. No, don't worry, I won't try to convert anyone tonight. I'm too, too drained because of my current work. What kind? Well, it really isn't a job-job, I mean where you make money, and all. I've started a shelter for homeless animals in my apartment; I cry so much when I see a stray that I can't stand it. Who? Ho, he left some time ago. Something about there being 'other fish in the sea.' What in the world do you suppose he meant by that? By the way, I'm a little short of cash. Do you think you could lend me . . . ?"

At this point, things are at a stalemate, but the situation will quickly resolve itself in one of twelve ways. Take your pick: This time *you* can choose the ending you like—and the one you think makes best astrological sense.

A. Aries gets in a fight with Leo and has to go to the emergency room.
B. Taurus gets really tired and hungry and decides to go home, cook a hamburger, and go to bed early.
C. Gemini runs out of note paper and gets laryngitis at the same time.
D. Cancer gets a call from the babysitter and is so worried she goes home to take care of her children.
E. Leo gets so irritated that no one is paying attention to the bruises Aries gave him that he leaves in a huff.
F. Virgo gets a stomach ache and decides to leave. Besides, it's time for her mineral bath.
G. Libra isn't able to make up his mind and gets a headache in the process.
H. Scorpio decides it's definitely a plot to humiliate her, and bows out less than graciously.
I. Sagittarius gets a little drunk and leaves early to get the plane.
J. Capricorn leaves as soon as she gets her petition filled up because there isn't anyone there *really* worth knowing.
K. Aquarius decides to go teach people at the shelter to use his stamp-sorting machine so they can get jobs.
L. Pisces remembers she has a date with her spiritual advisor and that she forgot to feed the animals.

5

Moods of the Moon

How to Successfully Navigate Its Day-by-Day Changes

Never underestimate the power of the moon. It is the closest planet to earth, and the only one whose effect on human life can actually be measured. Even the most skeptical antiastrology person has to admit that the moon rules the tides. If you stand on the beach for even a half hour or so, you can literally *see* how the moon works its magic as the water flows higher or lower, according to the time of day. There are places in the world where the tide rises as much as forty feet from its lowest to its highest point—that's *power*. If you think about the fact that humans are about 98 percent water in our chemical màkeup, it's much easier to accept the fact that the moon has the same powerful effect on us as it does on the tides.

Like the "female" she symbolically is, the moon also changes her mind—or her sign—more quickly than any other planet. If you look at the day-by-day predictions in this book, which gives the position of the moon for every day, you will see that this changeable planet moves into a different sign about every two days.

As it moves from sign to sign, the moon brings a different kind of energy to the earth's atmosphere. Those who are particularly sensitive—like Cancers—feel it most strongly. But even the most stolid types are often moved by the effect of the particular sign the moon occupies on any given day, though they may not want to admit it.

Are we then slaves to the moods of the moon? Not if we understand its energies and cooperate with them. If you work *with* the moon and not against her, you can actually make life a lot easier for yourself. For instance, there are certain activities that go more smoothly when the moon is in a particular sign, just as other activities are more difficult to accomplish. Scheduling things accordingly could prevent a lot of frustration. You don't have to become a complete "lunatic" (ancient meaning, "one ruled by the moon") to benefit from its positive vibes, but simply go with the flow. Keep in mind, however, that the moon's effect will be *modified* by your sun sign, so be sure to check out your individual daily prediction. For instance, for *any* sun sign, the days when the moon is in that sign should bring a surge of energy. Whether you handle that energy positively or negatively is up to you.

Here's a rundown of the moods of the moon and the human activities that go with them.

When the Moon Is in Aries There is a very *physical* tone to this day. People may be throwing their weight around in more ways than one. Impatience, independent action, and quick tempers can sprout up all over the place. The good news is that most people will be feeling rather decisive, so some things can be completed. The bad news is that decisions may be totally unilateral; what *you* want may be exactly what someone else *doesn't* want. Similarly, people may be invading each other's territories; "keep off the grass" signs won't mean much today. Rule-breaking is the order of the day, and so are the consequences that go along with it. However, if there's a big mountain to scale, today's the day to begin the climb. If there's a formidable task that requires a lot of get-up-and-go to accomplish, today's the day to plunge in with both feet. If there's something you've been hesitating to tell someone, today you'll get the nerve to say it, but it may be difficult to be tactful. Try, anyway. On the up side, people will be feeling in the mood for some fun and frolic—practical jokes are very "moon in Aries." Even the boss may get in the spirit of things. It's a good day to:

Make a sale	Sharpen knives
Do heavy housework	Stop worrying
Do some baking	Make a clean break
Start a diet	Start an exercise class
Buy a lottery ticket	Do something on your own
Get a haircut	Try a new recipe
Have your eyes checked	Throw a last-minute party

When the Moon Is in Taurus Today, the amber light goes on, and people start to proceed with more caution. Rather than being adventurous, most people will feel like sticking with routine tasks. It is not a good day to try something new. In this more conservative mood, people will tend to hold on to what they have; don't try to borrow money from a friend today. Concentrate on making your own money grow, instead. Speaking of increase, this is an excellent day to "make your garden grow" in every sense of the phrase. Along with a quieter mood of the day, you may feel like pampering yourself a bit; allow yourself at least one luxury. Chocoholics, beware, however; this is a day for food binges and all forms of dietary excess. Creature comforts are a lot on everyone's mind; in fact, it may be difficult to crawl out of that comfortable bed in the morning. And more than a few people will be crawling back into it fairly early—with their favorite person. Sexual cravings are high on the list of "moon moods" today. Enjoy!

It's a good day to:

Put something off until tomorrow	Put up preserves
Buy clothes or jewelry	Have a massage
Get your teeth filled	Start singing lessons
Start a savings account	Sell high on the market
Stick to your guns	Buy a plant
Buy candy	Buy real estate
Stay home and watch television	Hug somebody

When the Moon Is in Gemini There's a touch more energy in the air today, and people will begin moving around a lot more. For some, there will be a lot of nervous energy and the scattery feeling that goes along with it; don't force yourself to concentrate if you can avoid it. It's a day to make connections—call, write, or bump into both new and old friends. Wits are generally sharp today, and people could be cracking jokes all around you. On the other hand, they may also be spilling some secrets. Gossip is easy to start today, and it could spread like wildfire. Mind your mouth! Anything requiring manual dexterity can easily get done today; even those who are usually clumsy may find they have nimble fingers. The tendency today is to do things quickly, if a bit superficially. If there are a couple of things that require a once-over-lightly treatment, get them out of the way now. If you haven't been invited to a party, give your own—or at least plan to get together with some buddies for a little socializing; the time is definitely right.

It's a good day to:

Get your hair cut	Use your hands
Join a club	Pay bills
Have a tooth pulled	Eat out
Sign up for a new course	Take a walk/drive
Send a letter	Call your brother/sister
Try something new	Tell a fib
Learn a language	Do two things at once

When the Moon Is in Cancer In Cancer, the moon is in her very own sign—and you'll know it. All those "moon" characteristics—like changeableness, sensitivity, and the desire for security—will be heightened. Cancers, of course, will feel it most strongly; and the other water signs, Scorpio and Pisces, may be even moodier than usual. The general tendency today is to do things that make you feel comfortable and feel good. For some, that means eating a lot of food; for others, it could be hitting the bottle a bit. People tend to feel a bit sorry for themselves during the transit of the moon through Cancer. When two people who live together are both feeling that way, the result can be a rather touchy day—and evening. As much as you want the comfort of others, you are better off on your own and working off those anxious feelings by yourself. Not for safety, but for comfort's sake, the best place to go today is no farther than your own backyard. You'll probably be feeling very stay-at-home anyway. However, it's an excellent day for memories. Reminisce with somebody you love, or get out that old photo album by yourself. You might find yourself shedding a tear or two, but it's all in a good cause.

It's a good day to:

Bake something delicious	Hug your children
Buy something old	Take care of somebody
Put up preserves	Go without makeup
Buy property	Call your mother
Start a habit	Buy something for the house
Plant something	Entertain at home
Pamper yourself	Give your hair a treatment

When the Moon Is in Leo Today, everyone feels like "coming out of the woodwork." Just as Cancer moon makes you want to hide, Leo moon makes you want to get out there and be seen. Nothing but the best will do on this day, so it could be a rather expensive one. Most people will be more generous than usual—both with their money and their affections; many a new romance has started under a Leo moon. Leo is also one of the more playful signs, so a lot of you will be in the mood for fun and games. Eating out is very Leo moon—and so is picking up the check. Today, you may have to fight for it. However, the boss may be a lot stricter than usual, and even those with nobody to "boss" will try to push somebody around. If you've got children, today you will appreciate them very much—no matter what they do. Most people find themselves reaching for the newest thing in the closet under this transit of the moon. If they don't have anything new to wear, they'll probably go out and buy it—on credit. No matter what time of the year it is, you'll be looking for a little sunshine or at least a warm place. On the beaches or by the fireplaces are where most people would like to be today—wishing life were one long vacation.

It's a good day to:

Borrow money	Buy jewelry
Get a new hairstyle	Invest in the market
Start building something	Do something creative

Follow a hunch   Prepare a gourmet meal
Steal the spotlight   Dress up
Be brave   Kiss somebody new
Be waited on

When the Moon Is in Virgo Now it's back to work, and back to reality. There's a sharp distinction between the Virgo moon mood and what precedes it, so you may shock yourself. Perhaps by deciding it's really time to get organized and then actually *doing* it. On the home front it's a great day to rearrange all those sloppy closets and cupboards. On the job, you couldn't pick a better time to wrestle with that nasty detail work you've been avoiding. However, all is not good news under Virgo moon. For one thing, by contrast to Leo moon's generosity, people will be positively stingy today—both with their money and their love. Even the best of situations could deteriorate today when one or the other of the involved parties decides to point out the other's flaws. Your best course under the Virgo moon is to check that impulse to criticize. People can become highly self-critical during this transit, too. One extreme example of the going-over some people can give themselves during a Virgo moon is to develop mysterious maladies or to discover aches and pains they never felt before. Not to worry; they'll be all better by the time the moon moves into the next sign. Virgo moon is also inspection time, so the boss may be particularly sensitive to messy desks today and sloppiness in general. Keep things buttoned up and tidy for best results.

It's a good time to:

Start a diet   Start a new job
Get a physical   Sew or mend something
Bake bread   Read a good book
Quit smoking   Get a complete makeover
Buy a pet   Call your maiden aunt
Try to do without something   Feel like a martyr
Buy health food   Do a puzzle

When the Moon Is in Libra Now it's time to kiss and make up. Any relationships that suffered from the ragged nerves of Virgo moon time can be nicely patched up today. Pleasantries should be easy for one and all. In fact, even people who are normally rather gruff should smile a bit more today. Libra moon is one of the most social of moon periods; meeting and greeting should be prevalent activities. Most people will want to put their best foot forward, too, so the impulse to dress up and look your best may come upon you. You may feel rather self-indulgent as well; hard work is not as compatible with the Libra moon period as rest and relaxation are. It's definitely a time of togetherness, so even habitual loners may be looking for company. Most people will feel they need people—possibly one special person. Romance blossoms under the Libra moon in its purest form. It's not so much sex people want now as romantic love and companionship. No one's actually made a count, but it's a fair bet that more flowers get sent under the Libra moon than at any other time. Physical beauty is also highly important, so Libra moon is a great one under which to get yourself a whole new look or to redo anything that needs it. Something that's off-balance will bother you more at this time.

It's a good day to:

Be tactful	Forgive and forget
Redecorate	Add color to your life
Give a party	Luxuriate
Fall in love	Sign up for a dance class
Join a singing group	Buy a stereo
Buy something beautiful	Buy a down comforter
Try a new makeup	Learn about wine

When the Moon Is in Scorpio Things could easily get heavy today, and the tendency will be to go to extremes. Haters will hate more; lovers will love more passionately and physically. The sex drive is stimulated in many people during this transit of the moon. With all those intense emotions flying around, it's not surprising that people easily get hot under the collar—and/or imagine that somebody is out to get them. However, there is an up side to the Scorpio moon, and that is the extra jot of will power it gives the most weak-willed people. If you've got to dig in your heels and clench your teeth to get something done, today's the day you will be able to do it. People *endure* a lot under the Scorpio moon. The only problem is that they may develop some resentment toward those they believe should be enduring with them. However, the tendency is to keep silent. In spite of the intense emotionalism of the Scorpio moon, there isn't a lot of outright complaining. People will let the pressure build up inside of them and then burst out into violent rages. If your temper isn't good under the best of circumstances, control it during the Scorpio moon, by all means. It's also a time when people tend to feel a bit claustrophobic; a good walk in the fresh air can work wonders at this time.

It's a good day to:

See a psychiatrist
Buy a house
Open a secret bank account
Make a firm decision
Do your taxes
Throw away what you don't need
Do some strenuous exercise

Have good sex
Face up to a crisis
Read a good mystery
Take body-building
Get a prescription filled
Buy life insurance
Change your life

When the Moon Is in Sagittarius Things definitely lighten up when the moon moves into Sagittarius—and people loosen up, too. In fact, one danger under this moon is getting too relaxed—with your diet, your money, or your generous spirits. Moderation is not the mood of the day, so you may have to force it on yourself. It is not a good time to try to stop smoking—or to stop doing anything self-indulgent. There's definitely a "live and let live" attitude in the air when the moon is in Sagittarius, so bad relations should be easily improved. A spirit of good will is pervasive, as well as a lighthearted attitude. One thing that means is that even normally conservative people will be willing to take chances; those for whom a more liberal outlook is a natural state of affairs could really go too far out on a limb. If you gamble, bet *only* what you can afford to lose today. The place everyone will want to be today is outdoors. In fact, more than one person will simply disappear from the scene to do something either adventurous or relaxing. It's an excellent day to think big, but you may find the follow-through a bit difficult. The big picture is what's easiest to see right now; leave the fine brush strokes for another time. Enjoy the spirit of fun and generosity that should be in the air.

It's a good day to:

Make a long-distance call	Go to church
Plan a trip	Enjoy a hobby
Buy a dog (or a horse)	Learn a new language
Contribute to a wildlife-foundation	Do something charitable
	Borrow money
Try a new approach	Run away from it all
Sell anything to anybody	Get a bigger place
Try your luck/feel lucky	

When the Moon Is in Capricorn In sharp contrast to the "easy come, easy go" feeling of the Sagittarius moon, the moon in Capricorn brings on a much more serious mood. You could call it the "workaholic's moon," and even those whose work style is less intense will find themselves wanting to get a lot done. It's important to *accomplish something* when the moon is in Capricorn, if you are to feel comfortable. Most people want to tread only on solid ground at this time, so there could be a bit of distrust in the air. No one wants to waste time—and least of all on things or people from whom they are not likely to derive some kind of benefit. Another curious facet of the Capricorn moon mood is a tendency to feel older and more serious; some lighter types dislike the feeling so much they will go out of their way to look young. It's the kind of day that matronly secretary in the office is likely to appear in something rather frilly. People can really handle things under the Capricorn moon too; endurance is *very* Capricorn. That means those who exercise will work out harder and longer; those who normally do not push themselves will do at least a little self-prodding. A good image is paramount to many people when the moon is in this sign, and the tendency is for people to be quite status conscious. Self-control is the order of the day, in every respect.

It's a good day to:

Start a new job	Make a list
Buy antiques	Keep your money

Buy anything for investment	Go to the dentist
Wear anything with a good label on it	Start a diet
	Work late
Bet on a favorite	Ask for repayment of a debt
Go to the chiropractor	
Buy insurance	Clean house

When the Moon Is in Aquarius When the moon moves into the sign of Aquarius from the sign of Capricorn, it's as if somebody took the cork out of the bottle. Suddenly, the rather repressed mood bursts into a desire for change—a *need* for change. This is one of those days when people tend to make rash moves like quit a dull job, call it quits with a clinging person, throw out everything in their closet and start all over again. Reaching this point is easy to do under the Aquarian moon. However, it's usually very positive. What's important at this time is to try something new, not just get rid of something old. Some people decide to experiment with a new recipe, a new lover, or a new hair style. It's the kind of day when a woman with long hair will decide to get a crew cut. On the relationship side, the mood now is one of brotherly love and friendship rather than highly charged sexual encounters. Wanting to be with friends and feeling like part of a group is what's important now. No one is a stranger under the Aquarian moon, and talking to people on the street is very common. The thing to be careful of under this moon is doing something irreparable—like finally telling the boss what you really think of him. He/she could easily decide that it's time for a change of personnel.

It's a good day to:

Do something kinky	Buy/wear something crazy
Try a new food	Color your hair
Do something friendly	Contribute to a charity
Start flying lessons	Move to a new place
Do something impulsive	Buy a television/stereo
Join a club	Make a new friend
Make a speculative investment	Be fair

When the Moon Is in Pisces This is a time when people wear their hearts on their sleeves and feel *very* vulnerable. There's a lot of ultrasensitivity under the Pisces moon, and a lot of crying on shoulders—if you can find one that isn't already occupied. Mixed in with the emotionalism is a real feeling of empathy with others; now's the time people feel that everyone is in the same boat. However, it may be a bit difficult to keep things afloat today, because there isn't a lot of firm direction from anyone or anything. It's confusion time, and even the clearest of messages can get a little garbled. Indecisiveness will spread like the plague, so don't expect to get any clear-cut answers today. Creative people get more creative under the Pisces moon, and anyone could feel just a bit poetic. Romantic relationships are heavenly under the Pisces moon as long as they don't get out of control. Keeping certain other things under control—like drinking and other forms of escapism—is a wise precaution, too. The most satisfying and least dangerous escape is to hold hands with someone you love while you watch a real tearjerker movie. Lots of people call in sick under the Pisces moon, and there's a good reason: Most people don't like to cry in public.

It's a good day to:

Put on weight
Fall in love
Develop ESP
Find God
Buy flowers or perfume
Swear off something
Get hooked on something
Write a poem
Take in a stray dog or cat
Visit the sick
See a therapist
Stay home and read
Pamper yourself
Buy a camera

6

Venus and Mars

Love and Sex
Peace and War
Cooperating and Competing

Next to your sun sign, your moon sign, and your rising sign, the positions of Venus and Mars in your horoscope are probably the most important indicators of your personal psychology. This is because Venus shows your affectional nature and Mars shows your sexual nature. To put it another way, *Venus shows your wants and needs in romantic love while Mars shows your sexual style and your manner of expressing it.*

In a broader sense, Venus and Mars are the principles of peace and war. Venus wants to cooperate and relate to others, to share life experiences. Mars is totally concerned with self and getting what you want. Everybody's got a Venus and Mars in their horoscope because every human being has to both live with others and assert him-/herself. It's all a matter of degree. If you want to, you can think of Venus as the "higher" side of human relationships; Mars the "lower." However, you've got to keep in mind that—like all other opposites in the universe—both *cooperating* and *competing* are necessary if the world is to continue going round.

Because Venus has to do with the need to share, the sign in which it is placed will tell a lot about how you attract people you want to share with. It will also show what attracts you to others. Beyond the love arena, the position of Venus in your horoscope shows your attitudes toward money and personal possessions, creature comforts, and things of beauty. Venus is "feminine" in nature, and women tend to relate to their Venus sign more than men. But for *both* sexes, it is an available energy.

The good side of Venus is:
Sharing, beautifying, peacemaking
The bad side is:
acquisitiveness, self-indulgence, laziness

Because the position of Mars shows how you go about getting what you want, it will tell a lot about your personal drive—how *much* you want what you want. It is the desire principle, and will indicate just how passionate your passions are. Ambition, assertiveness, and anger are just a few steps away from each other, so Mars will also reveal what makes you angry or what gets you going. The planet Mars is "masculine" in nature—highly so—and men will find it easier to get in touch with their Mars energy. However, every woman's got a Mars too, and sooner or later a woman's Mars energy will present itself.

The "good" side of Mars is:
Dynamic energy, courage, sexual drive
The "bad" side is:
manipulation, cowardice, sexual abuse

No matter what area of life you are relating these planets to, it is useful to think of them in sexual terms, and of our human sexual organs. Venus is open and receptive; Mars thrusts forward and penetrates. Because we normally attract someone or are attracted to someone before we get sexually involved, Venus energy precedes Mars energy. In other words, Venus shows how *receptive* you are; Mars shows how *active* you are. Venus also has a lot to do with our ideas and images of romance, our romantic fantasies, while Mars is an indicator of sexual fantasies—which may or may not be acted out, depending on the individual's degree of inhibition.

Just as some combinations of people can coexist in constant harmony while others are in constant conflict,

Venus and Mars in an individual person can work well together, or at cross-purposes. When your Venus doesn't get along well with your Mars, you've got a problem. Sometimes a sexual problem, but always an inner conflict. How can you tell if your Venus and Mars are "friends" or "foes"? First, by looking up the positions of your personal Mars and Venus in the charts provided at the end of this chapter, reading the descriptions of those planets in the signs they fall in for you. But, just to make things a bit clearer, here's a rundown of easy Mars/Venus relationships and difficult ones. (By the way, you can also apply this principle in comparing your Venus/Mars positions to those of someone else, as well.)

Venus and Mars are "at war" when:

- One is in a fire sign, and one is in an earth sign. Here you've got a conflict between the practical and the experimental sides of yourself.
- One is in a fire sign and one is in a water sign. One part of you says "let's do it"; the other side says, "I might get hurt," so you might be stalled.
- One is in an earth sign and one is in an air sign. Air likes to think about things a little; earth needs to know it will work. Once again, it may hold you back.
- One is in an air sign and one is in a water sign. Yours is a conflict between the mental relationship and the emotional one; you may find it hard to decide what you want.

Venus and Mars are on good terms when:

- One is in a fire sign, one is in an air sign.
- One is in an earth sign and one is in a water sign.
- Both are in the same element.

Venus and Mars in The Signs

Venus in Aries (fire element)

While this position of Venus in a man or a woman indicates the kind of person who falls in love impulsively, both sexes want to be conquered, when they have Venus in Aries. They may be outrageously flirtatious, but can lead others on a merry chase before they give in. There is a tendency to look for trouble when Venus is in ths position; actually, it is excitement Venus in Aries people crave. Their personal likes and dislikes will be quite clearly defined, and they will be vocal about them. In matters of taste, there is less refinement than when Venus is in a softer sign. Both the males and the females may play up their sexuality in the way they dress; they like very loud things like rock music and bright colors. There is also an impish charm in these people and a tendency to play love games. The *real* goal is to be swept away by a romantic lover who lives up to a mediaeval code of chivalry and/or chastity.

Mars in Aries (fire element)

This is a highly competitive position for Mars; people with Mars in Aries leave no doubt about the fact that they want it, and they want it *now*—whatever "it" is. Mars in Aries can cut through a lot of life's red tape. When it comes to courtship, Mars in Aries people are equally able to disregard the small talk and get right down to business. However, this position of Mars often makes for a rather selfish lover—one who is so concerned with getting that he/she doesn't do an awful lot of giving. Mars in Aries people are likely to turn off as quickly as they turn on. Passion burns brightly, but is often short-lived. They are highly independent and likely to leave if a romantic partner gets too possessive or demanding. Mars in Aries is also always ready for a fight, so relationships are a bit stormy.

Venus in Taurus (earth element)

This is a highly sensual position for Venus to be in. People with Venus in Taurus are turned on by sweet words and soft music—and any form of touching. They like all kinds of nice and beautiful things, and will be attracted by someone who dresses well and has expensive taste. Venus in Taurus people can be a little self-indulgent, but in the main their desire is to make the object of their affection comfortable. And they will do it in very tangible ways; Venus in Taurus people of both sexes like to do things for others. When someone with Venus in Taurus is attracted, he/she is loyal. Love does not come in a flash, as it does with Venus in Aries people, but when it comes, it usually stays. At least as far as the person with Venus in Taurus is concerned. These people are generally so devoted that a breakup is extremely unsettling. You can always make a Venus in Taurus person happy with candy or flowers. The best kind of love feels good, tastes good, looks good, and smells good.

Mars in Taurus (earth element)

This Mars can express itself as ambition with a definite direction—or as controlled sexuality. Mars in Taurus people of both sexes can appear rather lazy, but actually their slow movements are usually on a deliberate course. Some people with Mars in Taurus are really looking for a safe position in a job or with a partner. Their manner of sexuality is highly sensual though they may be slow to get aroused. When a Mars in Taurus person enters into an affair, however, there is usually the intention to make it a long and serious one. These people are certainly capable of quick affairs, but they generally prefer a comfortable relationship where they do not constantly have to keep proving their love. There is a certain giving quality to Mars in Taurus, and the men are exceptionally considerate lovers. The women are fairly passive, but passionate and giving when they get going.

Venus in Gemini

Venus in Gemini people of both sexes tend to be turned on more by *talk* than by physical stimulation. Relationships have to have a mental dimension in order for them to get involved. In fact, Venus in Gemini people are likely to make better friends than lovers. When their affections *are* engaged, the connection is likely to be a little tenuous, and the Venus in Gemini's feelings may not run as deep as his/her partner's. Fickleness is a reality with these people— they like a lot of changes, and that goes for people as well as environments. Job-hopping is a trait of Venus in Gemini, and so is a constant changing of the guard in their romantic lives. However, Venus in Gemini people make wonderful romantic partners, because they are really *interested* in the people they get involved with. Never tell a Venus in Gemini person to "shut up and make love"; he/she will be very likely to shut the door on the relationship.

Mars in Gemini

Mars in Gemini people assert themselves rather erratically; there isn't a lot of staying power, in jobs or in relationships. The "alternating current" of Mars in Gemini energy makes for a rather on again, off again sexual life. People with Mars in this position are capable of having a number of purely mental relationships in between their sexual ones. These are the kind of people who talk their way into things, including a job and someone's bed. Their approach is a bit on the delicate side, and one may wonder when the Mars in Gemini person is really going to get started. However, once their passion is aroused, Mars in Gemini people like a lot of variety; sex can get quite original with these people. The tendency to bore easily goes both for their attitudes toward their sexual partners and the manner in which they have sex. Both sexes are real charmers, however, and sometimes get their way in a rather devious manner.

Venus in Cancer (water element)

The overriding thing that people with Venus in Cancer want is *security*, really the emotional kind, but since a secure home base goes along with their needs, the material kind is important too. Venus in Cancer people can be highly traditional in their romantic values—home, mother, and apple pie are symbols of the things that turn these people on. If you want to engage the emotions of a Venus in Cancer person, all you have to do is look as if you *need* somebody—preferably a mother. Venus in Cancer people need to be needed, but sometimes can go overboard by totally taking over the other person's life. With Venus in this sign, people respond strongly to all kinds of romantic things, from the card that says "I love you" to a little token of affection for no special occasion. However, Venus in Cancer people are highly self-protective, so you first have to break down their natural reserve and fear of getting hurt. Once you do, you won't find a more faithful lover. Except perhaps Taurus.

Mars in Cancer (water element)

Mars in Cancer people can sneak up on you when they've decided they want you; their approach is a bit sideways, like the locomotion of the crab that is the Cancer symbol. They are soft and subtle lovers and said by some to be among the best sexual partners in the zodiac. However, as sensitive and understanding as they tend to be in the sexual area, they can be overly possessive with people they love, and even turn rather cruel when they are rejected. Cancer is a water sign, and it is as if that water starts boiling—invisibly—then the lid totally pops off when the explosion comes. Mars in Cancer people tend to be a little blind to their sexual/ambition drive and can even pretend to themselves that it doesn't exist. For this reason, they make formidable enemies, because while they look as if they are asking for peace they are really preparing for battle.

Venus in Leo (fire element)

There's a pretty simple way to get a Venus in Leo person to like you. Give him/her a lot of attention—*positive* attention. Venus in Leo people do want love, but they want admiration and adulation to come along with it. A bit like Venus in Aries, Venus in Leo wants a *courtly* lover—someone who will swear absolute loyalty. When it's a Leo sun sign person who also has Venus in Leo, you've got the absolute monarch of them all. Venus in Leo also goes only for the best, and is attracted to what looks expensive or rewarding—in both jobs and people. Venus in Leo expects you to dress and look your best, no matter what the circumstances. It is not a "casual" Venus. Demonstrations of love are very important, too. Words are great, of course, and so is a lot of hugging and the rest of the physical love spectrum. However, candy—or some other tangible token of affection—is expected. Venus in Leo has fierce pride, so if you even slip once and appear not to *respect* this person, he/she is likely to brush you off—with a very grand gesture of course.

Mars in Leo (fire element)

Speaking of grand gestures, Mars in Leo wrote the book. This kind of person is the one who will lavish the object of his/her affection with all kinds of luxurious things. Mars in Leo is a real showy person and expects to be appreciated for it. Both the males and the females are aggressive about going after what they want, and once they are happily ensconced—with a lover or a job—they are loyal and steady. However, the down side of the Mars in Leo position is a violent temper: a *really* violent temper. Both sexes can get quite physical in expressing anger. This is the position of the female who throws plates and the man who slaps his faithless lover on the cheek. Mars in Leo is unrelentingly honest—and will expect you to be too. One devious move, and it's over

Venus in Virgo (earth element)

Venus in Virgo wants a love that *works*. Pure sex or romance may appeal to Virgo's desire for the unadulterated, but there's got to be an element of the practical in it too. People with Venus in Virgo often actually fall in love with their jobs faster than they do with people. When Venus is in the sign, you often find the dedicated, loyal, "number two" person who spends a lifetime catering to the needs of a powerful boss. He/she is likely to be just a little bit in love with that boss too. As for sex, the Venus in Virgo person has a very healthy attitude toward it—possibly too healthy in the sense that it is sometimes regarded as an excellent form of exercise. Venus in Virgo people are not really cold—in fact, when they love someone they can't do enough for them, particularly in attending to their physical comfort. The problem is that this position of Venus makes a person overly analytical in determining what he/she wants. If the Venus in Virgo person keeps his/her mouth shut, and doesn't openly criticize, there is a much better possibility that he/she will make good, solid relationships.

Mars in Virgo (earth element)

Virgo's inventive sexuality is one of the best-kept secrets in the zodiac; Mars in Virgo turns out some of the most experimental and skillful lovers of all. That is, if you can attract one of these people in the first place. Mars in Virgo people are far from promiscuous; in fact, their standards are likely to be a bit too high. They are constantly questioning their *own* desires and drives, picking them apart instead of acting upon them. Mars in Virgo is ideal for success in just about any job or profession. With any sun sign, it adds to the ability to cooly analyze problems and solve them with a reasonable amount of dispatch. When it comes to romantic involvement, this is not one of the more "romantic" Mars positions (unless the sun sign is Libra). You may feel as if your Mars in Virgo lover is checking you over first for anything that might turn him/her off. This is the sign that usually says "let's shower together" before he/she says "let's go to bed."

Venus in Libra (air element)

First off, remember that when the planet Venus is in Libra, it's in its "home sign." When it comes to beauty, harmony, and balance, Venus in Libra people want it all. When Venus is in Libra, the most attractive things in life are the *nicest*—people, places, jobs, clothes, you name it. Venus in Libra people want it nice, but they also want it *easy*. In fact, this sometimes "cold" position of Venus can make for a person who marries for status or money. If you look comfortable in every sense of the word, you've got a shot at attracting that Venus in Libra person who catches your eye. And he/she will, because this position of Venus usually confers a great-looking body. Even if the Venus in Libra person loves or marries for convenience, he/she gives an awful lot in return. Once you've engaged his/her love the Venus in Libra person considers you the best, the most beautiful/handsome, and the brightest person in the universe and will treat you accordingly.

Mars in Libra (air element)

This position of Mars often makes for a passive/aggressive type of individual—a specific psychological pattern. The Mars in Libra person rarely goes directly after what he/she wants, but more or less lingers in front of it, waiting for the other person to make the right move. Mars in Libra people don't get hired as quickly as other types because they don't seem to *care* enough about whether or not they get the job. When it comes to love, Mars in Libra can be quite frustrating. You really don't know what's going on here—does or doesn't he/she want to get involved? This is also a rather "refined" position for brash Mars. Mars in Libra people usually have excellent manners, and never appear to get ruffled. They will just sit and smile while you rant and rave. Suddenly, however, they can turn on their heel and walk out the door. The technique Mars in Libra people use to go about making their subtle conquests is *talk*—but it can easily fool you because it seems so casual.

Venus in Scorpio (water element)

A lot of people with sun sign Scorpio have Venus in Scorpio too; (one's Venus sign is often one's sun sign because Venus is so close to the sun in the solar system). These double-whammy Scorpios are extraordinarily intense in all their emotional needs, but anyone with Venus in Scorpio is going to be touched by the madness of this intense sign. The curious paradox is that Venus in Scorpio people are either totally *turned on* by someone or something—or totally *turned off*. There are very few halfway deals in their lives. Venus in Scorpio can also be highly manipulative, adjusting his/her emotions to suit other needs—like money. When Venus is in Scorpio, people are attracted to what seems mysterious, dangerous, or hard-to-get. They love puzzles, and can be a bit of a puzzle themselves to prospective romantic partners. When they do get involved, however, they have a great deal of staying power—emotionally at least. They can fairly easily separate their physical *actions* from their mental states, however.

Mars in Scorpio (water element)

People with Mars in Scorpio have a very strong "energy field" surrounding them; you can almost see it and feel it. What they want, they want passionately—and will seek in no uncertain terms. They are equally positive about what they *don't* want—so you will know whether you've got a shot with them right away. No waiting with *this* aggressive sign. The legendary supersexuality of Scorpio is real with Mars in Scorpio people. However, they may use their sexual power to control other people and situations. And, if they are rejected against their will (which doesn't happen too often) they are capable of the worst kind of venomous reactions. Jealous lovers who are violent to their former partners are a parody of the Mars in Scorpio type of intensity. One way Mars in Scorpio people can hurt or simply tease others is by withholding their love—and their physical passion. They have great powers of self-control.

Venus in Sagittarius (fire element)

People with Venus in the restless, mobile sign of the Centaur often get the reputation for being fickle, and there is more than a grain of truth in that label. But the reason a Venus in Sagittarius person may move around or not become committed is that he/she is so vulnerable to deceit and dishonesty. As the saying goes, "once burned, twice shy," and openhearted, friendly Sagittarius is likely to get burned very early in life. When Venus in Sagittarius people do get involved, they are absolutely delightful to love. Broadminded, unpossessive, full of fun, they really want to enjoy romance. Sagittarius is also a very intellectual sign, so in order to get Venus in Sagittarius people to stick with you for a while, you've got to keep them interested. Sex is great, but sex with talk is even greater for these people. Venus in Sagittarius is also highly idealistic, so you've got to be a higher type to appeal to someone with Venus in this sign. Love is gallantry and honor and all those things that are so hard to find in life.

Mars in Sagittarius (fire element)

Sagittarius is a sign that thinks in global terms, so when Mars is in the sign of Sagittarius, you find a person who wants it all—and often has to be satisfied with nothing. People with Mars in Sagittarius assert themselves bluntly and get right to the point. However, they tend to be so optimistic in their expectations that they may just as quickly decide they have made a mistake. Better luck next love. Mars in Sagittarius doesn't deliberately hurt people; this sign is kind to all—both animals and humans. Their sexual nature can also be rather "animalistic" because this is a lusty sign, and so fond of all outdoor sports that they often want to do it anywhere, anytime. One way Mars in Sagittarius people get to your heart is through your sense of humor; they really know how to make people laugh. It is a powerful weapon in their professional lives too; it's hard to fire someone who is such a delight to have around—even if he/she isn't around that much. The big problem with Mars in Sagittarius people is that they sometimes don't want to take responsibility for their own actions, and lay things on other people. Even if Mars in Sagittarius is the one to break things up, he/she will somehow or other get you to believe that it's *your* fault.

Venus in Capricorn (earth element)

Appearances count a lot to Venus in Capricorn people—in every sense of the word. In order to appeal to them, you've got to look solid and substantial—and fairly rich as well. Because there is a natural reserve to Capricorn, people with Venus in this sign will dislike public displays of affection; the cooler you are in your approach, the better. Their public image and their private one are not too far apart, either. Not that Venus in Capricorn isn't normal; he/she can be quite passionate in bed. But very, very *serious*, too. If you mistake this sign's sober approach to life for coldness, you will not be the first person who has. Once again, like those with Venus in Virgo, Venus in Capricorn is attracted to *practical* people—people who can really work for them in one way or another. While some do actually consciously go after a financially comfortable marital situation, what the vast majority will settle for is someone who is willing to help handle a lot of the more serious aspects of life. Male or female, Venus in Capricorn people want you to be *useful*. Unfortunately, some people with Venus in this sign have such a low sense of self-worth, that they will try to buy love—or sell it—because they don't feel anyone will accept them for what they are.

Mars in Capricorn (earth element)

Mars in Capricorn people always want to know the rules before they enter the game; they assert themselves with extreme caution. However, when they *know* what they want, they have incredible powers to help them get it. One is patience; Mars in Capricorn can wait very well. Another thing they have going for them is self-control; their timing is excellent because they can hold themselves back when they want to. All this makes for a rather sexually confusing type, and sometimes one who is sexually confused. Mars in Capricorn people can go without sex for amazing lengths of time if nothing seems worth the effort. When they do go for it, their approach can be extremely lusty and earthy, as befits the earth element of Capricorn. Even more than someone with Mars in Scorpio, the person with Mars in Capricorn can be a user. In love or business, he/she can easily fake it to get the carrot on the end of the stick. Then, before you know it, the person who seemed so hot for you has now turned stone cold. Sad, but true.

Venus in Aquarius (air element)

The best way to attract someone with Venus in Aquarius is to be a bit unconventional; these people love anyone or anything that is off-beat. However, you may find that you are considered a specimen rather than a romantic partner—or at least that's how it's likely to feel. People with Venus in Aquarius seem to have a real problem with deep involvement; often they really *want* it, but somehow or other their deepest wells of emotion are very difficult to tap.

Their habitual reaction to love is often "easy come, easy go." Are they cruel people? Generally not, and often Venus in Aquarius people suffer a lot from their difficulty with feeling. They will rarely tell you, however, because there is a real need for distance there. And distance is what they seek in one-on-one relationships. If you become possessive with, or jealous of a person with Venus in Aquarius, you will lose him/her very quickly. As with some of the other mental signs like Gemini and Libra, you have got to keep the affair or the marriage *interesting* in one way or another. This is a Venus position that often likes kinky sex, porno movies, and other forms of artificial stimulation. However, they usually don't care enough about sex-for-the-sake-of-sex to be unfaithful.

Mars in Aquarius (air element)

When Mars is in this erratic sign, people tend to go through periods of feast and famine, largely because they can fluctuate between being extremely assertive and sure about what they want or totally inactive. During the latter periods you could actually call the Mars in Aquarius person lazy. In love, the Mars in Aquarius person tends to go after the unusual or difficult; involvements with people who are already attached are quite common. In many cases it is because the Mars in Aquarius person really is terribly afraid of deep involvement. There is a detachment about Mars in Aquarius people that sometimes works against permanent attachment to people or professional situations. Mars in Aquarius really prefers to go it alone. Perhaps the reason is that they always want to be free to experiment with the new. In sex, the Mars in Aquarius person is hung up on technique; he/she likes intelligent sex, and sometimes wants to prove how clever he/she is via this rather bizarre route.

Venus in Pisces (water element)

For people with Venus in Pisces, what's attractive is often bound up with some kind of sacrifice. This is the position of Venus that leads to martyrdom of all kinds. Some Venus in Pisces people find it impossible to get involved with anything or anyone normal and healthy; their instinctive need is to care for the lame and needy. Therefore, many Venus in Pisces people are rather easily taken advantage of by unscrupulous types who use them or take them for all they're worth. By the same token, Venus in Pisces people can put a real *drain* on the object of their affections—demanding more and more proofs of undying love, soulful demonstrations, sometimes even more tangible support. However, in the broadest, most universal sense of the word, Pisces is the "best" position for Venus as it represents the principle of *true love*. True love is totally unselfish, totally self-sacrificing. Though few normal mortals are capable of such "divine" love, Venus in Pisces people come closest to being able to make it. On the more mundane side, people wth Venus in Pisces are attracted by all kinds of sentimental and often impractical things. They will love you most if you spend your last penny on a bouquet of violets rather than bread for the table. So what? You'll just live on love.

Mars in Pisces *(water element)*

Mars in Pisces people can easily lose their way; the sign of Pisces is not stable enough for the aggressive energy of Mars, so Mars in Pisces people tend to scatter their energies in too many places. On the other hand, they are the most subtle and devious people in the zodiac when it comes to going after what they really *do* want. Their come-on is usually to be rather weak and helpless. Both the males and the females snare you by making you think they really *need* you. There's a lot of poetry to Mars in Pisces people, so the start of an affair is likely to be all moonlight and roses. However, you may find that once you are entangled, you can't get yourself out when you want out. Mars in Pisces people have a way of snarling you up in their webs of erratic energy. Just when they've agreed that you should go, they'll become helpless again and make you feel you have to stay. However, Mars in Pisces people do offer a very wonderful kind of love—soft, sensitive, and caring. The object of their desires is often someone similar or someone involved with art or music in some way. However, Pisces types are best off hooking up with a strong partner—someone who can keep their Mars energy on a straight and even course. The best part of Mars in Pisces people is that they are rarely, if ever, cold.

VENUS SIGN 1910–1975

	Aries	Taurus	Gemini	Cancer	Leo	Virgo
1910	5/7-6/3	6/4-6/29	6/30-7/24	7/25-8/18	8/19-9/12	9/13-10/6
1911	2/28-3/23	3/24-4/17	4/18-5/12	5/13-6/8	6/9-7/7	7/8-11/8
1912	4/13-5/6	5/7-5/31	6/1-6/24	6/24-7/18	7/19-8/12	8/13-9/5
1913	2/3-3/6 5/2-5/30	3/7-5/1 5/31-7/7	7/8-8/5	8/6-8/31	9/1-9/26	9/27-10/20
1914	3/14-4/6	4/7-5/1	5/2-5/25	5/26-6/19	6/20-7/15	7/16-8/10
1915	4/27-5/21	5/22-6/15	6/16-7/10	7/11-8/3	8/4-8/28	8/29-9/21
1916	2/14-3/9	3/10-4/5	4/6-5/5	5/6-9/8	9/9-10/7	10/8-11/2
1917	3/29-4/21	4/22-5/15	5/16-6/9	6/10-7/3	7/4-7/28	7/29-8/21
1918	5/7-6/2	6/3-6/28	6/29-7/24	7/25-8/18	8/19-9/11	9/12-10/5
1919	2/27-3/22	3/23-4/16	4/17-5/12	5/13-6/7	6/8-7/7	7/8-11/8
1920	4/12-5/6	5/7-5/30	5/31-6/23	6/24-7/18	7/19-8/11	8/12-9/4
1921	2/3-3/6 4/26-6/1	3/7-4/25 6/2-7/7	7/8-8/5	8/6-8/31	9/1-9/25	9/26-10/20
1922	3/13-4/6	4/7-4/30	5/1-5/25	5/26-6/19	6/20-7/14	7/15-8/9
1923	4/27-5/21	5/22-6/14	6/15-7/9	7/10-8/3	8/4-8/27	8/28-9/20
1924	2/13-3/8	3/9-4/4	4/5-5/5	5/6-9/8	9/9-10/7	10/8-11/12
1925	3/28-4/20	4/21-5/15	5/16-6/8	6/9-7/3	7/4-7/27	7/28-8/21
1926	5/7-6/2	6/3-6/28	6/29-7/23	7/24-8/17	8/18-9/11	9/12-10/5
1927	2/27-3/22	3/23-4/16	4/17-5/11	5/12-6/7	6/8-7/7	7/8-11/9
1928	4/12-5/5	5/6-5/29	5/30-6/23	6/24-7/17	7/18-8/11	8/12-9/4
1929	2/3-3/7 4/20-6/2	3/8-4/19 6/3-7/7	7/8-8/4	8/5-8/30	8/31-9/25	9/26-10/19
1930	3/13-4/5	4/6-4/30	5/1-5/24	5/25-6/18	6/19-7/14	7/15-8/9
1931	4/26-5/20	5/21-6/13	6/14-7/8	7/9-8/2	8/3-8/26	8/27-9/19

VENUS SIGN 1910–1975

Libra	Scorpio	Sagittarius	Capricorn	Aquarius	Pisces
10/7-10/30	10/31-11/23	11/24-12/17	12/18-12/31	1/1-1/15	1/16-1/28
				1/29-4/4	4/5-5/6
11/19-12/8	12/9-12/31		1/1-1/10	1/11-2/2	2/3-2/27
9/6-9/30	1/1-1/4	1/5-1/29	1/30-2/23	2/24-3/18	3/19-4/12
	10/1-10/24	10/25-11/17	11/18-12/12	12/13-12/31	
10/21-11/13	11/14-12/7	12/8-12/31		1/1-1/6	1/7-2/2
8/11-9/6	9/7-10/9	10/10-12/5	1/1-1/24	1/25-2/17	2/18-3/13
	12/6-12/30	12/31			
9/22-10/15	10/16-11/8	1/1-2/6	2/7-3/6	3/7-4/1	4/2-4/26
		11/9-12/2	12/3-12/26	12/27-12/31	
11/3-11/27	11/28-12/21	12/22-12/31		1/1-1/19	1/20-2/13
8/22-9/16	9/17-10/11	1/1-1/14	1/15-2/7	2/8-3/4	3/5-3/28
		10/12-11/6	11/7-12/5	12/6-12/31	
10/6-10/29	10/30-11/22	11/23-12/16	12/17-12/31	1/1-4/5	4/6-5/6
11/9-12/8	12/9-12/31		1/1-1/9	1/10-2/2	2/3-2/26
9/5-9/30	1/1-1/3	1/4-1/28	1/29-2/22	2/23-3/18	3/19-4/11
	9/31-10/23	10/24-11/17	11/18-12/11	12/12-12/31	
10/21-11/13	11/14-12/7	12/8-12/31		1/1-1/6	1/7-2/2
8/10-9/6	9/7-10/10	10/11-11/28	1/1-1/24	1/25-2/16	2/17-3/12
	11/29-12/31				
9/21-10/14	1/1	1/2-2/6	2/7-3/5	3/6-3/31	4/1-4/26
	10/15-11/7	11/8-12/1	12/2-12/25	12/26-12/31	
11/3-11/26	11/27-12/21	12/22-12/31		1/1-1/19	1/20-2/12
8/22-9/15	9/16-10/11	1/1-1/14	1/15-2/7	2/8-3/3	3/4-3/27
		10-12/11-6	11/7-12/5	12/6-12/31	
10/6-10/29	10/30-11/22	11/23-12/16	12/17-12/31	1/1-4/5	4/6-5/6
11/10-12/8	12/9-12/31	1/1-1/7	1/8	1/9-2/1	2/2-2/26
9/5-9/28	1/1-1/3	1/4-1/28	1/29-2/22	2/23-3/17	3/18-4/11
	9/29-10/23	10/24-11/16	11/17-12/11	12/12-12/31	
10/20-11/12	11/13-12/6	12/7-12/30	12/31	1/1-1/5	1/6-2/2
8/10-9/6	9/7-10/11	10/12-11/21	1/1-1/23	1/24-2/16	2/17-3/12
	11/22-12/31				
9/20-10/13	1/1-1/3	1/4-2/6	2/7-3/4	3/5-3/31	4/1-4/25
	10/14-11/6	11/7-11/30	12/1-12/24	12/25-12/31	

VENUS SIGN 1910–1975

	Aries	Taurus	Gemini	Cancer	Leo	Virgo
1932	2/12-3/8	3/9-4/3	4/4-5/5 7/13-7/27	5/6-7/12 7/28-9/8	9/9-10/6	10/7-11/1
1933	3/27-4/19	4/20-5/28	5/29-6/8	6/9-7/2	7/3-7/26	7/27-8/20
1934	5/6-6/1	6/2-6/27	6/28-7/22	7/23-8/16	8/17-9/10	9/11-10/4
1935	2/26-3/21	3/22-4/15	4/16-5/10	5/11-6/6	6/7-7/6	7/7-11/8
1936	4/11-5/4	5/5-5/28	5/29-6/22	6/23-7/16	7/17-8/10	8/11-9/4
1937	2/2-3/8 4/14-6/3	3/9-4/17 6/4-7/6	7/7-8/3	8/4-8/29	8/30-9/24	9/25-10/18
1938	3/12-4/4	4/5-4/28	4/29-5/23	5/24-6/18	6/19-7/13	7/14-8/8
1939	4-25/5/19	5/20-6/13	6/14-7/8	7/9-8/1	8/2-8/25	8/26-9/19
1940	2/12-3/7	3/8-4/3	4/4-5/5 7/5-7/31	5/6-7/4 8/1-9/8	9/9-10/5	10/6-10/31
1941	3/27-4/19	4/20-5/13	5/14-6/6	6/7-6/1	7/2-7/26	7/27-8/20
1942	5/6-6/1	6/2-6/26	6/27-7/22	7/23-8/16	8/17-9/9	9/10-10/3
1943	2/25-3/20	3/21-4/14	4/15-5/10	5/11-6/6	6/7-7/6	7/7-11/8
1944	4-10/5-3	5/4-5/28	5/29-6/21	6/22-7/16	7/17-8/9	8/10-9/2
1945	2/2-3/10 4/7-6/3	3/11-4/6 6/4-7/6	7/7-8/3	8/4-8/29	8/30-9/23	9/24-10/18
1946	3/11-4/4	4/5-4/28	4/29-5/23	5/24-6/17	6/18-7/12	7/13-8/8
1947	4/25-5/19	5/20-6/12	6/13-7/7	7/8-8/1	8/2-8/25	8/26-9/18
1948	2/11-3/7	3/8-4/3	4/4-5/6 6/29-8/2	5/7-6/28 8/3-9/7	9/8-10/5	10/6-10/31
1949	3/26-4/19	4/20-5/13	5/14-6/6	6/7-6/30	7/1-7/25	7/26-8/19
1950	5/5-5/31	6/1-6/26	6/27-7/21	7/22-8/15	8/16-9/9	9/10-10/3
1951	2/25-3/21	3/22-4/15	4/16-5/10	5/11-6/6	6/7-7/7	7/8-11/9
1952	4/10-5/4	5/5-5/28	5/29-6/21	6/22-7/16	7/17-8/9	8/10-9/3
1953	2/2-3/13 4/1-6/5	3/4-3/31 6/6-7/7	7/8-8/3	8/4-8/29	8/30-9/24	9/25-10/18

VENUS SIGN 1910–1975

Libra	Scorpio	Sagittarius	Capricorn	Aquarius	Pisces
11/2-11/25	11/26-12/20	12/21-12/31		1/1-1/18	1/19-2/1
8/21-9/14	9/15-10/10	1/1-1/13	1/14-2/6	2/7-3/2	3/3-3/26
		10/11-11/5	11/6-12/4	12/5-12/31	
10/5-10/28	10/29-11/21	11/22-12/15	12/16-12/31	1/1-4/5	4/6-5/5
11/9-12/7	12/8-12/31		1/1-1/7	1/8-1/31	2/1-2/25
9/5-9/27	1/1-1/2	1/3-1/27	1/28-2/21	2/22-3/16	3/17-4/10
	9/28-10/22	10/23-11/15	11/16-12/10	12/11-12/31	
10/19-11/11	11/12-12/5	12/6-12/29	12/30-12/31	1/1-1/5	1/6-2/1
8/9-9/6	9/7-10/13	10/14-11/14	1/1-1/22	1/23-2/15	2/16-3/11
	11/15-12/31				
9/20-10/13	1/1-1/3	1/4-2/5	2/6-3/4	3/5-3/30	3/31-4/24
	10/14-11/6	11/7-11/30	12/1-12/24	12/25-12/31	
11/1-11/25	11/26-12/19	12/20-12/31		1/1-1/18	1/19-2/11
8/21-9/14	9/15-10/9	1/1-1/12	1/13-2/5	2/6-3/1	3/2-3/26
		10/10-11/5	11/6-12/4	12/5-12/31	
10/4-10/27	10/28-11/20	11/21-12/14	12/15-12/31	1/1-4/4	4/6-5/5
11/9-12/7	12/8-12/31		1/1-1/7	1/8-1/31	2/1-2/24
9/3-9/27	1/1-1/2	1/3-1/27	1/28-2/20	2/21-3/16	3/17-4/9
	9/28-10/21	10/22-11/15	11/16-12/10	12/11-12/31	
10/19-11/11	11/12-12/5	12/6-12/29	12/30-12/31	1/1-1/4	1/5-2/1
8/9-9/6	9/7-10/15	10/16-11/7	1/1-1/21	1/22-2/14	2/15-3/10
	11/8-12/31				
9/19-10/12	1/1-1/4	1/5-2/5	2/6-3/4	3/5-3/29	3/30-4/24
	10/13-11/5	11/6-11/29	11/30-12/23	12/24-12/31	
11/1-1/25	11/26-12/19	12/20-12/31		1/1-1/17	1/18-2/10
8/20-9/14	9/15-10/9	1/1-1/12	1/13-2/5	2/6-3/1	3/2-3/25
		10/10-11/5	11/6-12/5	12/6-12/31	
10/4-10/27	10/28-11/20	11/21-12/13	12/14-12/31	1/1-4/5	4/6-5/4
11/10-12/7	12/8-12/31		1/1-1/7	1/8-1/31	2/1-2/24
9/4-9/27	1/1-1/2	1/3-1/27	1/28-2/20	2/21-3/16	3/17-4/9
	9/28-10/21	10/22-11/15	11/16-12/10	12/11-12/31	
10/19-11/11	11/12-12/5	12/6-12/29	12/30-12/31	1/1-1/5	1/6-2/1

VENUS SIGN 1910–1975

	Aries	Taurus	Gemini	Cancer	Leo	Virgo
1954	3/12-4/4	4/5-4/28	4/29-5/23	5/24-6/17	6/18-7/13	7/14-8/8
1955	4/25-5/19	5/20-6/13	6/14-7/7	7/8-8/1	8/2-8/25	8/26-9/18
1956	2/12-3/7	3/8-4/4	4/5-5/7 6/24-8/4	5/8-6/23 8/5-9/8	9/9-10/5	10/6-10/31
1957	3/26/4-19	4/20-5/13	5/14-6/6	6/7-7/1	7/2-7/26	7/27-8/19
1958	5-6/5-31	6/1-6/26	6/27-7/22	7/23-8/15	8/16-9/9	9/10-10/3
1959	2-25/3-20	3/21-4/14	4/15-5/10	5/11-6/6	6/7-7/8 9/21-9/24	7/9-9/20 9/25-11/9
1960	4-10/5-3	5/4-5/28	5/29-6/21	6/22-7/15	7/16-8/9	8/10-9/2
1961	2-3/6-5	6/6-7/7	7/8-8/3	8/4-8/29	8/30-9/23	9/24-10/17
1962	3/11-4/3	4/4-4/28	4/29-5/22	5/23-6/17	6/18-7/12	7/13-8/8
1963	4/24-5/18	5/19-6/12	6/13-7/7	7/8-7/31	8/1-8/25	8/26-9/18
1964	2/11-3/7	3/8-4/4	4/5-5/9 6/18-8/5	5/10-6/17 8/6-9/8	9/9-10/5	10/6-10/31
1965	3/26-4/18	4/19-5/12	5/13-6/6	6/7-6/30	7/1-7/25	7/26-8/19
1966	5/6-6/31	6/1-6/26	6/27-7/21	7/22-8/15	8/16-9/8	9/9-10/2
1967	2/24-3/20	3/21-4/14	4/15-5/10	5/11-6/6	6/7-7/8 9/10-10/1	7/9-9/9 10/2-11/9
1968	4/9-5/3	5/4-5/27	5/28-6/20	6/21-7/15	7/16-8/8	8/9-9/2
1969	2/3-6/6	6/7-7/6	7/7-8/3	8/4-8/28	8/29-9/22	9/23-10/17
1970	3/11-4/3	4/4-4/27	4/28-5/22	5/23-6/16	6/17-7/12	7/13-8/8
1971	4/24-5/18	5/19-6/12	6/13-7/6	7/7-7/31	8/1-8/24	8/25-9/17
1972	2/11-3/7	3/8-4/3	4/4-5/10 6/12-8/6	5/11-6/11 8/7-9/8	9/9-10/5	10/6-10/30
1973	3/25-4/18	4/18-5/12	5/13-6/5	6/6-6/29	7/1-7/25	7/26-8/19
1974						
	5/5-5/31	6/1-6/25	6/26-7/21	7/22-8/14	8/15-9/8	9/9-10/2
1975	2/24-3/20	3/21-4/13	4/14-5/9	5/10-6/6	6/7-7/9 9/3-10/4	7/10-9/2 10/5-11/9

VENUS SIGN 1910–1975

Libra	Scorpio	Sagittarius	Capricorn	Aquarius	Pisces
8/9-9/6	9/7-10/22	10/23-10/27	1/1-1/22	1/23-2/15	2/16-3/11
	10/28-12/31				
9/19-10/13	1/1-1/6	1/7-2/5	2/6-3/4	3/5-3/30	3/31-4/24
	10/14-11/5	11/6-11/30	12/1-12/24	12/25-12/31	
11/1-11/25	11/26-12/19	12/20-12/31		1/1-1/17	1/18-2/11
8/20-9/14	9/15-10/9	1/1-1/12	1/13-2/5	2/6-3/1	3/2-3/25
		10/10-11/5	11/6-12/16	12/7-12/31	
10/4-10/27	10/28-11/20	11/21-12/14	12/15-12/31	1/1-4/6	4/7-5/5
11/10-12/7	12/8-12/31		1/1-1/7	1/8-1/31	2/1-2/24
9/3-9/26	1/1-1/2	1/3-1/27	1/28-2/20	2/21-3/15	3/16-4/9
	9/27-10/21	10/22-11/15	11/16-12/10	12/11-12/31	
10/18-11/11	11/12-12/4	12/5-12/28	12/29-12/31	1/1-1/5	1/6-2/2
8/9-9/6	9/7-12/31		1/1-1/21	1/22-2/14	2/15-3/10
9/19-10/12	1/1-1/6	1/7-2/5	2/6-3/4	3/5-3/29	3/30-4/23
	10/13-11/5	11/6-11/29	11/30-12/23	12/24-12/31	
11/1-11/24	11/25-12/19	12/20-12/31		1/1-1/16	1/17-2/10
8/20-9/13	9/14-10/9	1/1-1/12	1/13-2/5	2/6-3/1	3/2-3/25
		10/10-11/5	11/6-12/7	12/8-12/31	
10/3-10/26	10/27-11/19	11/20-12/13	2/7-2/25	1/1-2/6	4/7-5/5
			12/14-12/31	2/26-4/6	
11/10-12/7	12/8-12/23		1/1-1/6	1/7-1/30	1/31-2/23
9/3-9/26	1/1	1/2-1/26	1/27-2/20	2/21-3/15	3/16-4/8
	9/27-10/21	10/22-11/14	11/15-12/9	12/10-12/31	
10/18-11/10	11/11-12/4	12/5-12/28	12/29-12/31	1/1-1/4	1/5-2/2
8/9-9/7	9/8-12/31		1/1-1/21	1/22-2/14	2/15-3/10
9/18-10/11	1/1-1/7	1/8-2/5	2/6-3/4	3/5-3/29	3/30-4/23
	10/12-11/5	11/6-11/29	11/30-12/23	12/24-12/31	
	11/25-12/18	12/19-12/31		1/1-1/16	1/17-2/10
10/31-11/24					
8/20-9/13		1/1-1/12	1/13-2/4	2/5-2/28	3/1-3/24
		10/9-11/5	11/6-12/7	12/8-12/31	
			1/30-2/28	1/1-1/29	
10/3-10/26	10/27-11/19	11/20-12/13	12/14-12/31	3/1-4/6	4/7-5/4
			1/1-1/6	1/7-1/30	1/31-2/23
11/10-12/7	12/8-12/31				

MARS SIGN 1910–1975

	Jan.	Feb.	Mar.	Apr.	May	June	July	Aug.	Sept.	Oct.	Nov.	Dec.
1910	AR	TA	GE	GE	CA	CA	LE	VI	VI	LI	SC	SC
1911	SA	CP	AQ	AQ	PI	AR	TA	TA	GE	GE	GE	TA
1912	TA	GE	GE	CA	CA	LE	LE	VI	LI	LI	SC	SA
1913	CP	CP	AQ	PI	AR	AR	TA	GE	CA	CA	CA	CA
1914	CA	CA	CA	CA	LE	LE	VI	LI	LI	SC	SA	SA
1915	CP	AQ	PI	PI	AR	TA	GE	GE	CA	LE	LE	LE
1916	LE	LE	LE	LE	LE	VI	VI	LI	SC	SC	SA	CP
1917	AQ	AQ	PI	AR	TA	GE	GE	CA	LE	LE	VI	VI
1918	LI	LI	VI	VI	VI	VI	LI	LI	SC	SA	SA	CP
1919	AQ	PI	AR	TA	GE	CA	CA	LE	VI	VI	CP	LI
1920	LI	SC	SC	SC	LI	LI	SC	SC	SA	SA	LI	AQ
1921	PI	AR	AR	TA	GE	GE	CA	LE	LE	VI	LI	LI
1922	SC	SC	SA	SA	SA	SA	SA	SA	CP	CP	AQ	AQ
1923	PI	AR	TA	TA	GE	CA	CA	LE	VI	VI	LI	SC
1924	SC	SA	CP	CP	AQ	CA	PI	PI	AQ	AQ	PI	PI
1925	AR	TA	TA	GE	CA	AR	LE	VI	VI	LI	SC	SC
1926	SA	CP	CP	AQ	PI	AR	AR	TA	TA	TA	TA	TA
1927	TA	TA	GE	GE	CA	LE	LE	VI	LI	LI	SC	SA
1928	SA	SA	AQ	PI	PI	AR	TA	GE	GE	CA	CA	CA

MARS SIGN 1910-1975

	Jan.	Feb.	Mar.	Apr.	May	June	July	Aug.	Sept.	Oct.	Nov.	Dec.
1929	GE	GE	CA	CA	LE	LE	VI	VI	LI	SC	SC	SA
1930	CP	AQ	AQ	PI	AR	TA	GE	GE	CA	CA	LE	LE
1931	LE	LE	CA	LE	LE	VI	VI	LI	LI	SC	SA	CP
1932	CP	AQ	PI	AR	TA	TA	GE	CA	CA	LE	VI	VI
1933	VI	VI	VI	VI	VI	VI	LI	LI	SC	SA	SA	CP
1934	AQ	PI	AR	AR	TA	GE	GE	CA	LE	LE	VI	LI
1935	LI	LI	LI	LI	LI	LI	LI	SC	SC	SA	VI	AQ
1936	PI	PI	AR	TA	GE	GE	CA	LE	LE	SA	CP	LI
1937	SC	SC	SA	SA	SC	SC	SC	SA	SA	SA	AQ	AQ
1938	PI	AR	TA	SA	CP	AQ	AQ	CP	CP	VI	LI	SC
1939	SC	SA	SA	CP	GE	CA	LE	LE	VI	VI	AQ	PI
1940	AR	AR	TA	GE	GE	CA	AR	AR	VI	AR	LI	SC
1941	SA	SA	CP	AQ	AQ	PI	AR	VI	VI	LI	AR	AR
1942	TA	TA	GE	GE	CA	LE	LE	VI	VI	GE	SC	SC
1943	SA	CP	AQ	AQ	CA	AR	TA	TA	LI	SC	GE	GE
1944	GE	GE	GE	CA	CA	TA	TA	GE	LI	CA	SC	SA
1945	CP	AQ	AQ	PI	AR	TA	VI	LI	CA	CA	LE	LE
1946	CA	CA	CA	CA	LE	LE	VI	CA	LI	SC	SA	SA
1947	CP	AQ	PI	AR	AR	TA	GE	CA	CA	LE	LE	VI

77

MARS SIGN 1910–1975

	Jan.	Feb.	Mar.	Apr.	May	June	July	Aug.	Sept.	Oct.	Nov.	Dec.
1948	VI	LE	LE	LE	LE	VI	VI	LI	SC	SC	SA	CP
1949	AQ	PI	PI	AR	TA	GE	GE	CA	LE	LE	VI	VI
1950	LI	LI	LI	VI	VI	LI	LI	SC	SC	SA	CP	CP
1951	AQ	PI	AR	TA	TA	GE	CA	CA	LE	VI	VI	LI
1952	LI	SC	SC	SC	SC	SC	SC	SC	SA	CP	CP	AQ
1953	AR	AR	AR	TA	GE	GE	CA	LE	VI	VI	LI	LI
1954	SC	SA	SA	CP	CP	CP	SA	SA	CP	CP	AQ	PI
1955	PI	AR	TA	GE	GE	CA	LE	LE	VI	LI	LI	SC
1956	SA	SA	CP	AQ	AQ	PI	PI	PI	PI	PI	SC	AR
1957	AR	TA	TA	GE	CA	CA	LE	VI	VI	LI	SC	SC
1958	SA	CP	CP	AQ	PI	AR	AR	AR	TA	GE	TA	TA
1959	TA	GE	GE	CA	LE	LE	LE	TA	TA	LI	SC	SA
1960	CP	CP	AQ	CA	CA	AR	TA	VI	LI	CA	CA	SA
1961	CA	CA	AQ	PI	PI	AR	VI	VI	GE	SC	SA	CA
1962	CP	AQ	PI	PI	AR	TA	GE	GE	CA	LE	LE	SA
1963	LE	LE	LE	LE	LE	LE	VI	LI	SC	SC	SA	LE
1964	AQ	AQ	PI	AR	AR	TA	GE	LI	LE	LE	SA	CP
1965	VI	VI	VI	VI	VI	VI	LI	LI	SC	SA	VI	VI
1966	AQ	PI	AR	AR	TA	GE	CA	CA	LE	VI	VI	LI

78

MARS SIGN 1910–1975

	Jan.	Feb.	Mar.	Apr.	May	June	July	Aug.	Sept.	Oct.	Nov.	Dec.
1967	LI	SC	SC	LI	LI	LI	LI	SC	SA	SA	CP	AQ
1968	PI	PI	AR	TA	GE	GE	CA	LE	LE	VI	LI	LI
1969	SC	SC	SA	SA	SA	SA	SA	SA	SA	CP	AQ	PI
1970	PI	AR	TA	TA	GE	CA	CA	LE	VI	VI	LI	SC
1971	SC	SA	CP	CP	AQ	AQ	AQ	AQ	AQ	AQ	PI	PI
1972	AR	TA	TA	GE	CA	CA	LE	LE	VI	LI	SC	SC
1973	SA	CP	CP	AQ	PI	PI	AR	TA	TA	TA	AR	AR
1974	TA	TA	GE	GE	CA	LE	LE	VI	LI	LI	SC	SA
1975	SA	CP	AQ	PI	PI	AR	TA	GE	GE	GE	CA	GE

AR—Aries
TA—Taurus
GE—Gemini
CA—Cancer
LE—Leo
VI—Virgo
LI—Libra
SC—Scorpio
SA—Sagittarius
CP—Capricorn
AQ—Aquarius
PI—Pisces

9

The Planets As "Stars"

The Astrological Cast of Characters in Order of Their Appearance

As you learned in the chapter "Defining Terms," the planets are the *sine qua non* of astrology—the factor without which there would be no such study. It is the placement of the planets in the signs of the zodiac that give those signs meaning in human terms, and the placement of the planets in an individual horoscope that "spell out" that individual's character/personality. As for forecasting, it is the movement (transits) of the planets throughout our lifetime that activate one part of our chart or another and bring out certain life conditions.

Those planets are moving bodies and not "stars" in the astrological sense, though they are sometimes referred to with that word. In Shakespeare's play, *Julius Caesar*, Cassius, one of the conspirators, states, "The fault, dear Brutus, is not in our stars but in ourselves that we are underlings." Shakespeare (Cassius) actually knew what he was talking about because astrology was part and parcel of daily life in Elizabethan times when the play was written, as well as in Caesar's ancient Rome. However, Shakespeare seems to have preferred "stars" as a more poetic word than "planets." He also was right about another thing: The "stars" (planets) don't push people around unless you let them. The key is to understand the role each planet plays in your basic astrological makeup through your natal chart and to get to know yourself via this ancient and pragmatic science. Then you will better understand how the transits of the different planets are most likely to affect you.

Though the planets are not stars by astronomical definition (except for the sun), they do play the starring roles in the great cosmic drama that is acted out every day of our lives, and has been since the beginning of life on earth. There are other heavenly bodies—like the asteroids—that play supporting roles, but most astrologers take the Big Ten into consideration when they do a chart or a personal forecast: the sun, the moon, Mercury, Venus, Mars, Jupiter, Saturn, Uranus, Neptune, and Pluto. (Some of these planets, like the Moon, Venus, and Mars, are touched on in other parts of this book, and you may want to read those sections to get a better understanding of their characteristics.)

Each planet rules one or more signs of the zodiac—i.e., is very closely associated with that sign or signs. The one that rules your sun sign is your own personal planet, so to speak, and its description will fill in more of the background of your sign.

The following is a rundown of the planetary cast of characters, presented in their order of appearance, their actual position in our solar system As you know, the sun is the center of our solar system, and the orbits of the planets form rings around it. Looking at the planets this way underscores the fact that the *closer* planets influence us much more strongly as individuals. Planets farther out in the solar system are not only farther away, they also move much more slowly. While a transit of the moon lasts two days, for instance, a transit of Uranus (which takes eighty-four years to circle the zodiac) may influence your life for many months. However, even with these distant planets, their position in a specific *house* of your own horoscope will greatly influence your astrological makeup.

The Sun

Vital Statistics: 864,000 miles in diameter; average distance from earth, 93 million miles; gaseous nature. Appears to circle the zodiac in 365 days.

Rules: The sign of Leo
Fourth period of life: ages 23 to 41
Role: The true "star" . . . the male lead . . . the doer . . . the activator.
Facts and Foibles: The position of the sun in anyone's horoscope is the central fact about that person, astrologically speaking. Your sun sign is your core—your individuality. It is your ego in the best sense of the word, the part of you that moves you in a certain life direction. No matter what your sun sign is, true self-development means developing the highest potential of that sign. People really grow into their sun signs as they mature, and the sun symbolically governs that stage of life (23 to 41) at which we are (or should be) mature individuals who are concerned with creating something in our own right. The sun is considered a masculine planet, because it is the fiery, animating force of life. We are meant to *express* our sun sign; those who do not can literally have a lifeless quality about them.

Those born under the sign of Leo have been said to be favored because of their rulership by the most important "planet" of them all. In ancient times, the sun was often the chief deity and was worshipped for its extraordinary power. It was recognized that without the sun, life on earth could not exist, and the dimming of its light via an eclipse was a terrifying experience for early civilizations that recognized their dependence upon its warmth and vitalizing nature. Whether or not Leo is a special sign is debatable, but there is no doubt that there is a tendency in some Leo sun sign people to become overly self-centered. Perhaps even unconsciously, they sense that it is a heady destiny to be ruled by the sun, but they are unable to handle its tremendous energies properly.

The Moon

Vital Statistics: 238,857 miles from the earth; 2,160 miles in diameter (one-fourth earth's size). Revolves around the earth (circles the zodiac) in about 27 ½ days
Rules: The sign of cancer
The first four years of human life

Role: The leading lady ... the "feeler" ... the mother ... the reactor.

Facts and Foibles: The moon is not exactly a planet, either; it is a satellite of our own planet, earth. However, it is the largest satellite with respect to its parent planet anywhere in the solar system that we know of. It has a tremendous gravitational pull, which is demonstrated on earth by the changing of the tides and other natural phenomena.

The moon has no light of its own, and we can see it shining only because it reflects the sun. Therefore, the moon is considered a *receptive* or "feminine" planet, rather than an active one like the sun. The moon in mythology has always been a woman—often the "Great Mother" to ancient peoples who saw the sun as the "Great Father." Accordingly, the moon rules the first four years of human life, when we are totally dependent on our mothers, and the motherly sign of Cancer, which is closely associated with nurturing and growth. In an individual horoscope, the position of the moon indicates our ability to feel and to respond emotionally. It is our impressionability and sensitivity, i.e., our subjective rather than our objective sign. The moon reacts to experience and remembers it. All our memories are stored in our subconscious, which is the part of the human psyche the moon signifies. In a sense, as the moon rules the night, it rules our dark or hidden side. As it takes some time for us to develop or grow into our sun sign, the moon sign manifests itself much more strongly in young children than the sun sign does. The moon represents the instinctual nature connected with infantile responses; our moon sign acts from habit, often without thinking.

Mercury

Vital Statistics: 36 million miles away from the sun; 2,900 miles in diameter; orbits sun at 108,000 miles per hour; goes through zodiac in 88 days.

Rules: The signs of Gemini and Virgo
Age of curiosity: 4 through 14

Role: The young male lead ... the observer ... the messenger ... the communicator.

Facts and Foibles: Mercury is the hottest, quickest, and smallest of the planets, and is closest to the sun. It is so closely associated with the sun in an astronomical sense, that Mercury is very often in the same sign as the sun in a natal chart. In any horoscope, it is never more than two signs away from your sun sign.

In ancient times Mercury was regarded as the sun's messenger, and the gods with whom it was associated always had some kind of communicating function. In Egypt, Mercury was Thoth—scribe to the gods, keeper of the divine books. The Greeks called him Hermes, the messenger; the Romans renamed him Mercury, but assigned similar functions. Hermes/Mercury always had a golden tongue, and was regarded as the great persuader. Quickness and deftness also associate Mercury with all kinds of human skills requiring manual and mental dexterity.

Mercury has a double role to play as ruler of the signs of Gemini and Virgo. In a sense, Mercury is two-faced; the communicative side in Gemini, his precise specialist side in Virgo. No matter what your sun sign is, in your horoscope Mercury symbolizes your style of thinking and communicating—not so much how intelligent you are as how you tend to put things together mentally.

Mercury is a very human planet, and has a very human foible; occasionally he gets things all mixed up and causes a lot of trouble. About three times a year, for about three weeks at a time, Mercury seems to be going *backwards*. (That appearance is caused by the varying rates of speed of various planets—like two trains traveling in the same direction that can seem as if they are traveling in two different directions.) During these periods Mercury is said to be *retrograde,* it is known to cause problems in all kinds of human interactions. People get the wrong message, or don't get it at all. People who are supposed to meet on a street corner never find each other. Trains and planes are missed, luggage is lost, orders simply never get transmitted or seem to vanish in thin air. There has been quite a bit of research on Mercury retrograde, and it all proves out. Even if people don't know *why* retrograde Mercury

makes things go wrong, they sure know it does. In 1986 Mercury will be retrograde during these periods:
March 7 through March 30.
July 9 through August 3.
November 2 through November 22.

Venus

Vital Statistics: 67.2 million miles from the sun; 26 million to 160 million miles from earth; approximately the same size and volume as earth. Goes through all twelve signs of the zodiac in about 225 days.

Rules: The signs of Taurus and Libra
Period of developing sexuality: ages 14 to 21

Role: The young, nubile female lead . . . the love interest . . . the artist.

Facts and Foibles: Like Mercury, Venus follows the sun very closely, so in anyone's horoscope it is never very far away from your sun sign. Symbolically, Venus represents your capacity to love and relate, and the capacity to appreciate beauty. In ancient myth, Venus was seen as the daughter of the moon, a feminine planet associated with many of the earthly things traditionally associated with women: the providing of food and shelter, the beautifying of the home, the harmonizing of opposites and settler of strife. Venus is a peaceful planet in every sense of the word. Aphrodite to the Greeks, Venus to the Romans, this goddess/planet was seen as the bounteous giver of life's gifts and pleasures—the personification of beauty. She is supposed to inspire us with the desire for both material and spiritual growth.

Like Mercury, Venus has two faces, but, strangely, one rules a feminine sign, Taurus, and one rules a masculine sign, Libra. In Taurus, Venus shows her earthier side, more concerned with creature comforts, sex, and material prosperity. In Libra, a more refined Venus shines forth as the graceful "hostess," the one who beautifies things and relates to others.

Though most Libra males are quite virile, their rulership by the planet Venus often manifests itself in extremely good looks and a great appreciation of beauty. The virile male hairdresser or interior decorator is the personification of this side of Venus. Because Venus seeks peace rather than war, harmony rather than discord, she rules lawyers, mediators, and arbitrators.

Since Venus rules one feminine earth sign and one masculine air sign, she is sometimes seen as a symbol for the fact that all things in the universe can be made to work in harmony—even the incompatible elements of air (Libra) and earth (Taurus) and the often antagonistic principles of male and female—in real life as in astrology. Divorce courts come under the rulership of Venus.

Mars

Vital Statistics: 14 million miles from the sun; 35 million miles from earth; 10 percent of earth's size; circles the zodiac in about 687 days.
Rules: The sign of Aries
Ages 42 to 56
Role: The virile male antagonist . . . the lover . . . the warrior.
Facts and foibles: Mars is a rather small planet and has sometimes been called "Earth's little brother." However, since ancient times Mars has been attributed with great powers—possibly because of its fiery red color. Even the earliest peoples associated Mars with strife and sex and a warriorlike attitude. In fact, Mars has had a rather bad reputation in astrology and was sometimes known as the "lesser malefic." But some groups assigned Mars another role and gave him a different dimension. The Egyptians called Mars Artes, and connected him with personal creative expression; to the Hebrews he played a similar role. When you think about it, sex, strife, and creative expression are only a few steps away from each other. Certainly, the act of procreation is a creative one, as it gives new life. War and strife are divisive, but often a new order comes out of them as well.

Mars is pure masculine energy—sometimes a bit rough, but always determined. In a personal horoscope, the sign position of Mars tells how you tend to assert yourself, how aggressive you are likely to be when going after what you want, even how much you will want it. Mars is our desire nature. (See the chapter on Venus and Mars to find out more about Mars in your own horoscope.) As the god of war, Mars is associated with courage and bravery, traits that are available to the Aries sun sign person if he/she cares to develop them. Mars is moral courage too, and the Mars-ruled Aries sun sign person at his/her best will never desert a cause or a person—no matter how rough the going gets.

About once every two years Mars returns to the same place it occupied on the day of your birth; to astrologers this is known as the "Mars return." It is a period of time during which one can make great strides, because Mars is stimulating that area of the natal chart connected with taking on the world. People often feel a great surge of energy during their Mars return, but if that energy is not directed in a productive channel, it can cause a lot of problems in relationships. You are far better taking out your Mars return aggressiveness on another job or another creative project rather than another person.

Jupiter

Vital Statistics: Largest planet in the solar system, 318 times larger than earth; 365 million to 600 million miles from earth; gaseous nature; circles the zodiac in about 12 years.
Rules: The sign of Sagittarius
　　　　Ages 57 to 68
Role: The hero ... the "father confessor" ... the one who saves the day.
Facts and Foibles: From earliest times, Jupiter was assigned a role in the "cosmic drama" almost as important as that of the sun. Huge and luminous, Jupiter was easily visible to the naked eye eons before the age of the telescope. The sun may have been god in the all-encompassing sense, but Jupiter was *the* god who could make things happen, even interfere in human affairs if he was needed. And he has always been a "good guy." The Hindus, whose roots lie in antiquity, call him Vishnu, the preserver. To the Greeks, he was Zeus, the god

who reigned supreme on Mount Olympus; he became Jupiter under the Romans. The important thing about this masculine god-planet is that it has always been very godly but very human at the same time. Zeus frequently came down from Mount Olympus to bestow his favors on people—particularly women who caught his fancy (causing his wife Hera to become jealous). Jupiter-Zeus is the god who keeps one foot in heaven and one foot firmly planted on the earth. Since the planet itself is large and impressive-looking, it has always been associated with benevolence and expansiveness. Our English word "jovial" has its roots in the name Jove, by which name Jupiter was sometimes called.

Joviality is one of the characteristics that is available to people born under the sign of Sagittarius, which Jupiter rules. Some Sagittarians are jovial, they spend all their money and all their energy on making life one long party.

But Jupiter has a serious side, too. Jupiter is associated with the divine law, and the ability to make that law known to men on earth. The higher Sagittarian, ruled by Jupiter, has a sense of this mission, and often takes the real-life role of priest-missionary or teacher of higher studies. While Venus and Libra, the sign Venus rules, are associated with the *practice* of law, Jupiter and Sagittarius are connected with the *making* and *interpretation* of laws.

Saturn

Vital Statistics: 75,000 miles in diameter, 95 times as big as earth; 886 million miles from the sun; takes 29 years to circle the zodiac.
Rules: The sign of Capricorn
Ages 68 on
Role: The "older man" ... the taskmaster ... the disciplining father.
Facts and Foibles: Like Jupiter, Saturn is so large it can be seen with the naked eye from earth and was watched carefully by early peoples. It was quickly observed that certain transits of Saturn brought trials and troubles on earth and so the planet earned itself the name of the

"greater malefic" by the time astrologers had begun to record their findings. Is Saturn really a "bad guy" as so many astrology books will tell you? There is no question that Saturn represents the principle of limitation; when you go too far out on a limb or get over expansive, Saturn is always there to teach you that there are rules and restrictions. However, as Saturn also represents the principle of contraction, this planet can and does bring periods of time in which we can consolidate our forces and make a secure place for ourselves in this world.

Saturn is also sometimes called the "lord of Karma." Translated into human terms, that means that Saturn represents our inevitable responsibilities, our "fated" duties in this world. Once again, there is a positive side. When Saturn is strongly placed in an individual's chart, that individual is exceptionally able to handle responsibility and achieve worldly success. As ruler of the sign of Capricorn, Saturn brings to that sign an extraordinary talent for working long and hard as well as reaping the material rewards that come with dedication to a task.

Kronos (or Chronos) was the ancient Greek god who is generally regarded as the prototype for Saturn's particular personality or role, and his story sheds a lot of light on the perceptions of this planet. Kronos was born to the very highest ancient god, Ouranos, and to the original earth mother, Ge. Kronos got a little carried away with this position and overthrew his father (castrating him) to take over the throne. When Kronos was told one of his own children would do the same to him, he swallowed them all—except Zeus, who was miraculously saved and became the "avenger." Later on, Zeus banished Kronos into exile. We know Kronos as Father Time—that shadowy old man who reminds us that it's later than we think. Kronos/Saturn also cautions against runaway ambitions, which is often punished by a downfall like his.

One of the most fascinating aspects of Saturn is that it is an uncannily accurate cosmic clock. Taking about 29 years to make a full circle of the zodiac, Saturn returns to the same place it occupied in your horoscope at your birth when you are about 29 years old. The "Saturn return" is regarded by astrologers as the true end of childhood (astrology is kind to us weak mortals by giving us more time to "grow up" than conventional earthly wisdom does). When Saturn begins to creep up on us in our late twenties, we generally begin to feel that it's time to settle down and do something big in the way of taking on earthly responsibility. Many people go through a "life crisis" at this time, because they feel the push that Saturn is giving them, but have trouble knowing what to do about it. Many, many people resolve the dilemma by getting married, buying a home, having a child, or getting divorced. The point is that it is time to *do something decisive* and to take responsibility for our own lives and actions. There are an incredible number of "Saturn return babies" because having a child is probably the most joyful as well as the biggest responsibility a person can assume.

On its second return—at about the human age of 58—people are generally ready to start relaxing their responsibilities and enjoying the fruits of their labors. It is a wise precaution to make ready for the second Saturn return, because just as Saturn tells us we have to *work*, he also tells us when it is time to *stop* working. But remain a productive human being, with real interests and the wherewithal to pursue them.

Uranus

Vital Statistics: 1.7 billion miles from earth; 29,300 miles in diameter, 15 times larger than earth; takes 84 years to circle the zodiac; has an erratic orbit.
Rules: The sign of Aquarius
Teenagers
Role: The rebel ... the home-wrecker ... the visionary.
Facts and Foibles: Uranus is the first of the "modern" planets, i.e., those unknown to the ancients, and only discovered via the telescope. Uranus, the first planet to be discovered in this manner, was thus a shock to both astronomers and astrologers. Both groups believed the orbit of Saturn defined the limits of our solar system,

and both had to revise their thinking at this discovery. Astrologers took things in their stride by calling Uranus a "planet of the higher octave" and interpreting it as a breakthrough from the realm of purely earthly influences (with Saturn as the dividing line) to the "cosmic" or "higher" order of things. They decided that Uranus—an unconventional planet in many respects—must be the ruler of the quirky sign of Aquarius (which had been formerly ruled by Saturn). In a way it is uncanny that the sudden discovery of Uranus in 1781 heralded all the breakthrough discoveries of the 19th and 20th centuries. In a sense, Uranus ushered in the modern world; it also rules our current Age of Aquarius. As that age (approximately 2000 years long) will continue to shock us with discovery after discovery, it hopefully will also bring us the sense of brotherhood of humanity that is the hallmark of the sign of Aquarius.

As Uranus takes 84 years to circle the zodiac, it stays in each sign about seven years. (It is currently about two-thirds of the way through the sign of Sagittarius.) Whatever Uranus touches as it transits a person's natal chart gets a real jolt. Sometimes very suddenly. Uranus hates the status quo and almost always shakes it up. That means that a lot of changes take place when Uranus comes along, but for most people those changes are eventually positive ones. Uranus gets you out of whatever rut you happen to be in and does it quite forcefully. However, those who resist the changes Uranus "suggests" can cause themselves a lot of trouble. If you aren't willing to bend, Uranus can really "break you up."

Uranus is appropriately associated with the teen years, during which young people are often in a state of rebellion. However, here too, it is a *necessary* fact of life that people must eventually rebel against the strictures of childhood in order to become separate individual human beings. Uranus is associated not only with teenagers, but also with many of the things that represent their rebellion, like rock music, blaring radios, and all that goes with them. In essence, Uranus is the symbol of the electronic modern world.

Neptune

Vital Statistics: 2.6 billion miles from earth; 2.7 billion miles from the sun; takes about 165 years to circle the zodiac.

Rules: The sign of Pisces
No specific age.

Role: The fascinating stranger ... the poet ... the one who confuses the issue... the dreamer of great dreams.

Facts and Foibles: As it is difficult to get a handle on people heavily influenced by Neptune (like Pisceans), it took astronomers a while to figure out what Neptune really was. At first they observed nothing but some rather weird abberations in the orbit of Uranus as they began to plot that planet's orbit. In the early 1840s, some of them proved mathematically that there *must* be another planet out there, although it couldn't be seen. Finally, using all the data at hand, a German astronomer spotted Neptune in 1846.

There is a rather "sneaky" character to Neptune, but what this nebulous planet really symbolizes is the love that passes all understanding, the all-encompassing universal love that is virtually impossible for mortals to feel and give. Venus represents two-way love, the sharing kind. Neptune's love goes only in one direction. Neptune gives in a sense of self-sacrifice, and takes nothing in return.

There is evidence that even though no one really *saw* Neptune until 1846, the ancients knew all about its principles, and embodied them in the mythical figure of Poseidon (later called Neptune), the lord of the seas, master of the deep. When you think that more than three-quarters of the earth's surface is covered by water, you realize that Neptune was pretty important in the overall scheme of things. In fact, according to the Greeks, when the universe was created, it was divided among Zeus-Jupiter, who took the heavens, Hades-Pluto who took the underworld, and Poseidon-Neptune who took the oceans.

Just as water is difficult to contain, it is difficult for many people to get in touch with Neptune's higher qualities in their own charts. Water is soul and spirit, metaphysically speaking, so Neptune should make us aspire to much higher things. Not only universal love, but poetry, music and art in its purest forms. However, what Neptune touches in most people's natal charts often turns into an area of confusion rather than creativity. Neptune rules liquid in all its forms and, unfortunately, some people react to Neptune's confusing vibes by turning to alcohol or drugs. For many drug and alcohol abusers, however, the real goal of their vice is to attain a kind of "cosmic consciousness" which is the real realm of Neptune.

Since Neptune takes 165 years to circle the zodiac, it stays in one sign for 13 years or more. Therefore, it is the zodiacal *sign* Neptune makes to the "personal planets" in your chart that really count. People positively influenced by Neptune make the true artists and poets of this world—as well as the visionaries who interpret its meaning in more philosophical and metaphysical terms.

Pluto

Vital Statistics: 3,666 billion miles from the sun; takes about 242 years to circle the zodiac.
Rules: The sign of Scorpio
Prenatal
Role: The "heavy" . . . the transformer . . . the tragic hero.
Facts and Foibles: As you will note, Pluto is a little light on vital statistics. That's because this immensely distant planet, only discovered in 1930, has yet to reveal some of its secrets to astronomers. Like Neptune, it was discovered only because of the erratic nature of the orbit of Uranus. But, even when Pluto was conclusively sighted in 1930, its small size relative to its extremely strong gravitational pull didn't make sense to astronomers. Either Pluto is much larger than we now think or it is so dense that it exerts a force much greater than its size should account for.

Either way, there's no doubt that Pluto represents *power*. In fact, many astrologers connect the discovery of Pluto with the discovery by man of the extraordinary power in matter itself—the power of the atom. As with Neptune, Pluto's "realm" had been staked out in myth and astrology long before its actual discovery. Pluto is Hades, lord of the underworld—the place of darkness that all men fear. However, since most older religions regard life and death as a cycle, Pluto represents rebirth as well. We die only to be reborn. One of the symbols for Pluto is the Phoenix that rises triumphantly from its own ashes. Pluto—and the sign of Scorpio that it rules—hold onto their secrets, but have an incredible power to endure and triumph over life's circumstances. The extremes of life and death that Pluto/Scorpio is associated with connect neatly with the extremism of this astrological sign. "Plutonic" Scorpios often regard the world as totally black and white, with very few grays in between. They can also be the "best" of people, like reformers and religious leaders, or the "worst" of people, like criminals and those who manipulate others for their own purposes.

10

Astrotrivia

How Do You Rate in the Best Game in Town?

The ancient art of astrology is loaded with bits and pieces of miscellaneous information—all of it fascinating, and some of it more useful than you may think. For instance, did you know that every zodiac sign has a special day of the week and certain colors assigned to it? And, how good are you at guessing sun signs of celebrities—those larger-than-life models of sun signs in the flesh? The Astrotrivia that follows is partly in quiz form, partly in short-take astrological facts. In the first part, you can test your own astrological perceptivity; in the second, you can add a lot to your fund of astrological information—and maybe even learn a few things, you can use in your daily life.

Astrotrivia Part I
Sun Signs of the Rich and Famous

Try to answer the following questions yourself; if you're stumped you'll find the answers on page 103–104.

1. What famous stripper and the famous actress who played her mother in a Broadway show have the sign of Capricorn in common?

2. What two show biz buddies—who run in the same pack—are both Sagittarians?

3. What do these people have in common: Joseph Stalin, Richard Nixon, Herman Goering, Al Capone, and Mao Tse Tung?

4. What two handsome male movie stars, both known for their progressive ideas, have the same sun sign? And, what is it?

5. What highly Scorpionic actor had an on-again, off-again lifetime romance with a glamourous Pisces actress?

6. What two female tennis pros are both athletic Sagittarians?

7. What U.S. president had a "show-me-I'm-from-Missouri" personality, and what was his sun sign?

8. What two famous "lonely hearts" columnists get their soft Cancerian shoulders cried on all the time?

9. What two "greats" of American popular music were both thoroughly American, and both born on the Fourth of July?

10. Under what sign were these warrior peacemakers all born: Dwight D. Eisenhower, David Ben Gurion, Jimmy Carter, Mohandus Ghandi, and Eleanor Roosevelt?

11. What anti-American villainess of World War II was born on the Fourth of July?

12. What sun sign do these people have in common: Oscar Wilde, Truman Capote, and Gore Vidal?

13. What two famous rock stars—one early, one late—were born not only under the same sign, but on the same day?

14. Which of the following is/was not a Scorpio?
    Charles Manson   Robert Kennedy
    Bo Derek   Pablo Picasso
    Katherine Hepburn   Indira Ghandi
    Princess Grace   Johnny Carson
    Henry Kissinger   Billy Graham

15. All of the following were born under the two most musical signs of the zodiac. What are they?

Judy Collins	Michael Jackson
Barbra Steisand	George Gershwin
Stevie Wonder	Luciano Pavarotti
Fred Astaire	Paul Simon
Irving Berlin	Julie Andrews
Bing Crosby	Anthony Newly
Beverly Sills	John Lennon
Bobby Darin	Guiseppe Verdi

16. All the following ladies of the stage and screen are masters of their craft. Which craftsman-like sun sign were they all born under?

Lauren Bacall	Celeste Holm
Anne Bancroft	Greer Garson
Ingrid Bergman	Twiggy
Greta Garbo	Jo Ann Worley
Sophia Loren	Claudette Colbert
Lilly Tomlin	Raquel Welch

17. What sun sign do the following famous rebels and rule-breakers have in common: Marlon Brando, Warren Beatty, Eddie Murphy, Charlie Chaplin, Hugh Hefner?

18. What sun sign do these medical and research geniuses have in common: Madame Curie, Jonas Salk, Christian Bernard?

19. What present-day famous Leo "princess" lived in Camelot with her Gemini "prince"?

20. What two great ballet stars were both born in the same country, and share the graceful sun sign, Pisces?

Answers on p. 103–104

Astrotrivia Part II
More Celebrity Sun Sign Lore

Just a handful of the many, many stage/screen-struck Leos:

Robert DeNiro	Julia Child
Mike Jagger	Arlene Dahl
Lucille Ball	Alfred Hitchcock
Dustin Hoffman	Mae West
Cecil B. Demille	George Bernard Shaw
John Derek	Dino D. Laurentis
Mike Douglas	Robert Mitchum
Robert Redford	Peter O'Toole
Jason Robards Jr.	Roman Polanski
Esther Williams	Jill St. John
Stanley Kubrick	Robert Taylor
Shelly Winters	Keenan Wynn

And here are some Leos who make/made the international scene their stage:

Fidel Castro	Henry Ford
Jackie Onassis	Alex Haley
Coco Chanel	Lawrence of Arabia
Benito Mussolini	Mata Hari
Rasputin	Napoleon
Neil Armstrong	Andy Warhol
Mike Conners	

Librans are often lovely, like Catherine Deneuve and Brigitte Bardot. Barbara Walters is the ultimate "cool" Libra.

Cancer is the second fame sign, because Cancer rules the public. Cancers who have made it somehow or other are:

Bill Cosby	Ringo Starr
Jimmy Cagney	John Glenn
Ernest Hemingway	Arthur Ashe
Gerald Ford	The Mayo brothers (of the Mayo clinic)

Some outspoken, inventive Aquarians whose opinions have not always been popular, but were always ahead of their time:

Norman Mailer
Charles Darwin
Jules Verne
Ayn Rand
Galileo

Ralph Nader
Thomas Edison
Betty Friedan
Vanessa Redgrave
Franklin D. Roosevelt

Astrotrivia Part III
Fascinating Facts About the Signs

Here are the colors that, by tradition, match each of the signs of the zodiac:

1. Aries: bright red, scarlet, magenta

2. Taurus: pastels in most shades, especially pink and turquoise

3. Gemini: beiges and light gray

4. Cancer: shimmery and irridescent shades of gray and silver; anything luminous

5. Leo: bright golds and yellows

6. Virgo: dark navy, brown, gray

7. Libra: cloudy pales, especially blue-green

8. Scorpio: murky colors, especially blood red and black

9. Sagittarius: rich blues, purples, greens

10. Capricorn: black, "no-color" colors

11. Aquarius: checks, stripes, patterns, electric blue

12. Pisces: deep lilac, mauve, sea green

Each Sign/Planet owns a day of the week:

Sunday = Sun/Leo

Monday = Moon/Cancer

Tuesday = Mars/Aries, Mars/Scorpio

Wednesday = Mercury/Gemini, Mercury/Virgo

Thursday = Jupiter/Sagittarius, Neptune/Pisces

Friday = Venus/Taurus, Venus/Libra

Saturday = Saturn/Capricorn, Saturn/Aquarius

(Since there are only seven days and twelve signs, some of the signs double up. Also, since the ancients only knew seven planets, there are only enough days to match seven of the ten planets we now recognize.)

Astrotrivia Part IV
Where Do You Belong?

Each sign is said to have certain places where it belongs. Long ago, the world was divided up according to astrological tradition, so there are certain countries, cities, and areas that have the vibrations of certain signs. Tradition divides up other kinds of spaces, too, as you will see.

- *Aries places:* In the world: Birmingham, Oldman, Leicester, and Blackburn, *England* ... Florence, Naples, Verona and Padua *Italy* ... Marseilles and Burgundy *France* ... *Denmark, Germany, Palestine, Syria, Japan.*

    Anywhere: sheepfolds, forges, tool houses, fireplaces, on sandy soil, kilns, ceilings, fire houses, emergency rooms.

- *Taurus places:* In the world: Dublin, *Ireland* ... Mantua, Parma, Palermo, *Italy* ... St. Louis, *U.S.A.* ... *The Greek Islands, Asia Minor,* the *Caucasus.*

    Anywhere: banks, dairies, pastures, shady places, corn fields, middle rooms of houses, altars, maypoles.

- *Gemini places:* In the world: San Francisco, *U.S.A.* ... London and Plymouth, *England* ... Bruges, *Belgium* ... Versailles and Louvaine, *France* ... Nurenburg, *Germany* ... *Lower Egypt, Armenia, Wales.*

    Anywhere: buildings with pillars, bookcases, hills and mountains, upper back rooms, graineries.

- *Cancer places:* In the world; St. Andrews, *Scotland* ... Amsterdam, *Holland* ... New York City, *U.S.A.* ... Stockholm, *Sweden* ... Genoa, Venice, Milan, *Italy* ... *Paraguay, North and West Africa.*

Anywhere: lakes and brooks, salt marshes, pubs, kitchens, cellars, corner houses facing north.
- *Sagittarius places:* In the world: Avignon, *France* ... Stuttgart, Cologne, *Germany* ... Nottingham, Sheffield, Bradford, *England* ... Provence, *France* ... *Hungary, Arabia, Tuscany.*

  Anywhere: highest place around, topmost room in house, stables for racing horses, obelisks, places near fire, where incense is burned.
- *Capricorn places:* In the world: Brussels, *Belgium* ... Port Said, *Egypt* ... *India, Afghanistan, Mexico, Lithuania, Orkney Islands, Macedonia.*

  Anywhere: vaults, convents, thick forests, gates and hinges, old trees, jails, cattle barns, door knockers, game preserves.
- *Aquarius places:* In the world: Brighton and Trent, *England* ... Salszburg, *Austria* ... Hamburg, *Germany* ... the Piedmont, *Italy* ... *Prussia, Red Russia, Westphalia.*

  Anywhere: buses, bridges, ladders, garages, airplanes, power transmitters, fountains, springs and streams, sleds, ice caps.
- *Pisces places:* In the world; Alexandria, *Egypt* ... Seville, *Spain* ... Southport, Lancaster, Bournemouth, Tiverton, *England* ... *Portugal, Calabria, Normandy, Sahara.*

  Anywhere: fish ponds, oceans, oil fields, submarines, séances, flooded areas, bars, aquariums, boat yards, swimming pools, hospitals.
- *Leo Places:* In the world: Rome, Ravenna, *Italy* ... Bath, Bristol, Portsmouth, Blackpool, *England* ... Philadelphia, Chicago, *U.S.A.* ... *Bohemia, Sicily, the Alps, Damascus.*

  Anywhere: wild animal preserves, deserts and forests, castles, furnaces, gold mines, porches, forts.
- *Virgo places:* In the world: Paris, Lyons, Toulouse, *France* ... Boston, Los Angeles, *U.S.A.* ... Heidelberg, *Germany* ... *Turkey, West Indies, Brazil, Silesia, Switzerland.*

  Anywhere: pantries, restaurants, refrigerators, medicine cabinets, desks, malt houses.

- *Libra places:* In the world: Dover, Liverpool, Newcastle, *England* ... Messina, *Italy* ... Halifax, *Nova Scotia* ... *China, Norway, The Transvaal, the Barbary coast.*
  Anywhere: windmills, wood sheds, harbors, tops of mountains, garrets and lofts, guest rooms, tops of dressers, domed buildings.
- *Scorpio places:* In the world: Copenhagen, *Denmark* ... Leeds, Nottingham, *England* ... Johannesburg, *South Africa* ... Burma, *India* ... *Tibet, North China, Argentina.*
  Anywhere: junk yards, meat markets, laboratories, low gardens and streams, vineyards, deepest part of ocean.

Astrotrivia Part V
Which Animal Best Suits You?

Each sign is said to have an affinity with certain kinds of pets. Here's the rundown.

Aries: No animal that needs a lot of taking care of; but if Aries has one pet, he/she will usually have two, so the animals can take care of each other.

Taurus: Almost any kind of soft, warm creature. Taurus is a great nature lover, so even a skunk would be welcome.

Gemini: Anything with fascinating habits, like bees or ants, or anything that talks, like a parrot or a minah bird.

Cancer: Anything in need of a mother is welcome in Cancer's house, no matter how sloppy or in need of care.

Leo: Cats, of course, preferably with good breeding. Peacocks or anything with bright colors or plumage are fine too.

Virgo: Cats are preferable, because they are clean animals, but any animal in distress brings out Virgo's warmth.

Libra: This sign would just as soon do without, but if a pet is preferred, it's the perfectly groomed poodle or other refined breed of dog or cat.

Scorpio: This sign goes for rather dangerous pets, such as snakes, or anything with a sting. Basically, animals are creatures to be observed, not coddled.

Sagittarius: Horses—at home or at the race track. Any very large dog in the city, almost anything of immense size in the country.

Capricorn: Capricorns *need* pets to help pull them out of their frequent depressions. The friendliest kind of animals are the best bet, like sheepdogs.

Aquarius: This sign needs a very smart animal, so is picky about the breed of dog or cat. Actually, birds are preferable to this cool sign.

Pisces: Many people born under this sign will take in any stray that strays into their path, no matter how scraggly or ugly. They often put animals before humans in their scheme of things.

Astrotrivia Part I answers

1. Gypsy Rose Lee and Ethel Merman (who played Gypsy's mother in *Gypsy*).
2. Frank Sinatra and Sammie Davis, Jr.
3. They were all born under the calculating sign of Capricorn.
4. Paul Newman and Alan Alda were both born under the sign of Aquarius.
5. Richard Burton was the Scorpio; Liz Taylor the Pisces.
6. Billie Jean King and Chris Evert.
7. Harry S. Truman, a Taurus.
8. Abigail Van Buren ("Dear Abby") and Ann Landers.

9. George M. Cohan ("Yankee Doodle Dandy") and Louis "Satchmo" Armstrong.
10. Libra.
11. Tokyo Rose.
12. Libra.
13. Elvis Presley and David Bowie (January 5—Capricorn).
14. Henry Kissinger. He's a wily Gemini, but he could easily fool you, because his moon sign is Scorpio.
15. The column on the left are Taureans; those on the right are Librans.
16. Virgo.
17. Aries.
18. Scorpio.
19. Jackie Kennedy Onassis is a Leo; John F. Kennedy was a Gemini.
20. Rudolph Nureyev and Vaslav Nijinsky.

11

Sun Sign Changes. 1920–1975

If you were born "on the cusp" (very near the end or the beginning of a sign) you can find out what your sign really is by using the chart that follows. Many people do not realize that the sun does not "change signs" on the same day every year—or, for that matter, at the same time. For this reason the chart of sun sign changes is calculated to the minute.

How to Use the Chart

Locate your year of birth, then the month in which you were born. Let's say you were born in April of 1942. In the box for that month and year you will see

20–Tau
12:30 P.M.

That means if you are born *after* 12:30 p.m. on April 20 in 1942, you are a Taurus. If you were born before that date and time, your sun sign is the preceding one, Aries.

In this chart (as well as in the rising-sign chart) the signs are abbreviated as follows:

Ar = Aries
Tau = Taurus
Gem = Gemini
Can = Cancer
Leo = Leo
Vir = Virgo
Lib = Libra
Sc = Scorpio

Sag = Sagittarius
Cap = Capricorn
Aq = Aquarius
Pis = Pisces

NOTE: All times given in the sun sign changes chart are Eastern Standard. You must correct for daylight savings time (subtract one hour) and for time zone. For Central Standard Time subtract one hour; for Mountain Standard Time subtract two hours; for Pacific Standard Time subtract three hours.

	1920	1921	1922	1923	1924	1925	1926	1927	1928	1929
Jan	21–Aq 4:05 am	20–Aq 8:55 am	20–Aq 2:48 pm	20–Aq 8:35 pm	21–Aq 2:29 am	20–Aq 8:20 am	20–Aq 2:13 pm	20–Aq 8:12 pm	21–Aq 1:57 am	20–Aq 7:42 am
Feb	19–Pis 5:29 pm	18–Pis 11:21 pm	19–Pis 5:16 am	19–Pis 11:00 am	19–Pis 4:51 pm	18–Pis 11:43 pm	18–Pis 4:35 am	19–Pis 10:35 am	19–Pis 4:20 pm	18–Pis 10:07 pm
Mar	20–Ar 5:00 pm	20–Ar 10:51 pm	21–Ar 4:49 am	21–Ar 10:29 am	20–Ar 4:20 pm	20–Ar 11:13 pm	21–Ar 4:01 am	21–Ar 11:59 am	20–Ar 3:44 pm	20–Ar 9:35 pm
Apr	20–Tau 4:39 am	20–Tau 10:32 am	20–Tau 4:29 am	20–Tau 10:06 pm	20–Tau 3:59 am	20–Tau 10:51 am	20–Tau 3:36 pm	20–Tau 9:32 pm	20–Tau 3:17 am	20–Tau 9:11 am
May	21–Gem 4:22 am	21–Gem 10:17 am	21–Gem 9:11 am	22–Gem 9:45 pm	21–Gem 3:41 am	21–Gem 10:33 am	21–Gem 3:15 pm	21–Gem 9:08 pm	21–Gem 2:53 am	21–Gem 8:48 am
June	21–Can 12:40pm	21–Can 6:36 pm	22–Can 12:27 am	22–Can 6:03 am	21–Can 12:noon	21–Can 5:50 pm	21–Can 5:21 am	22–Can 11:30 pm	21–Can 11:07 am	21–Can 5:01 pm
July	22–Leo 11:40 pm	23–Leo 5:31 am	23–Leo 11:20 am	23–Leo 5:01 pm	22–Leo 11:58 pm	23–Leo 4:45 am	23–Leo 10:25 am	23–Leo 4:17 pm	22–Leo 11:02 pm	23–Leo 3:54 am
Aug	23–Vir 6:22 am	23–Vir 12:15 pm	23–Vir 6:04 pm	23–Vir 11:52 pm	23–Vir 5:48 am	23–Vir 11:33 am	23–Vir 5:14 pm	23–Vir 11:06 pm	23–Vir 4:53 am	23–Vir 10:41 am
Sept	23–Lib 3:25 am	23–Lib 11:20 am	23–Lib 5:10 am	23–Lib 9:04 pm	23–Lib 2:58 am	23–Lib 8:43 am	23–Lib 2:25 pm	23–Lib 8:17 pm	23–Lib 2:36 am	23–Lib 7:52 am
Oct	23–Sc 12:31 pm	23–Sc 6:03 pm	23–Sc 11:53 pm	24–Sc 5:51 am	23–Sc 11:44 am	23–Sc 5:31 pm	23–Sc 11:18 pm	24–Sc 5:07 am	23–Sc 10:55 am	23–Sc 4:41 pm
Nov	22–Sag 9:15 am	22–Sag 3:21 pm	22–Sag 8:55 pm	23–Sag 2:54 am	22–Sag 8:46 am	22–Sag 2:36 pm	22–Sag 8:28 pm	23–Sag 2:14 am	22–Sag 8:00 am	22–Sag 1:48 pm
Dec	21–Cap 10:17 pm	22–Cap 4:08 am	22–Cap 9:57 pm	22–Cap 3:53 pm	21–Cap 10:45 pm	22–Cap 3:37 am	22–Cap 9:34 am	22–cap 3:18 pm	21–Cap 9:04 pm	22–Cap 2:53 am

	1930	1931	1932	1933	1934	1935	1936	1937	1938	1939
Jan	20—Aq 1:33 pm	21—Aq 7:18 pm	20—Aq 1:07 am	20—Aq 6:53 am	20—Aq 10:37 am	20—Aq 6:29 pm	21—Aq 12:12am	20—Aq 6:01 am	20—Aq 11:59 am	20—Aq 5:51 pm
Feb	19—Pis 4:00 am	19—Pis 9:06 am	19—Pis 3:29 pm	19—Pis 9:16 pm	19—Pis 3:02 am	19—Pis 8:52 am	19—Pis 2:33 pm	18—Pis 3:21 pm	19—Pis 2:20 am	19—Pis 8:10 am
Mar	21—Ar 3:30 am	21—Ar 9:40 am	20—Ar 2:54 am	21—Ar 8:43 pm	21—Ar 2:28 am	21—Ar 8:19 am	20—Ar 1:58 am	20—Ar 7:45 am	21—Ar 1:43 am	21—Ar 7:29 am
Apr	20—Tau 3:06 pm	20—Tau 8:40 pm	20—Tau 2:28 am	20—Tau 8:19 am	20—Tau 2:00 pm	20—Tau 7:50 pm	20—Tau 1:31 pm	20—Tau 7:20 pm	20—Tau 1:15 pm	20—Tau 6:55 pm
May	21—Gem 2:42 pm	21—Gem 8:15 pm	21—Gem 2:07 am	21—Gem 7:57 am	21—Gem 1:35 pm	21—Gem 7:25 pm	21—Gem 1:08 pm	21—Gem 6:57 pm	21—Gem 12:51 pm	21—Gem 6:27 pm
June	21—Can 11:53 pm	23—Can 4:28 am	21—Can 10:23 am	21—Can 4:12 pm	21—Can 9:48 pm	22—Can 3:32 am	21—Can 9:22 am	21—Can 3:12 pm	21—Can 9:04 pm	22—Can 2:40 am
July	23—Leo 10:42 am	23—Leo 3:21 pm	22—Leo 9:18 pm	23—Leo 3:06 am	23—Leo 8:42 am	23—Leo 2:33 pm	22—Leo 8:18 am	23—Leo 2:07 am	23—Leo 7:57 am	23—Leo 1:37 pm
Aug	23—Vir 4:27 pm	23—Vir 10:10 pm	23—Vir 4:06 am	23—Vir 9:53 am	23—Vir 3:32 pm	23—Vir 9:24 pm	23—Vir 3:11 am	23—Vir 8:58 am	23—Vir 2:46 pm	23—Vir 8:31 pm
Sept	23—Lib 1:35 pm	23—Lib 7:23 pm	23—Lib 1:16 am	23—Lib 7:01 am	23—Lib 10:45 am	23—Lib 6:38 am	23—Lib 12:26 pm	23—Lib 6:13 am	23—Lib 12:noon	23—Lib 5:50 pm
Oct	23—Sc 11:25 pm	24—Sc 4:15 am	23—Sc 10:04 am	23—Sc 3:48 pm	23—Sc 9:35 pm	24—Sc 3:29 am	23—Sc 10:18 am	23—Sc 3:06 pm	23—Sc 8:54 pm	24—Sc 2:46 am
Nov	22—Sag 7:34 pm	23—Sag 1:25 am	22—Sag 7:10 am	22—Sag 10:53 am	22—Sag 6:44 pm	23—Sag 12:35 am	22—Sag 6:25 pm	22—Sag 12:17 pm	22—Sag 6:06 pm	22—Sag 11:59 pm
Dec	22—Cap 8:40 am	22—Cap 2:30 pm	21—Cap 8:14 pm	22—Cap 1:58 am	22—Cap 5:49 pm	22—Cap 1:37 pm	21—Cap 7:27 pm	22—Cap 1:22 am	22—Cap 7:13 am	22—Cap 1:05 pm

	1940	1941	1942	1943	1944	1945	1946	1947	1948
Jan	20–Aq 11:44 pm	20–Aq 5:34 am	20–Aq 11:16 am	20–Aq 5:20 pm	20–Aq 11:09 pm	20–Aq 4:55 am	20–Aq 10:44 am	20–Aq 4:23 pm	20–Aq 10:18 pm
Feb	19–Pis 2:04 pm	18–Pis 7:59 pm	19–Pis 1:39 am	19–Pis 7:41 am	19–Pis 1:28 pm	18–Pis 7:15 pm	19–Pis 1:10 am	19–Pis 6:53 am	19–Pis 12:37 pm
Mar	20–Ar 1:24 pm	20–Ar 7:21 pm	21–Ar 1:03 am	21–Ar 7:03 am	21–Ar 12:49 pm	20–Ar 6:38 pm	21–Ar 12:34 am	21–Ar 6:13 am	20–Ar 11:57 am
Apr	20–Tau 12:51 pm	20–Tau 6:51 am	20–Tau 12:30 pm	20–Tau 6:32 pm	20–Tau 12:18 am	20–Tau 6:08 am	20–Tau 12:03 pm	20–Tau 5:40 pm	19–Tau 11:25 pm
May	21–Gem 12:23 am	21–Gem 6:23 am	21–Gem 12:01 pm	21–Gem 6:03 pm	20–Gem 11:51 pm	22–Gem 5:41 am	21–Gem 12:03 pm	21–Gem 5:04 pm	20–Gem 10:58 pm
June	21–Can 8:37 am	21–Can 2:33 am	21–Can 12:01 am	22–Can 2:13 am	21–Can 9:03 am	21–Can 1:52 pm	21–Can 7:45 pm	22–Can 1:19 am	21–Can 7:11 am
July	22–Leo 8:37 am	23–Leo 2:33 am	23–Leo 8:08 pm	23–Leo 1:05 pm	22–Leo 6:55 pm	23–Leo 12:48 am	23–Leo 6:37 am	23–Leo 12:12 pm	22–Leo 6:06 pm
Aug	23–Vir 7:34 pm	23–Vir 1:26 am	23–Vir 6:59 am	23–Vir 1:05 pm	23–Vir 6:55 pm	23–Vir 7:36 am	23–Vir 1:23 pm	23–Vir 7:09 pm	23–Vir 1:03 am
Sept	23–Lib 2:21 am	23–Lib 8:30 am	23–Lib 1:50 pm	23–Lib 7:55 pm	23–Lib 1:47 am	23–Lib 7:36 am	23–Lib 1:23 pm	23–Lib 7:09 pm	23–Lib 1:03 am
Oct	23–Sc 11:46 pm	23–Sc 5:33 am	23–Sc 11:10 am	23–Sc 5:12 pm	23–Sc 11:02 pm	20–Sc 4:50 am	23–Sc 10:41 am	24–Sc 4:29 pm	23–Sc 10:22 pm
Nov	22–Sag 8:39 am	22–Sag 2:22 pm	22–Sag 8:01 pm	24–Sc 2:09 am	23–Sc 7:57 am	20–Sc 1:45 pm	23–Sc 7:37 pm	24–Sc 1:27 am	23–Sc 7:19 am
Dec	21–Cap 5:49 am	22–Sag 11:38 am	22–Sag 5:23 am	22–Sag 11:22 pm	22–Sag 5:09 am	22–Sag 10:56 am	22–Sag 4:47 am	22–Sag 10:38 pm	22–Sag 4:29 am
	21–Cap 6:55 pm	22–Cap 12:44 am	22–Cap 6:31 am	22–Cap 12:30 pm	21–Cap 6:15 pm	22–Cap 12:04 am	22–Cap 5:54 pm	22–Cap 11:44 pm	21–Cap 5:23 pm

	1949	1950	1951	1952	1953	1954	1955	1956	1957
Jan	20–Aq 4:11 am	20–Aq 10:00 am	20–Aq 3:53 pm	20–Aq 9:38 pm	20–Aq 3:22 am	20–Aq 9:14 am	20–Aq 3:03 pm	20–Aq 8:49 pm	20–Aq 2:43 am
Feb	18–Pis 6:27 pm	19–Pis 12:16 am	19–Pis 6:10 am	19–Pis 11:57 am	18–Pis 5:41 pm	19–Pis 11:33 pm	19–Pis 5:19 am	19–Pis 11:05 am	18–Pis 5:01 pm
Mar	20–Ar 5:49 pm	20–Ar 11:30 pm	21–Ar 5:26 am	20–Ar 11:14 am	20–Ar 5:01 pm	20–Ar 10:54 pm	21–Ar 4:36 am	20–Ar 10:21 am	20–Ar 4:17 pm
Apr	20–Tau 5:18 am	20–Tau 11:00 am	20–Tau 4:49 pm	20–Tau 10:37 pm	19–Tau 4:26 am	20–Tau 10:20 am	20–Tau 3:58 pm	19–Tau 9:44 pm	20–Tau 3:45 am
May	21–Gem 4:51 am	21–Gem 10:27 am	21–Gem 4:15 pm	20–Gem 10:04 pm	21–Gem 3:53 am	21–Gem 9:48 am	21–Gem 3:25 pm	20–Gem 9:13 pm	21–Gem 3:09 am
June	21–Can 1:03 pm	21–Can 6:37 pm	22–Can 12:25 am	21–Can 6:13 am	21–Can noon	21–Can 5:55 pm	21–Can 11:32 pm	21–Can 5:24 am	21–Can 11:21 am
July	22–Leo 1:58 am	23–Leo 5:30 am	23–Leo 11:29 am	22–Leo 5:05 pm	22–Leo 10:53 pm	23–Leo 4:45 am	23–Leo 10:25 am	22–Leo 4:20 pm	22–Leo 10:13 pm
Aug	23–Vir 6:49 pm	23–Vir 12:24 pm	23–Vir 6:22 pm	23–Vir 12:03 am	23–Vir 5:46 am	23–Vir 11:37 am	23–Vir 5:19 pm	22–Vir 11:15 pm	23–Vir 5:07 am
Sept	23–Lib 4:05 am	23–Lib 9:44 am	23–Lib 3:38 pm	22–Lib 9:24 pm	23–Lib 3:07 am	23–Lib 8:56 am	23–Lib 2:42 pm	22–Lib 8:30 pm	23–Lib 2:27 am
Oct	23–Sc 1:04 pm	23–Sc 6:48 pm	23–Sc 12:37 am	23–Sc 6:22 am	23–Sc 12:07 pm	23–Sc 5:58 pm	22–Sc 11:44 pm	23–Sc 5:35 am	23–Sc 11:33 am
Nov	22–Sag 10:17 am	22–Sag 4:03 pm	22–Sag 9:52 pm	22–Sag 3:36 am	22–Sag 9:23 am	22–Sag 3:14 pm	22–Sag 9:02 pm	22–Sag 2:51 am	22–Sag 8:45 am
Dec	21–Cap 11:24 am	22–Cap 5:14 am	22–Cap 11:01 am	21–Cap 4:44 pm	21–Cap 10:22 pm	22–Cap 4:25 am	22–Cap 10:12 am	21–Cap 4:00 pm	21–Cap 9:49 pm

	1958	1959	1960	1961	1962	1963	1964	1965	1966
Jan	20–Aq 2:20 pm	20–Aq 2:20 pm	20–Aq 8:11 pm	20–Aq 2:02 am	20–Aq 7:49 am	20–Aq 1:55 pm	19–Aq 7:43 pm	20–Aq 1:30 am	20–Aq 8:21 am
Feb	18–Pis 10:49 pm	19–Pis 4:38 pm	19–Pis 10:26 am	18–Pis 6:27 pm	18–Pis 10:16 am	19–Pis 4:09 am	19–Pis 10:25 am	18–Pis 3:49 pm	18–Pis 9:39 pm
Mar	20–Ar 10:06 pm	21–Ar 3:55 pm	20–Ar 9:43 am	20–Ar 5:27 pm	20–Ar 9:30 am	21–Ar 3:20 am	20–Ar 9:43 am	20–Ar 3:05 pm	20–Ar 8:53 pm
Apr	20–Tau 9:28 am	20–Tau 3:17 pm	20–Tau 10:06 pm	20–Tau 2:33 am	20–Tau 8:51 am	20–Tau 2:37 pm	19–Tau 9:00 pm	20–Tau 2:27 am	20–Tau 8:12 am
May	21–Gem 8:52 am	21–Gem 2:38 pm	20–Gem 8:33 pm	21–Gem 1:51 am	21–Gem 8:17 am	21–Gem 1:59 pm	20–Gem 8:33 pm	21–Gem 1:27 am	21–Gem 7:33 am
June	21–Can 4:57 pm	21–Can 10:50 pm	21–Can 4:43 am	21–Can 10:12 am	21–Can 4:24 pm	21–Can 11:04 pm	21–Can 4:43 am	21–Can 9:56 am	21–Can 3:33 pm
July	23–Leo 3:51 am	23–Leo 9:45 am	22–Leo 5:38 pm	22–Leo 9:12 pm	23–Leo 3:19 am	23–Leo 9:00 am	22–Leo 3:38 pm	22–Leo 8:49 pm	23–Leo 2:24 am
Aug	23–Vir 10:47 am	23–Vir 4:44 pm	22–Vir 10:35 pm	23–Vir 3:46 am	23–Vir 10:13 am	23–Vir 3:58 pm	22–Vir 10:35 pm	23–Vir 3:43 am	23–Vir 9:18 am
Sept	23–Lib 5:10 am	23–Lib 2:09 pm	22–Lib 8:00 pm	23–Lib 1:26 am	23–Lib 7:35 am	23–Lib 1:24 pm	22–Lib 8:00 pm	23–Lib 1:06 am	23–Lib 6:43 am
Oct	23–Sc 5:12 am	23–Sc 11:12 pm	23–Sc 5:03 am	23–Sc 10:46 am	23–Sc 4:41 pm	23–Sc 11:30 pm	23–Sc 5:03 am	23–Sc 10:11 am	23–Sc 3:52 pm
Nov	22–Sag 2:30 am	22–Sag 8:23 pm	22–Sag 2:19 am	22–Sag 8:10 am	22–Sag 2:02 pm	22–Sag 7:50 pm	22–Sag 2:19 am	22–Sag 7:30 am	22–Sag 1:15 pm
Dec	22–Cap 3:40 am	22–Cap 9:35 am	21–Cap 5:27 pm	21–Cap 9:25 pm	22–Cap 3:15 am	22–Cap 9:02 am	21–Cap 3:27 pm	21–Cap 8:41 pm	22–Cap 2:29 pm

	1967	1968	1969	1970	1971	1972	1973	1974	1975
Jan	20–Aq 1:05 pm	20–Aq 6:54 pm	20–Aq 12:30 am	20–Aq 6:25 am	20–Aq 12:14 pm	20–Aq 6:00 pm	19–Aq 11:49 pm	20–Aq 5:47 am	20–Aq 11:37 am
Feb	19–Pis 3:25 am	19–Pis 9:11 am	18–Pis 2:47 pm	18–Pis 8:43 pm	19–Pis 2:28 am	19–Pis 8:12 am	18–Pis 2:02 pm	18–Pis 8:00 pm	19–Pis 1:51 am
Mar	21–Ar 2:37 am	20–Ar 8:22 am	20–Ar 2:08 pm	20–Ar 7:59 pm	21–Ar 1:28 am	20–Ar 7:22 am	20–Ar 1:13 pm	20–Ar 7:08 pm	21–Ar 12:58 am
Apr	20–Tau 1:56 am	19–Tau 7:42 pm	20–Tau 1:18 am	20–Tau 5:16 am	20–Tau 12:54 pm	19–Tau 6:38 pm	20–Tau 12:31 am	20–Tau 5:19 am	20–Tau 12:08 pm
May	21–Gem 1:19 pm	20–Gem 7:07 pm	21–Gem 12:41 am	21–Gem 6:32 am	21–Gem 12:16 pm	20–Gem 6:00 pm	20–Gem 11:54 pm	21–Gem 5:37 am	21–Gem 12:08 pm
June	21–Can 1:13 am	21–Can 7:07 pm	21–Can 1:13 am	21–Can 2:43 pm	21–Can 12:16 pm	21–Can 2:07 am	21–Can 8:01 am	21–Can 1:38 pm	21–Can 1:25 pm
July	23–Leo 4:23 am	22–Leo 1:13 am	22–Leo 6:55 am	22–Leo 12:43 pm	22–Leo 6:21 pm	22–Leo 1:03 am	22–Leo 6:56 pm	23–Leo 12:30 am	23–Leo 7:23 am
Aug	23–Vir 3:13 pm	22–Vir 9:52 pm	23–Vir 2:35 am	23–Vir 6:35 am	23–Vir 2:16 pm	22–Vir 8:04 pm	23–Vir 1:55 am	23–Vir 7:29 am	23–Vir 1:24 pm
Sept	23–Lib 12:38 pm	22–Lib 6:26 pm	23–Lib 12:07 am	23–Lib 5:59 am	23–Lib 11:47 am	22–Lib 5:34 pm	22–Lib 11:22 pm	23–Lib 4:59 am	23–Lib 10:56 am
Oct	23–Sc 9:44 pm	23–Sc 1:30 am	23–Sc 9:03 am	23–Sc 3:05 pm	22–Sc 8:53 pm	23–Sc 2:42 am	23–Sc 8:31 am	23–Sc 2:12 pm	23–Sc 8:07 pm
Nov	22–Sag 7:05 pm	22–Sag 12:59 am	22–Sag 6:23 am	22–Sag 12:25 pm	22–Sag 6:15 pm	22–Sag 12:04 am	22–Sag 5:55 am	22–Sag 11:39 am	22–Sag 5:32 pm
Dec	22–Cap 8:17 am	21–Cap 2:00 pm	21–Cap 7:44 pm	22–Cap 1:36 am	22–Cap 5:26 am	21–Cap 1:14 pm	21–Cap 7:09 pm	22–Cap 12:57 am	22–Cap 7:47 am

12

Leo: The Big Picture

Because the twelve signs of the zodiac represent twelve ways of being in the world, you will know more about yourself and why you tend toward certain types of behavior and attitudes by knowing more about Leo. If you read about the elements and qualities in "Defining Terms," for instance, you'll find out that you are one of the outgoing, active *fire signs*, and, as one of the *fixed signs*, you are able to hold your own quite well. You can "meet yourself" in the Leo prototype described in "Twelve Places at the Table," and your regal, "fiery," planetary ruler, the sun, provides some excellent clues about the Leo style.

However, even with these broad brush strokes, your Leo portrait is still a bit abstract; to see yourself in totality, you need more of the background filled in. That means going back to some very important basics: your fifth place position in the zodiac, your picture symbol, the lion, and the shorthand figure, or glyph, that astrologers use to indicate Leo when they draw up a horoscope. In Leo, as in every astrological sign, these three factors link together, forming a strong chain of meaning that holds together everything that is Leo.

The fire sign Leo—which follows the water sign Cancer—begins the second round of the fire-earth-air-water sequence of elements. As the second of the fire signs, Leo represents a stage of human existence that is a bit more mature than that represented by first place fire sign Aries—though both share many of the same naive, beginner qualities. When the sun reaches zero degrees Leo on or about July 22, the northern hemisphere begins high summer—the hottest period of the year, when the sun burns brightly with a steady, unrelenting heat, and there are few refreshing breezes to break the scorching stillness. The fruits of the earth are full grown and overwhelming in their abundance. The earth is at a maximum, virtually showing off how much it can produce.

As there is a magnificence about the earth at this time of year, so is there a magnificence about people born under the sign of Leo. These people have a tendency to live as if their resources will never run out. To upbeat, optimistic Leo, the winter is a long way off, and life is to be enjoyed *now*. High summer is the time when many people take vacation and take time out, reveling in the beautiful weather; for many Leos, too, life is just one long vacation. Though it is not really a lazy sign, Leo loves the good life, and has no problem treating him-herself to the best there is. But the most significant point about Leo's position in the zodiac is the correlation between the steady heat of the summer, and the unflagging intensity of people born under this sign. Leo's loyalty is legendary, and once this sign warms up to someone or something, it takes a hurricane to put out the fires of Leo's passion.

Leo's picture symbol, the lion, has many layers of meaning and many reflections in myth and legend. One of the original great lions was sent by the gods to challenge Hercules. It was said that nothing could harm the coat of this divine lion except its own claws, so Hercules strangled it to death and took the lion's skin to wear as a coat of armor during his other battles. Though people born under the sign of Leo are thin-skinned in the sense that they are easily slighted, Leo is one of the sturdiest signs of the zodiac—in both the physical and the psychological senses. The best lions are rarely daunted, and have great moral courage. The so-called "cowardly lion" of the Wizard of Oz ultimately demonstrated this quality.

The Royal Lion—king of beasts—turns up everywhere, including the Bible. In the Old Testament, the favored tribe of Judah was symbolized by the lion and was given the royal sceptre. In Rome, the lion was a symbol of the power of the empire, and the feeding of Christians to the lions symbolized the overcoming of any challenge to the authority of the state. On the other hand, King Richard the Lionhearted of England rode into the Crusades to recapture the Holy Land under the banner of the "Lion of Christ." A latter day ruler, Emporer Haile Selassie of Ethiopia, had "Lion of Judah" as well as "King of Kings" among his many titles. People born under the sign of Leo sense their "royalty" and their "divine right," but can use it either for great good or for much less noble causes.

The human heart, which is our physical center, is the part of the body ruled by the sign of Leo. In many ways, Leo is the sign most synomymous with living, breathing human life. In the glyph or shorthand symbol astrologers use to indicate Leo (see illustration) some people see the small open semicircle as the vein leading to the main coronary chamber of the heart, while the small curl at the right is the main artery that takes newly pumped blood and circulates it to the rest of the body. Though there are more esoteric meanings for Leo's symbol, this one captures the special importance of the sign and the central meaning of Leo as the sign in which the divine spark ignites human life.

13

Leo: Objectives and Obstacles

A Game Plan for Being the Most Successful Leo Under the Sun

Every astrological sign is a set of possibilities; being born under a particular sign does not guarantee you *are* or *will be* all those things that sign is capable of being. Nor would you want to. There are positive characteristics to be cultivated, as well as negative ones you can avoid or overcome. Living "à la carte"—selecting what you want from all the options available—is open to you, within the overall context of your sign.

You can, of course, order the "prix fixe" dinner by living your life as it comes without attempting to direct it. The choice is yours, which is one good reason it is incorrect to regard your astrological destiny as preordained. You are responsible for how you emobdy your sign, and what results from that embodiment.

Astrologically speaking, your life as a sign is a journey with a starting point, the raw or "primitive" end of the sign, and a destination, the evolved or "ideal" realization of that sign. Once again, you don't have to take the full trip; there are plenty of exits if you choose to use them. Few people are ever totally "finished." But if you at least know where you are going, and what potential booby traps lie along the way, you will be way ahead of the game.

Regard the following as a map, and use it in charting your course. The most successful way to be the best of your astrological sign is to work with it, in full knowledge of its up side and its down side. The happiest people of any astrological sign are those who aim high and are not afraid to stretch their understanding of themselves in order to reach their goal.

Where Leo Sarts

Leo is one of the "extremist" signs of the zodiac, so you are most likely to encounter Leos who are very good or very bad. However, even the latter type bears no malice toward anyone; he/she is simply too self-centered to make anyone else that important. The steady fires of Leo in the unevolved type merely burn to inflame Leo's ego. Instead of warming others with benevolence and generosity, this lesser type of Leo commands them to do his/her bidding—but is rarely very effective in getting true loyalty and support. There is no sadder sight in the zodiac than a magnificent Leo whose mighty roar is nothing but a purr. Once in a while this type goes into a full-scale temper tantrum to get people's attention, but the reaction is usually: "There he/she goes again." The primitive Leo bears a great resemblance to the tame housecat; in fact, many of them turn into classic fat cats who live for nothing but to be fed and stroked. And, oh, the stroking Leo demands! For many, the desire for adulation is a real trap, because they easily fall prey to conniving types who know exactly which buttons to push to get naïve Leo to come across. Some very cruel types will even coax Leo to "perform" so that they can laugh at the sorry spectacle a clowning but ill-advised Leo can be. But, in the end, the unevolved Leo is his/her own worst enemy because Leo has taken his natural gifts and wasted them—usually by refusing to try to figure out what makes him/her tick.

Here are some buzz words by which you can recognize the primitive Leo type:

Pompous	Bossy
Snobbish	Primadonna
Intolerant	Arrogant
Vain	Thoughtless
Power-hungry	Opinionated

Where Leo Can Go

In many ways, Leo is the most personal sign of the zodiac, relating everything in the world at large to his/her own world. While in the primitive Leo this can become mere self-centeredness, in the evolved Leo it is self-expression in the best sense of the word. It is Leo's symbolic function in the zodiac to bring unconsciousness into the conscious and to express it clearly and dramatically, thereby enriching the rest of humanity. Simply put, the sign of Leo is the sign of the creative artist. Whether a particular Leo is a great artist or manages a successful commercial enterprise, he/she is living up to the Leo destiny. Most Leos, however, will have to do their self-expressing on a much more ordinary level, but they can be equally effective examples to others. The best Leos *dare* to express their powers and do not care whether or not the world applauds them for it. In their heart of hearts, this kind of Leo knows he/she is the best it can be. It is not vanity or conceit, but a calm acceptance of the fact that they've been given a lot more than other people and must use it to the fullest. It is uncanny how many talented and gifted Leos you will find, and there are those who believe Leo is really a favored sign. The evolved Leo knows it but doesn't lord it over other people. He/she simply goes out and does, or is, "the best." Here are some buzz words by which you can recognize the evolved Leo type:

Magnanimous	Good organizer
Creative	Forceful
Enthusiastic	Dignified

Supportive of others   Loyal
Broadminded   Self-confident

How Leo Can Get There

Among Leo's greatest resources are a sense of play and a love of life. Used properly, these assets can make Leo much beloved and extremely successful. One obvious way, of course, is through the performing arts, because if you scratch any Leo, you will find a would-be singer, dancer, actor, or some other type of performer. However, all the creative life force these things represent can be used off-stage to make Leo a focal point for a group of people to rally round and trust. Leo instinctively believes that life is good and that today should be happy; if he/she isn't simply a Polyanna, this upbeat attitude toward anything the world brings can inspire others to fight the good fight, no matter what the odds.

However, in order for Leo to teach others to trust, Leo him-herself must first learn to do so. That means that one of Leo's life strategies should be to take risks in the area of self-expression. If Leo fears laughter instead of applause, he/she is all too likely to suppress his/her creative instincts, thereby going through life feeling underdeveloped. To get where Leo can go, this sign has got to put him-herself out on a limb once in a while—and possibly take some falls as well. Leo is anything but a quiet sign, and when a Leo begins to keep silent for fear of what others' reactions will be, Leo should take it as a signal. No matter what Leo's sex, the motto "faint heart ne'er won fair lady" should be kept in mind. Underneath it all, Leo is brave in the best sense of the word. In order to develop true self-confidence, this sign above all must put him-herself on the firing line of life, in order to get the best that life has to offer. And to learn to trust.

Potential Pitfalls

The evolved Leos give a lot of love, and give it unstintingly; however, they need love in equal measure as well. The problem with Leo is that he/she can sometimes *appear* so self-confident and self-sufficient that others take it at face value and jump to the conclusion that this person doesn't need anyone else. It is far from the truth. Once again, Leo must avoid falling into the trap of being afraid to express emotional needs for fear of rejection. Unfortunately, too many Leos go through life believing that if they laugh the world will laugh with them, but they must cry alone. Leo is a highly emotional sign, and should express the full range of genuine emotions to others. If Leo continually tries to impress people with his/her superiority, those people are going to come to the conclusion that Leo doesn't need anything or anyone. Going hand in hand with this potential pitfall for Leo is the sign's tendency to substitute self-love for love from others. It is all too easy for proud Leo to put others off while putting him-herself on an emotional pedestal.

14

Pairing Off With Leo

Your Compatibility with Other Signs of the Zodiac

Since there are only twelve signs of the zodiac, it would be unusual to go through life without having to interact with each of them at one time or another. Obviously, your astrological makeup is more complex than your Leo sun sign, but there are some basic truths about how you tend to react when face to face with someone of another sun sign. If you have read about "The Geometry of Relationships," you already know that being a fire sign means Leo relates more easily to certain elements than to others. Now, getting more specific, you will see what the odds are on your match-ups with each of the other signs, including your own.

When most people talk about "relationships," they are usually referring to the romantic kind, and there is no doubt that since time immemorial love has been observed to have a great deal to do with keeping the earth revolving in its orbit. However, we also have a lot of other personal interactions, from important ones, like boss-employee and parent-child to more casual ones, like waitress-patron, cabdriver-rider, and buddy-buddy. The general "rules" that follow apply in all cases; just change the language a little and do a bit of interpretation. You will find that there is more truth than poetry in the matter of astrological compatibility.

Leo with Aries   You two might be a little like Hansel and Gretel wandering bravely through the "forest of life." You are both childlike in the ways you want to trust both other people and the world. From this point of view, you are compatible, but some difficulties will arise about who the leader is in this relationship. If you can carefully carve out each other's territory, there will be a lot of love and mutual respect here—as well as a lot of marvelous times together. You both can be brutally honest, so learn to let some things slide.

Leo with Taurus A lot of Taurus' good points will be totally lost on you, which is a shame. As a freewheeling fire sign, you need the stability that earth sign Taurus can provide. However, you could all too easily regard it as a curb on your freedom of expression. You both love creature comforts, but your taste is a little more lavish than Taurus'. Actually, this combination is much better in business than in romance. Taurus will be willing to let you take over the reins.

Leo with Gemini Be careful with Gemini; he/she could approach you full of curiosity, and you could pour out your heart's secrets, only to find that Gemini isn't as serious as you are. This is a potentially good combination, but you should keep your eyes wide open. Gemini's bubbly personality will appeal to your frivolous nature, but between the two of you you could create financial disaster. That's why, if you decide to go into business together, you should make it a top priority to hire an earth sign to keep the books.

Leo with Leo This rarely works well, for obvious reasons. Even if you are able to resolve the fact that both of you want to be the boss, you will still have other problems. One is that you will be each other's "mirror" and "audience"; you may waste a lot of time and talent simply impressing each other instead of expressing yourself to the fullest in the outer world. However, since you are both such genuine and warm people, your love would not be lost on each other.

Leo with Virgo You are most likely to have a hard time figuring out what Virgo really wants from you; maybe it is too much. The self-abnegating sign Virgo may want you to bolster his/her ego all the time, so that yours gets left out in the cold. Speaking of cold, you may find Virgo's brand of practical love a bit chilly for your taste. You do have a rather high opinion of yourself, and you certainly won't be happy about the well-meant criticism Virgo usually gives out. From Virgo's point of view, you are far too sensitive.

Leo with Libra Libra has just the right kind of "cool" to keep your fires banked properly and you provide Libra with the loyal love that makes him/her feel confident. This is an excellent combination for both a romantic fling and a lifetime relationship. However, you are both going to have to watch out for a tendency to live as if there is no tomorrow, and that life will always be easy. Keep reminding yourselves to take a daily dose of realism, and all will go well. In business, too, this is a good duo.

Leo with Scorpio Though both you and Scorpio have a love of drama, you certainly don't have the same taste. Scorpio's intense emotionalism is far too murky for you; you want to live on the light side. In some cases, Leo could get drawn into a potentially devastating affair with Scorpio. Scorpio could initially attract Leo with unflagging attention and sexual wiles. Eventually, however, Leo will realize he/she is being possessed and will want to break away. And it's not that easy with Scorpio.

Leo with Sagittarius Sagittarius may "call your bluff," but you will love it. The sincere Sagittarian knows right off that you share the same high ideals—in personal relationships as in other things. Regardless of age, Sagittarius is likely to play the role of teacher with the more naïve Leo. Among the many wonderful things you will learn from this sign is the ability to admit that you are not always right. Sagittarius may give you reason to be jealous at times, but you couldn't find a better mate to come home to.

Leo with Capricorn Capricorn has a subtlety that unsubtle Leo lacks, so this sign could be an excellent manager for you. However, in your emotional life Capricorn might not be able to provide the all-enveloping love and adulation you desire. He/she will regard you as a wonderful possession but might tend to undervalue your idealistic qualities and love of life. You need someone who reaches for the stars, not for the next material possession. However, in the business area you two would balance each other off nicely, you providing the creative ideas, Capricorn the master plan to carry them out.

Leo with Aquarius Aquarius tends to be as pure in heart as you are—but this cool air sign is coming from quite a different place. As personal in your feelings as you are, Aquarius is quite the opposite, and you want a much more involved and involving lover. You would definitely respect each other a lot, however, so you could be the best of friends—or business associates.

Leo with Pisces As impulsive and overly generous as you are, you are a lot more emotionally stable than Pisces. This sign could absolutely fascinate you by its ethereal qualities, but in the end you will be simply confused by the Pisces convoluted brand of love. You need someone a lot more forthright. An affair with Pisces might do you some good, however, because this is one sign that may make you look deep inside yourself and stop taking things at face value. It is definitely a different dimension than you live in.

15

The Leo Sex Role Dilemma

One of the most important ways in which the twelve signs of the zodiac are divided is into "masculine" signs and "feminine" signs, and there are six of each. The reason is simple: As one sign follows the other in the zodiac, they alternate energies, much like the Yin/Yang principle of eastern philosophy. The universe is made up of opposites that complement each other: light and dark, hot and cold, black and white, hard and soft. One is not better than the other; rather, each is essential to the existence of its opposite. In other words, you can't have one without the other.

The six fire and air signs are "masculine," since fire and air are connected with *active, assertive, outgoing* energy.

Aries	Gemini
Leo	Libra
Sagittarius	Aquarius

The six water and earth signs are "feminine," because water and earth represent *reactive, inner-directed, receptive* energy.

Taurus	Cancer
Virgo	Scorpio
Capricorn	Pisces

To put it simply, *the masculine fire and air signs are positive, while the earth and water signs are negative.* To remain neutral and avoid placing a higher value on one or the other kind of energy (or sign) it is useful to think of a battery with positive and negative poles. Without both, it simply doesn't work.

Though the masculine/feminine division of the signs has nothing whatever to do with human physical sexuality or sexual preference, it has very important implications for human behavior. Bluntly put, women born into male signs can be more "masculine"/achieving/competitive than men born into female signs. On the other hand, men born in female signs can be more "feminine"/nurturing/cooperative than women born into male signs. Both men and women born into signs that match their own sex may overemphasize behavior and attitudes connected with that gender. The "ideal" person, psychologically and metaphysically speaking, has a healthy mix of both masculine and feminine attitudes. Without at least some of both, we cannot be whole people, able to encompass and understand the total range of human emotions, desires, drives, and goals. Since none of us is perfect, just about everyone could stand a bit more "gender blending." Your astrological sign offers some excellent clues about how you can accomplish that.

Leo is one of the most masculine of the masculine signs because it is the most powerfully self-expressive—the ultimate manifestation of the *conscious* side of human life. Leo's drive to achieve recognition and praise is an extremely strong motivation that thrusts people born under this sign out into the world. There is little that is shy and retiring about Leo, even if he/she feigns it.

This means that Leo men tend to be superachievers: some are even capable of being ruthless (although mildly) to attain the status and power they want. However, it is particularly hard for Leo men to get in touch with the feeling part of their natures. Leo men often mistake sentimentality for real emotion and their own sensitivity to hurts for an ability to feel.

Leo women are some of the most successful people in the zodiac; those who enter the world of competition seem to rise to the top almost effortlessly. It is extraordinary how many female executives are born under the sign of Leo. And it is sad how many unhappy women this sign turns out as well. The Leo sex role dilemma is this: The men must make an effort to soften their hard edges and learn to recognize true compassion if they are to become whole people. Leo women have it even tougher. Unconsciously, they have a bit of contempt for that soft inner core of womanliness that is their natural birthright. Their first task is to make friends with their feminine nature and realize they have nothing to fear from the kind of softness it gives. In effect, Leo women have to stop competing with themselves if they are to have a happy, fulfilling life.

16

The Leo Female

Boss Lady

No matter what else is going on in a Leo woman's horoscope to give her one particular talent or another, the Leo woman is *competent*. No matter what she does or where she does it, the Leo woman does it well. Leo Julia Child does it in the kitchen—and also displays Leo's famous flair for showmanship. Ethel Barrymore did it on the stage; Jackie Kennedy displayed her competence first as a gracious and lovely first lady, later as a woman able to function quite well in the business world. However, for the Leo female, her competence is both a blessing and a curse. For one thing, many Leo women appear so self-sufficient no man would dare approach her, thinking she doesn't need *anyone*. Unfortunately, that is far from the truth. Leo women often desparately desire love and companionship, but fail to get it because their pride will not let them show their needs. Outwardly, Leos can be the most feminine of women and usually know how to turn themselves out quite stunningly. However, many also give off a "look, but do not touch" signal that people—particularly men—take literally.

The Leo woman typically grows up in a household where the father was an extremely dominant force; even if he is absent for one reason or another, his influence is very strong. The high standards of achievement a Leo woman's father sets stay with her for a lifetime—as does the desperate need for approval that came along with them. It is extremely important for the Leo woman to hold her head high no matter what her life circumstances.

As a child, the typical Leo girl is an angel and may even look like one—as long as she gets the praise and approval she so desperately needs. The Leo girl does not want to be treated like a princess for nothing, however. She simply wants her successes to be noticed and given loud rounds of applause. If this doesn't happen, the typically happy Leo girl can turn very sulky and pouty or turn inward. Many Leo girls grow up willing to do *anything* to get a nod of approval, and it can have a disastrous effect on their sex lives later on. Among her peers, the Leo girl is generally the leader, and all is well until someone challenges her authority. Then she is quite capable of "fighting for her turf," physically, if necessary. In school she is generally well above average and is often singled out by teachers for leadership roles. The Leo girls challenge to be the best and still be one-of-the-crowd starts very early.

As a young woman, Leo females start out on what for many is the happiest period of their lives. That is because they often achieve quick success in their career life by applying both their competence and their high standards of performance to whatever problem is put before them. Leo women are willing to work very hard, and aren't even afraid to get their hands dirty if it means they will be recognized—and promoted. Success means many things to the Leo female, and among them are the resources to afford the luxuries of life. Many Leo women gravitate toward the fashion and beauty fields, where they become their own best advertisements for lavish clothes and jewelry.

By wearing her success so beautifully, however, the Leo woman sets herself up for a very rocky romantic life. She wants someone who is better than she is in every way, and her standards are often ridiculously high. From some Leo women, this is their own reason for remaining unattached; as a fire sign, Leo does like freedom. For others, however, their constant search for perfection in a man leads to another unfortunate scenario. Some Leo women simply give up and enter into a series of tawdry affairs with men they would not consider marrying or who are already married. Young Leo women who are not as fanatically interested in their jobs and careers can spend an inordinate amount of time—and money—on "the hunt" for a man. These "pretty lions" often end up chasing their tails, because they too fall into the double bind of desperately wanting love and companionship while looking as if they couldn't care less.

As a mate, the Leo woman can be perfection itself, particularly for a man who wants everything done perfectly. She is quite capable of running a career, a home, and a batch of children all at the same time and all equally well. However, like everything else in Leo's life, this is the ideal and rarely the reality. One reason is that the Leo woman sometimes chooses a mate who is her inferior in some respect and attempts to play the role of masculine head of the household—a situation which neither she nor her husband will be happy with in the long run.

But if her partner doesn't walk out, her marriage will last, because the Leo woman is loyal. Even in these times, separation and divorce are particularly difficult for people born under the sign of Leo. One good reason is that divorce signals some kind of failure, which is anathema to the Leo woman.

No matter how good or how bad her marriage, the Leo woman will make sure that she maintains her self-respect. It is very unlike her to let anyone else know her problems, even her husband. Leo women are pretty good at living out their fantasies, and some even do it in a marriage that is far from what they would like to believe it is. The Leo woman who has come to terms with herself and her needs can be a delight to her mate, however, because her tendency to look on the sunny side will keep her smiling through many a crisis.

As a mother, the Leo woman must take care not to pass on her rigid standards to her children. It is possible to maintain discipline without demanding perfection. The Leo woman's heart is very warm and full, however, so once again, most Leo women excel in the role of mother. The best of them know how to play with, teach, and take care of their children all at the same time. The sign of Leo has a built-in connection with everything connected with the young, so in many cases, the Leo woman really comes into her own only when she bears children. In fact, for many Leo females, their relationships with their children can make up for whatever is lacking in their marriage and can be the element that binds the family together.

17

The Leo Male

The Kindly King

No matter how high or low his station in life, the Leo man is king of all he surveys—at least in his mind. Leo men who do not excel can turn into very boring people who are constantly bragging about minor successes or even mythical ones. But since Leo males have a lot of energy and a built-in desire both for money and the things it can buy, most end up at least moderately successful. Many rise to high positions, and some actually become famous. Through it all, however, the Leo man remains a child at heart with a childish desire to be "king of the mountain," King Arthur, and the king in his own home castle all rolled into one. The Leo man is extremely unhappy without a mate because he needs someone constantly at his side to applaud his every move. To his opposite number, he will be loving and generous, but there will be no question of what her role is. In many ways, the Leo male's whole life scenario is conditioned by his early relationship with his father. From him he has a very strong sense of responsibility and an equally sturdy sense of ethics; the Leo man is the ultimate idealist. Unfortunately, many attempt to become the ideal person but, since perfection is never possible, some simply talk themselves into believing that they are. The vanity and conceit of Leo men is real, though it is usually forgiven them because they have so many other good qualities.

As a child, the Leo boy can be very reckless. For one thing, he is exploring his maleness; for another, he is trying to do everything better than everyone else. More than one Leo boy has broken a limb falling out of that tree he managed to climb the highest in. Leo boys also worship their fathers; "my dad can beat your dad" is a very Leo-male statement. Like his sister the female Leo, the Leo boy generally leads the pack, but may not fare as well at school as she does. Many Leo boys become the smart aleck or the class clown. What their antics are designed to do is get attention, which is what they desire more than anything else at this stage of their lives. Some Leo boys never grow out of this stage and continue clowning around throughout their entire lives. Depending on how well they handle other things, the tendency can be very charming, or very disastrous.

As a young man, the Leo male is a real hustler in the job world. In fact, some throw themselves into their careers so hard that they cut out everything else—for a while, at least. But no matter how bent on success a Leo man is, he will eventually start looking around for that perfect woman to share his life with. Acceptance by a woman is so important to the Leo man that if he "fails" in a relationship, it is a severe blow to his self-respect. As a fire sign, Leo is very ardent, and he can be extremely passionate. When he is rejected, a Leo man can really go into a full-scale decline. Some will say he is suffering from a broken heart; others will see that it is his wounded pride that is hurting.

It's a lucky woman who has a romantic fling with a Leo male, because she will be treated to all kinds of earthly delights. Wining and dining is the Leo man's style, and he is enormously sentimental. By the same token, if she forgets a special day in their romantic lives, the Leo man will go into a real sulk and it may take weeks for her to pull him out of it. He is also extremely jealous, but here again the emotion springs from his innate sense of "kingship." Who would *dare* to think that his woman could choose another male over Leo? Some young Leo men are more tame than the roaring lion type, but they too want to be the center of a woman's universe. This kind of Leo male may do a lot of crying—even literally—and will hold on to the object of his affection more through emotional blackmail than tough-guy tactics.

As a mate, many Leo men are very old-fashioned, particularly in wanting their wives to stay at home. Heaven forbid if a Leo male's wife ventured out into the career world and did as well—or even better—than he! The Leo man generally treats his wife well, however, and expects to spend a lot of money on her—as he does on his physical surroundings. If you are willing to give the Leo man all the respect and adulation he requires, married life is not at all bad. Like Leo women, Leo men are fairly loyal to their wives in the sexual area. However, their "macho" streak will always surface; some work it out by having "boys' night out" quite regularly. If there is trouble in his marriage, the Leo man has a lot of trouble facing up to it. Once again, his high standards get in the way of even considering the possibility that he isn't up to snuff. Also, Leo men are very proud of their standing and status in the community. They do not like to admit the fact that all is not the best in the best of all possible households. The woman who marries a Leo man must be prepared to do quite a bit for her mate; she must also be prepared to suffer with him when he suffers a slight to his ego— even if she knows he is exaggerating the situation. The Leo husband tends to use his own home ground as his stage where he can display the full range of emotions that he must often suppress in order to be successful in the business world. Leo men don't cry—except in front of their wives.

As a father, the Leo man is extremely affectionate and playful. He will love his "cubs" fiercely, and want them to have the best of everything. He may also expect too much of them too soon, and begin to push them before they are ready to be pushed. The children of a Leo father will quickly find out what tactics bring dad into line; if they give him a lot of respect and a few "yes sirs," they can usually get away with murder. In the best of Leo males, fatherhood gives them a new perspective on life and may be the catalyst that turns him from an egocentric individual into the truly protective head of a family.

18

Leo Help Wanted

Selecting a Career/Your On-the-job Style

A vitally important aspect of a successful Leo game plan is making sure you land in the "right" job or career—i.e., the one that best suits your native talents and tendencies. It is more than a truism that people perform better doing what comes naturally. There are some natural careers for Leo, and they have several common denominators. One important one is the principle of organization at which Leo excells. Another is connected with the things and activities that bring pleasure to others. It is not possible to list *all* the specific jobs a Leo should do well at, but there are some "Leo images" that provide useful guidelines. Though you may not end up literally *doing* any of these things, try to conjure up an idea of what it takes to do the following jobs, and you'll have a better handle on what kind of inner resources Leo people have available to them for career success.

Dancer/choreographer

Public school teacher/administrator

Venture capitalist

Fashion editor

Department store sales/management

Child psychiatrist

Fund raiser

Public relations

Interior designer/architect

Restaurant/nightclub owner/manager

Chef

Actor/actress or musical performer

Equally important to finding the best job slot for you is understanding how your Leo sun sign affects your modus operandi on the job and your potential for moving up. Every sun sign has certain success skills that can smooth and widen the career path, as well as blind spots that can cause readblocks. The more you know about both, the better off you will be.

Sincere, passionate about what he/she does, and well-organized, Leo has an almost unbeatable combination of qualities for an extremely successful on-the-job style and a very bright future. Then why isn't every Leo a standout in the working world? With such a well-equipped sign as Leo, the most useful tack is to point out a couple of the dangers inherent in the Leo personality that can keep people born under this sign from achieving their full potential.

Leo's famous temper tantrums may be appropriate in the childhood years, but they have no place in the business world. Unfortunately, too many hot-headed Leos never learn to control their tempers, and display a counter-productive tendency to show them to their bosses and their employees. What is particularly unsettling to the people such Leos work with is the unpredictability of Leo's ups and downs. While Leo is not an essentially moody sign like Cancer, many people born under it lack the necessary calm to control their very strong emotions. When it comes to promotion time, this kind of Leo can easily be passed over by the management; what they want is someone who is much steadier at the helm.

Another potential pitfall for the success-oriented Leo is excessive partisanship. Leo has very strong likes and equally strong dislikes. If Leo is his/her usual honest self, he/she makes no secret of them in the workplace. The result: Leo often chooses the "wrong side" and suffers because of it. It is all well and good to be loyal, but it is not necessary to go down with the ship, as many Leos do. Subtlety does not come easily to people born under this sign, they have to learn it. Remember, Leo: Don't play favorites, don't take sides, and do at least try to *appear* neutral in office politics.

When Leo has got his/her temper under control and has learned to play it cool in other respects as well, there is little that can hold this sign back. A natural leader and a creative thinker, Leo has few excuses for not going right to the top of the ladder. However, there is one more cautionary note: Some people born under this sign can get a bit lazy when things seem to be rolling along well. If you fall into this category, just make sure you keep your Leo fires banked properly, so that you can quickly find the energy when it is needed.

19

How "Pure" A Leo Are You?

Your Moon Sign ... Your Rising Sign

No one is a "pure Leo"—or pure anything, for that matter—when it comes to astrological signs. As you will learn when you read "Defining Terms," there are many other factors in a horoscope that add up to the total person that is "you." Yes, there are twelve basic personality types according to the zodiac, but within those broad groups there are almost infinite variations.

Though you are a Leo at the core and can count on the portrait of your sun sign to define you in essence, the two other horoscope factors that count most are in your personality profile: your moon sign and your rising sign. Many people know their moon sign; anyone can quickly determine it via an ephemeris. If you know your birthtime at least within one hour, you can use the table in this book to find out what your rising sign is.

The Moon—Your "Dark Side"
Almost more than your sun sign, your moon sign indicates what makes you run. Most of the time, you do not know it yourself, because the moon is your subconscious, your "dark side" not because it is bad, but because it is hidden. When the meaning of your moon sign is added to your Leo sun sign, it is a fuller picture and a better indicator of your probable personality. Here's how a Leo sun sign mixes with each of the moon signs.

Leo sun sign/Aries moon sign   Your sense of honor should be very strong, and you could be loyal to a fault; learn to look at others a bit more realistically. There is a tendency toward willfulness with this combination, and a lot of impatience. With both your sun and your moon in fire signs, you could be burning up most of the time. Cool it!

Leo sun sign/Taurus moon sign   Nobody but nobody can change your mind once you've made it up. It's great to be strong-minded but not so great to be absolutely pigheaded. Back off a little. Your love of luxury could be extreme, and there is the possibility that you overindulge in life. However, you are equally generous with others as you are with yourself.

Leo sun sign/Gemini moon sign   You tend to be a bit more subtle than the typical Leo sun sign person, who often is almost too direct. You are also more agreeable about adapting to others' plans. However, you could be a bit too well versed in the technique of manipulating people; let your strong Leo conscience be your guide. You would make an excellent teacher—especially of teenagers.

Leo sun sign/Cancer moon sign   With this combination, you could easily become one of the Leo sun sign "fat cats," meaning you could easily treat yourself too well to everything in life—including a lot of leisure. Sometimes it takes a lot to get you going, but when you do, you can really turn out some good work. You are far too sensitive to slights from others, and should make an attempt to let more things simply roll off your back.

Leo sun sign/Leo moon sign   Your sense of self could be a bit exaggerated, and you may have to keep reminding yourself that the world does not really revolve around what you say, do or think. You are self-expressive in the extreme; be careful that your frequent scenes do not become so frequent that they become totally ineffective. However, you are the most loyal of friends who really goes to bat for those you love.

Leo sun sign/Virgo moon sign   You most likely are an uncharacteristically subdued Leo who is more comfortable in the number two spot than the boss position. However, there are times when your lack of self-confidence rankles you and makes you a rather cranky and dissatisfied type. Try being more self-expressive and live up to your Leo nature a bit more. You'll be a lot happier.

Leo sun sign/Libra moon sign   You are among the sweetest of Leo types, regardless of your sex, in the sense that you are very open and affable with others. Many of you will find your greatest success in some aspect of the arts, but chances are you will do well anywhere. Not the least of your virtues is a willingness to listen to the other side of the story; sometimes you do it for your own purposes, but it's still okay.

Leo sun sign/Scorpio moon sign   This is a potentially explosive combination; when this kind of Leo roars he/she can really damage other peoples' feelings. Try to keep your considerable passions under control and learn to apply reason to a situation before you overreact to it. You are absolutely made for worldly success and are an excellent manager; however, your "people skills" need a little working on.

Leo sun sign/Sagittarius moon sign   Easy come, easy go, is your motto; the more you make, the more you spend—a lot of it on others. This is one of the most generous combinations in the zodiac, in every sense of the word. You are the eternal optimist, but maybe you should get a little more skeptical—particularly about people who try to get something out of you. You are also entirely too free with your emotional enthusiams, but everyone loves you.

Leo sun sign/Capricorn moon sign You always know exactly what your return on investment is going to be for your time and money—whether you count it in dollars or other kinds of favors. This is the combination of the ultimate politician; you could quite literally do well in public office. Unfortunately, some people with this combination are overly concerned with outward appearances. Those who know the price of everything often know the value of nothing.

Leo sun sign/Aquarius moon sign You are among the most sincere of God's creatures, but you are sometimes such a big thinker that you think yourself right out into the stratosphere. Try to bring your ideas down to earth. Your sociable nature makes you loved by many. Fortunately, you are able to be fairly objective about people, even though you usually give them the benefit of the doubt.

Leo sun sign/Pisces moon sign This makes for a supersubtle Leo—almost too subtle for your own good. In fact, you dislike trouble so intensely that you might even shade the truth to get out of it. You tend to be highly partisan, believing the people you like are all good and the people you dislike are all bad. Try to see a little more of the gray tones in life and in people. Your creativity is exceptional.

Your Rising Sign—Know Your "Cover"
The third of the "big three" astrological factors is your rising sign, which you can think of as an *overlay* to your sun sign. Although it does not carry the psychological weight your moon sign does, your rising sign is also "unconscious" because it is a mode of external behavior that comes so naturally to you that you may not be aware of it. In a sense, your rising sign is your "cover." It can never totally obscure the "real you" of your sun sign, but it can temporarily mask that sign, especially

when people first meet you. Here's what happens to Leo when you lay a rising sign over typical Leo behavior.

Leo with Aries rising You could easily be one of the world's gruffer Leos. It's possible for you to scare people off without meaning to. Soften up your edges.

Leo with Taurus rising Chances are you are a real stunner with an excellent physical appearance. Your come-on is fairly soft, and people fall for it. A great act!

Leo with Gemini rising It would be very easy for you to monopolize any group you find yourself in. Even if you are bursting to say something, give others a chance.

Leo with Cancer rising You are probably a real smoothie with a line a mile long; people could literally line up for you. Just don't play too many games.

Leo with Leo rising You are all things Leo, and then some! If you play your cards right, you can dazzle everyone you see. Just don't *overplay* it.

Leo with Virgo rising With this combination you should be one of the more reserved Leos of the world. Make sure people sense your natural warmth under that facade.

Leo with Libra rising This is a potentially beautiful combination in many respects. Your charm could be absolutely devastating. Don't take too much advantage of it.

Leo with Scorpio rising Vanity could be your middle name, and you may give new meaning to the word proud. Come down to earth with the rest of us.

Leo with Sagittarius rising An outgoing friend to all you meet, you could be so effusive you appear phoney. Try to curtail your tendency to overstate things.

Leo with Capricorn rising This combination often

makes for the classic "clothes horse"; no matter what your status you look rich. Don't come off as a snob.

Leo with Aquarius rising   You are quite warm and yet a bit distant at the same time, and it's an excellent combination. However, you could tend to be rather dogmatic with strangers.

Leo with Pisces rising   It's easy for Leo to hide under this rising sign. Pity those who don't realize what strengths and fires lie under your exterior.

20

Find Your Rising Sign

It is easier than many people think to find out your rising sign. One reason is that it is based on "universal" or "sidereal" time—the measure used in space travel. To ascertain your rising sign, look through the following chart and locate the birthdate nearest your birth date; look across and locate the time nearest your brith time. Remember that if daylight saving time was in effect at your birth, you must subtract one hour from the time stated on your birth certificate. In the section for your date and time, you will find an abbreviation for the sign that was rising when you were born. For instance, if your birthdate is June 12 at 9:30 a.m., your rising sign is Leo; if you were born on the same date at 9:30 p.m., your rising sign is Capricorn.

You will notice that the *year* you were born does not affect your rising sign. However, the geographical latitude does. These tables are calculated for the middle latitudes of the United States. If you were born far to the south, it is wise to look at the sign that *follows* your rising sign as well. If you were born far to the north, check out the *previous* sign.

Rising Signs—A.M. Births

	1 AM	2 AM	3 AM	4 AM	5 AM	6 AM	7 AM	8 AM	9 AM	10 AM	11 AM	12 NOON
Jan 1	Lib	Sc	Sc	Sc	Sag	Sag	Cap	Cap	Aq	Aq	Pis	Ar
Jan 9	Lib	Sc	Sc	Sc	Sag	Sag	Sag	Cap	Cap	Aq	Pis	Ar	Tau
Jan 17	Sc	Sc	Sc	Sag	Sag	Cap	Cap	Aq	Aq	Pis	Ar	Tau
Jan 25	Sc	Sc	Sag	Sag	Sag	Cap	Cap	Aq	Pis	Ar	Tau	Tau
Feb 2	Sc	Sc	Sag	Sag	Cap	Cap	Aq	Pis	Pis	Ar	Tau	Gem
Feb 10	Sc	Sag	Sag	Sag	Cap	Cap	Aq	Pis	Ar	Tau	Tau	Gem
Feb 18	Sc	Sag	Sag	Cap	Cap	Aq	Pis	Pis	Ar	Tau	Gem	Gem
Feb 26	Sag	Sag	Sag	Cap	Aq	Aq	Pis	Ar	Tau	Tau	Gem	Gem
Mar 6	Sag	Sag	Cap	Cap	Aq	Pis	Pis	Ar	Tau	Gem	Gem	Can
Mar 14	Sag	Cap	Cap	Aq	Aq	Pis	Ar	Tau	Tau	Gem	Gem	Can
Mar 22	Sag	Cap	Cap	Aq	Pis	Ar	Ar	Tau	Gem	Gem	Can	Can
Mar 30	Cap	Cap	Aq	Pis	Pis	Ar	Tau	Tau	Gem	Can	Can	Can
Apr 7	Cap	Cap	Aq	Pis	Ar	Ar	Tau	Gem	Gem	Can	Can	Leo
Apr 14	Cap	Aq	Aq	Pis	Ar	Tau	Tau	Gem	Gem	Can	Can	Leo
Apr 22	Cap	Aq	Pis	Ar	Ar	Tau	Gem	Gem	Gem	Can	Leo	Leo
Apr 30	Aq	Aq	Pis	Ar	Tau	Tau	Gem	Can	Can	Can	Leo	Leo
May 8	Aq	Pis	Ar	Ar	Tau	Gem	Can	Can	Can	Leo	Leo	Leo
May 16	Aq	Pis	Ar	Tau	Gem	Gem	Can	Can	Can	Leo	Leo	Vir
May 24	Pis	Ar	Ar	Tau	Gem	Gem	Can	Can	Leo	Leo	Leo	Vir
June 1	Pis	Ar	Tau	Gem	Gem	Can	Can	Can	Leo	Leo	Vir	Vir
June 9	Ar	Ar	Tau	Gem	Gem	Can	Can	Leo	Leo	Leo	Vir	Vir
June 17	Ar	Tau	Gem	Gem	Can	Can	Can	Leo	Leo	Vir	Vir	Vir
June 25	Tau	Tau	Gem	Gem	Can	Can	Leo	Leo	Leo	Vir	Vir	Lib
July 3	Tau	Gem	Gem	Can	Can	Can	Leo	Leo	Vir	Vir	Vir	Lib
July 11	Tau	Gem	Gem	Can	Can	Leo	Leo	Leo	Vir	Vir	Lib	Lib
July 18	Gem	Gem	Can	Can	Can	Leo	Leo	Vir	Vir	Vir	Lib	Lib
July 26	Gem	Gem	Can	Can	Leo	Leo	Leo	Vir	Vir	Lib	Lib	Lib
Aug 3	Gem	Can	Can	Can	Leo	Leo	Vir	Vir	Vir	Lib	Lib	Sc
Aug 11	Gem	Can	Can	Leo	Leo	Leo	Vir	Vir	Lib	Lib	Lib	Sc
Aug 18	Can	Can	Can	Leo	Leo	Vir	Vir	Vir	Lib	Lib	Sc	Sc
Aug 27	Can	Can	Leo	Leo	Leo	Vir	Vir	Lib	Lib	Lib	Sc	Sc
Sept 4	Can	Can	Leo	Leo	Leo	Vir	Vir	Vir	Lib	Lib	Sc	Sc
Sept 12	Can	Leo	Leo	Leo	Vir	Vir	Lib	Lib	Lib	Sc	Sc	Sag
Sept 30	Leo	Leo	Leo	Vir	Vir	Lib	Lib	Sc	Sc	Sc	Sc	Sag
Sept 28	Leo	Leo	Leo	Vir	Vir	Lib	Lib	Lib	Sc	Sc	Sag	Sag
Oct 6	Leo	Leo	Vir	Vir	Vir	Lib	Lib	Sc	Sc	Sc	Sag	Sag
Oct 14	Leo	Vir	Vir	Vir	Lib	Lib	Lib	Sc	Sc	Sc	Sag	Cap
Oct 22	Leo	Vir	Vir	Lib	Lib	Lib	Sc	Sc	Sc	Sag	Sag	Cap
Oct 30	Vir	Vir	Vir	Lib	Lib	Sc	Sc	Sc	Sag	Sag	Cap	Cap
Nov 7	Vir	Vir	Lib	Lib	Lib	Sc	Sc	Sc	Sag	Sag	Cap	Cap
Nov 15	Vir	Vir	Lib	Lib	Sc	Sc	Sc	Sag	Sag	Cap	Cap	Aq
Nov 23	Vir	Lib	Lib	Lib	Sc	Sc	Sag	Sag	Sag	Cap	Cap	Aq
Dec 1	Vir	Lib	Lib	Sc	Sc	Sc	Sag	Sag	Cap	Cap	Aq	Aq
Dec 9	Lib	Lib	Lib	Sc	Sc	Sag	Sag	Sag	Cap	Cap	Aq	Pis
Dec 18	Lib	Lib	Sc	Sc	Sc	Sag	Sag	Cap	Cap	Aq	Aq	Pis
Dec 28	Lib	Lib	Sc	Sc	Sag	Sag	Sag	Cap	Aq	Aq	Pis	Ar

Rising Signs—P.M. Births

	1 PM	2 PM	3 PM	4 PM	5 PM	6 PM	7 PM	8 PM	9 PM	10 PM	11 PM	12 MIDNIGHT
Jan 1	Tau	Gem	Gem	Can	Can	Can	Leo	Leo	Vir	Vir	Vir	Lib
Jan 9	Tau	Gem	Gem	Can	Can	Leo	Leo	Leo	Vir	Vir	Vir	Lib
Jan 17	Gem	Gem	Can	Can	Can	Leo	Leo	Vir	Vir	Vir	Lib	Lib
Jan 25	Gem	Gem	Can	Can	Leo	Leo	Leo	Vir	Vir	Lib	Lib	Lib
Feb 2	Gem	Can	Can	Can	Leo	Leo	Vir	Vir	Vir	Lib	Lib	Sc
Feb 10	Gem	Can	Can	Leo	Leo	Leo	Vir	Vir	Lib	Lib	Lib	Sc
Feb 18	Can	Can	Can	Leo	Leo	Vir	Vir	Vir	Lib	Lib	Sc	Sc
Feb 26	Can	Can	Leo	Leo	Leo	Vir	Vir	Lib	Lib	Lib	Sc	Sc
Mar 6	Can	Leo	Leo	Leo	Vir	Vir	Vir	Lib	Lib	Sc	Sc	Sc
Mar 14	Can	Leo	Leo	Vir	Vir	Vir	Lib	Lib	Lib	Sc	Sc	Sag
Mar 22	Leo	Leo	Leo	Vir	Vir	Lib	Lib	Lib	Sc	Sc	Sc	Sag
Mar 30	Leo	Leo	Vir	Vir	Vir	Lib	Lib	Sc	Sc	Sc	Sag	Sag
Apr 7	Leo	Leo	Vir	Vir	Lib	Lib	Lib	Sc	Sc	Sc	Sag	Sag
Apr 14	Leo	Vir	Vir	Vir	Lib	Lib	Sc	Sc	Sc	Sag	Sag	Cap
Apr 22	Leo	Vir	Vir	Lib	Lib	Lib	Sc	Sc	Sc	Sag	Sag	Cap
Apr 30	Vir	Vir	Vir	Lib	Lib	Sc	Sc	Sc	Sag	Sag	Cap	Cap
May 8	Vir	Vir	Lib	Lib	Lib	Sc	Sc	Sag	Sag	Sag	Cap	Cap
May 16	Vir	Vir	Lib	Lib	Sc	Sc	Sc	Sag	Sag	Cap	Cap	Aq
May 24	Vir	Lib	Lib	Lib	Sc	Sc	Sag	Sag	Sag	Cap	Cap	Aq
June 1	Vir	Lib	Lib	Sc	Sc	Sc	Sag	Sag	Cap	Cap	Aq	Aq
June 9	Lib	Lib	Lib	Sc	Sc	Sag	Sag	Sag	Cap	Cap	Aq	Pis
June 17	Lib	Lib	Sc	Sc	Sc	Sag	Sag	Cap	Cap	Aq	Aq	Pis
June 25	Lib	Lib	Sc	Sc	Sag	Sag	Sag	Cap	Cap	Aq	Pis	Ar
July 3	Lib	Sc	Sc	Sc	Sag	Sag	Cap	Cap	Aq	Aq	Pis	Ar
July 11	Lib	Sc	Sc	Sag	Sag	Sag	Cap	Cap	Aq	Pis	Ar	Tau
July 18	Sc	Sc	Sc	Sag	Sag	Cap	Cap	Aq	Aq	Pis	Ar	Tau
July 26	Sc	Sc	Sag	Sag	Sag	Cap	Cap	Aq	Pis	Ar	Tau	Tau
Aug 3	Sc	Sc	Sag	Sag	Cap	Cap	Aq	Aq	Pis	Ar	Tau	Gem
Aug 11	Sc	Sag	Sag	Sag	Cap	Cap	Aq	Pis	Ar	Tau	Tau	Gem
Aug 18	Sc	Sag	Sag	Cap	Cap	Aq	Pis	Pis	Ar	Tau	Gem	Gem
Aug 27	Sag	Sag	Sag	Cap	Cap	Aq	Pis	Ar	Tau	Tau	Gem	Gem
Sept 4	Sag	Sag	Cap	Cap	Aq	Pis	Pis	Ar	Tau	Gem	Gem	Can
Sept 12	Sag	Sag	Cap	Aq	Aq	Pis	Ar	Tau	Tau	Gem	Gem	Can
Sept 20	Sag	Cap	Cap	Aq	Pis	Pis	Ar	Tau	Gem	Gem	Can	Can
Sept 28	Cap	Cap	Aq	Aq	Pis	Ar	Tau	Tau	Gem	Can	Can	Can
Oct 6	Cap	Cap	Aq	Pis	Ar	Ar	Tau	Gem	Gem	Can	Can	Leo
Oct 14	Cap	Aq	Aq	Pis	Ar	Tau	Tau	Gem	Can	Can	Can	Leo
Oct 22	Cap	Aq	Pis	Ar	Ar	Tau	Gem	Gem	Can	Can	Leo	Leo
Oct 30	Aq	Aq	Pis	Ar	Tau	Tau	Gem	Can	Can	Can	Leo	Leo
Nov 7	Aq	Aq	Pis	Ar	Tau	Tau	Gem	Can	Can	Can	Leo	Leo
Nov 15	Aq	Pis	Ar	Tau	Gem	Gem	Can	Can	Can	Leo	Leo	Vir
Nov 23	Pis	Ar	Ar	Tau	Gem	Gem	Can	Can	Leo	Leo	Leo	Vir
Dec 1	Pis	Ar	Tau	Gem	Gem	Can	Can	Can	Leo	Leo	Vir	Vir
Dec 9	Ar	Tau	Tau	Gem	Gem	Can	Can	Leo	Leo	Leo	Vir	Vir
Dec 18	Ar	Tau	Gem	Gem	Can	Can	Can	Leo	Leo	Vir	Vir	Vir
Dec 28	Tau	Tau	Gem	Gem	Can	Can	Leo	Leo	Vir	Vir	Vir	Lib

21

Leo Astro-Outlook for 1986

Leo's polar-opposite sign is unorthodox Aquarius, and 1986 is a year in which you could easily take on some of that sign's unconventional traits. For one thing, you might well adopt a more independent, nonconformist attitude about life in general and decide to go your own way—no matter what others think or feel. In addition, you could become especially fascinated with something scientific, unusual subjects, and/or humanitarian causes. More than one Leo will end 1986 with a whole new kit of knowledge, some of it involving the "occult" or unknown.

Get set for a love-at-first-sight romance—maybe even more than one. You'll be attracting a lot of attractive people who are as bright and brainy as you, and definitely individuals in their own right. In love and all other interpersonal relationships (such as with a roommate) you are going to have to excercise control not to get involved in power struggles in the coming months. In trying to make constructive changes, adopting a spirit of compromise will work a lot better than attempting to dominate the scene.

When your mind is in the work mode, you'll be brimming with original, inventive ideas that will benefit you greatly. Those involved in communications or in the computer field will find things go especially well. Others will derive both inspiration and a career direction from the desire to improve the world in some way.

A chance to travel could come your way in January

or October, and you should grab it. Romance is particularly wonderful in March and December, while June is an excellent month to make an enterprising move. To learn more about your life in 1986, consult the day-to-day forecasts in the following pages.

22

Fifteen Months of Day-by-Day Predictions

OCTOBER 1985

Tuesday, October 1 (Moon in Taurus) You may find yourself on the road—possibly in search of a new career opportunity. Don't limit your thinking to one situation, however; there are lots of possibilities out there. Ask some new social contacts whom they know, and if they are willing to introduce you. It's a smart approach.

Wednesday, October 2 (Moon in Taurus) Realize you are in danger of getting sidetracked and appearing less businesslike than you should. You can get in some fun, but you should make it later in the day. Stick to the work at hand and be willing to revise and rebuild something.

Thursday, October 3 (Moon Taurus to Gemini 8:26 a.m.) Be ready to show how interested you are and you will impress some higher-ups. The more questions you ask, the more impressed they will be. Read between the lines of a written communication you get today; there may be a hidden message. The lucky number is 5.

Friday, October 4 (Moon in Gemini) You may be the instigator in getting a group together that hasn't been together in a while. It could be family or friends. The harmony is sweet and makes you feel very good about having thought of it. Someone is stubborn, and you will have to be tactful.

Saturday, October 5 (Moon Gemini to Cancer 8:42 p.m.) Someone is puzzling you by his/her actions. When you know the whole story, you understand. In another situation, it is wise to play the waiting game rather than plunging in. Once again you may find yourself in a group. The lucky number is 7.

Sunday, October 6 (Moon in Cancer) Resist the urge to spill the beans today; you could do yourself a great disservice. Instead, pledge your loyalty to an association and announce that you see it as a long-term relationship. A solid person—possibly a Capricorn—will have some good advice.

Monday, October 7 (Moon in Cancer) You are probably feeling compassionate for those less fortunate than you. Put the feeling to work in a substantial way. That might mean visiting or calling someone who is confined in some way. An Aries provides a note of levity in the day. The lucky number is 9.

Tuesday, October 8 (Moon Cancer to Leo 6:38 a.m.) The sky's the limit today and you should reach as high as you like. Whatever happens, you will find yourself making an exciting new start in a new direction. Even if it is in a minor way, be innovative today. Indulge that urge to be showy; you can always carry it off. Some new contacts are very exciting.

Wednesday, October 9 (Moon in Leo) With the moon in your sign you should be in closer sync with your own feelings and with the feelings of the persons around you. If you feel helpless in a certain situation, it is far from the truth. Everything is on your side right now and you should use the good vibes. A warmhearted individual proves how much he/she cares about you.

Thursday, October 10 (Moon Leo to Virgo 1:24 p.m.) Today you trim your sails a bit by putting some dieting and exercise program into effect. You know you are looking good these days, but you would like to look even better. You may find yourself making a "personal appearance"; it may not be on television, but is important to you.

Friday, October 11 (Moon in Virgo) Don't expect something for nothing—that almost never happens. The luck that you have you should realize came from your hard work. You proved yourself to someone who was counting on you, and you reaped the rewards. Good for you. The lucky number is 4.

Saturday, October 12 (Moon Virgo to Libra 2:38 p.m.) Keep a tight hold on your cash and your heart today; someone may try to steal either or both of them. You have an irresistible urge to go shopping, and you could find some bargains; just remember that nothing's a bargain if you don't need it. A spendthrift Gemini may try to lead you astray.

Sunday, October 13 (Moon in Libra) A family gathering may be part of today's scenario. If it is, it may lead to some kind of a reconciliation that should make you feel very good. No matter whom you interact with today it should go smoothly. The lucky number is 6.

Monday, October 14 (Moon Libra to Scorpio 2:50 p.m.) Wherever you are today, you should be feeling particularly sociable and "in sync" with the people around you. It is an excellent time to exchange information and ideas—of all kinds. If you feel yourself flagging later in the day, realize that the best thing to do is get back to home base to "refuel." Spend as much time as possible later in the day with people who are supportive of what you think and do.

Tuesday, October 15 (Moon in Scorpio) Stay put for now, and you are in a very strong position. The roots you put down give you great strength—plus the respect of others. A rise in status is coming soon, and you should be ready for it.

Wednesday, October 16 (Moon Scorpio to Sagittarius 2:25 p.m.) A cycle is definitely coming to a close, and you should be ready to move on to new things. That means all your thinking should be big thinking; refuse to participate in petty disagreements. Follow the lead of someone who has a pioneering attitude. The lucky number is 9.

Thursday, October 17 (Moon in Sagittarius) Be daring—the time for action has arrived. Don't be afraid to try doing things in a new way, because it will work. You are feeling creative, and you are. You may even find yourself in on the ground floor of something very exciting.

Friday, October 18 (Moon Sagittarius to Capricorn 3:37 p.m.) Your affectionate Leo nature should get a chance to display itself. Children or young people should be the lucky recipients of your generosity. Another possible scenario has you using diplomacy with loved ones in order to avoid conflict. Whatever happens, be willing to follow rather than lead.

Saturday, October 19 (Moon in Capricorn) You may not be feeling in tiptop shape today. And you may realize that it is your own fault, and resolve to do something about it. If you put some restrictions on yourself, you really will feel better. Meanwhile remember that laughter is the best medicine. Keep looking on the bright side of things.

Sunday, October 20 (Moon Capricorn to Aquarius 8:04 p.m.) Throw yourself into your work and show how reliable you can be. Someone may be watching, and you may have to prove yourself. There will be time later for relaxation—and possibly even a social evening in which you are involved with very compatible people.

Monday, October 21 (Moon in Aquarius) Today you will find yourself exchanging ideas with someone who is as opinionated as you are. Concentrate on a free flow of information and opinion—don't allow yourself to force your views on the other person. There is an exciting development in some area of your life, and it could involve a relationship.

Tuesday, October 22 (Moon in Aquarius) You or someone else may feel like celebrating today, even if there is no official reason. At any rate, it is a day filled with music, laughing, and good company. You may run into someone who attracts you with an appealing voice and manner; Prepare to be intrigued.

Wednesday, October 23 (Moon Aquarius to Pisces 3:35 a.m.) There is an aura of romance about this day. Realize that it could all be in your head—and the result of a recent meeting. If you are free and truly interested, do not hesitate to contact the person. He/she may be trying to send you a message via some kind of mental telepathy. Even if you don't believe in it, investigate it. The lucky number is 7.

Thursday, October 24 (Moon in Pisces) Sometimes you feel as if you have no sense of money management at all; that is far from true. If you concentrate, you can be good at it. And now you should take advantage of some good information someone is willing to give you. Listen carefully, and even take notes. You can improve your financial standing.

Friday, October 25 (Moon Pisces to Aries 2:09 p.m.) Money for a trip appears as if from the blue; or perhaps you had put it aside for just some possibility like this. At any rate, someone offers an exciting suggestion that could broaden your horizons immensely. Go ahead and do it—it will be good for you. The lucky number is 9.

Saturday, October 26 (Moon in Aries) Today someone brings some sunshine into your life—and it may be in the form of an expression of affection. Don't get carried away by the drama of the situation, because you may want to retain a degree of independence in this relationship. Also, you should be sure you are both speaking the same language. It may all be very romantic, but is it practical?

Sunday, October 27 (Moon in Aries) Don't close your mind to a new opinion—even if it differs from yours. You must be willing to examine the other viewpoints if you are to learn anything. Your ability to see into the future will vastly affect your professional life. You don't have to be psychic, but you should let your intuition examine what is happening. Watch and wait.

Monday, October 28 (Moon Aries to Taurus 2:11 a.m.) Fortunately you are a very social person, and now you realize that who you know can help you a lot. It is one way to get ahead, but you should also rely on what you know. Enjoy the contact with important people, and be sure to look your best. You will be on display. The lucky number is 3.

Tuesday, October 29 (Moon in Taurus) If you want to get ahead, you must be willing to revise something you have already put together. You should be aware of the fact that some details are not quite pinned down. And—keep in mind that someone who could help you is waiting to see how you handle things. A practical approach will win the day.

Wednesday, October 30 (Moon Taurus to Gemini 2:36 p.m.) A change in your work environment puts you on the winning side. Be ready to say what you want and what you will do for it in return. This is a time for constructive change, and you are on your way up. Do not allow yourself to appear aloof, because free communication is important.

Thursday, October 31 (Moon in Gemini) You may find yourself in a circle of admirers today. They may bask in your glow that comes from a recent accomplishment. Don't forget to give special thanks to those who backed you up along the way. Even Leos have to admit they need help. The lucky number is 6.

NOVEMBER 1985

Friday, November 1 (Moon in Gemini) If you had your way, life would be a constant circus. Since it is not, don't be tempted away from your tasks by the promise of a social event. If you are going to get ahead, you are going to have to consolidate your recent gains. Pitch in and enjoy the companionship of a helpful co-worker—possibly an Aquarian. The lucky number is 4.

Saturday, November 2 (Moon Gemini to Cancer 3:12 a.m.) Sometimes you have a way of blurting out things you should keep to yourself. It is not really that you are a gossip; you just find confidential information very exciting. Remember that this bit of information has been placed in your trust. A fast-talking person may talk romance, but it may not be serious. Be realistic. The lucky number is 5.

Sunday, November 3 (Moon in Cancer) You may have to cast about for some clues on how to rescue a relationship. It may be one that exists right under your own roof. Perhaps some attention to your surroundings could work wonders; a small adjustment might lead to greater harmony. Someone makes a confession to you and you should be very compassionate.

Monday, November 4 (Moon Cancer to Leo 3:25 a.m.) You are beginning to think in terms of new values now and it helps you take a fresh look at your whole life. Try to get away by yourself today and do more thinking—you are on a great road. Soon you will be coming out into the sunshine.

Tuesday, November 5 (Moon in Leo) The moon in

your sign makes it easy for you to wheel and deal in both business and love. The power of your personality makes it hard for anyone to ignore you—or refuse you support. Enjoy your time in the driver's seat, and take some lesson from a Capricorn who does it all the time. The lucky number is 8.

Wednesday, November 6 (Moon Leo to Virgo 9:34 p.m.) You are much more able to express yourself now and should begin to see your full potential. Realize it is foolish to think with a limited viewpoint or to deal with petty people. Open up and use all your talents—for they are many. An Aries may play a prominent role today.

Thursday, November 7 (Moon in Virgo) You may be attracted to some high-risk activities today, either physical or financial. You are not generally foolish, so you need not worry. However, realize that a bit of caution never hurt anyone. Your self-esteem is on the rise.

Friday, November 8 (Moon in Virgo) An old debt will be repaid to you and you may find yourself reminiscing with someone about the old days. Don't let sentiment blind you to reality; you must always protect yourself, particularly in financial matters. The lucky number today is 2.

Saturday, November 9 (Moon Virgo to Libra 1:14 a.m.) You search for answers today and find yourself in touch with some intellectual types. You have an inquiring mind, so you find it a stimulating interlude. You even get a chance to display your own wit—and you experience some good feelings about yourself. Some upbeat news makes you feel optimistic.

Sunday, November 10 (Moon in Libra) Try to cut through as much redtape as possible today in order to get necessary communications out of the way. Paper work is a bore for you, but it is necessary. Meanwhile check out some details and be willing to revise some words if they do not get your message across effectively. Talk to another Leo today.

Monday, November 11 (Moon Libra to Scorpio 1:53 a.m.) You may be feeling rather confined today, but it is only temporary. Take this quiet time to have a quiet talk with someone who has the same interests you do in terms of property and real estate. These are weighty matters and they deserve a lot of attention. The lucky number is 5.

Tuesday, November 12 (Moon in Scorpio) Your talk of yesterday results in greater harmony today. It makes you able to start planning a very special evening with some very special people. You may even be thinking of doing a gourmet dinner. Make sure you plan ahead so no one will be disappointed. In another matter you should be willing to forgive and forget.

Wednesday, November 13 (Moon Scorpio to Sagittarius 1:12 a.m.) Slow down to a walk and try to figure out what is really going on. There is a puzzle that is baffling you, and it may involve a relationship with another person. You should learn the story behind the story before you go any further. It may be glamorous and mysterious, but is it real?

Thursday, November 14 (Moon in Sagittarius) This is a day to make permanent gains. You can achieve results on several fronts, as long as you are willing to go all the way. Whenever you talk with another person—about love, marriage, or business—you mean what you say. A significant person is on the scene today and plays a major role.

Friday, November 15 (Moon Sagittarius to Capricorn 1:10 a.m.) You may be involved with someone from a totally different background today. What you learn enlarges your viewpoint and makes you realize just how it is out there. You may make a definite decision about further studies and/or travel. Good going, Leo!

Saturday, November 16 (Moon in Capricorn) Don't overdo anything today. In fact, you might even do something about looking into some health matters that have been bothering you. On the other hand, your personal magnetism is quite high, and you can influence those around you who think the way you do. Make it a balanced day. The lucky number is 1.

Sunday, November 17 (Moon Capricorn to Aquarius 3:54 a.m.) Make yourself accessible today—particularly to those who depend on you for warmth and affection. If you are receptive, you will be able to smooth over the rough edges of the relationship. Spend some time just hanging around; it will show your concern.

Monday, November 18 (Moon in Aquarius) You run into someone who tells you in no uncertain terms that he/she totally disagrees with your point of view. It may startle you, but don't let it rattle you. Keep your sense of humor at the ready, and wait it out. Sooner or later you will have your say. The lucky number is 3.

Tuesday, November 19 (Moon Aquarius to Pisces 10:04 a.m.) You may have been planning a rather big bash; you may have to put those plans aside for a while. Patience and self-discipline are the key words now. After you have seen something through to its completion, you can focus on more frivolous things. Don't let the restrictions get you down.

Wednesday, November 20 (Moon in Pisces) Keep on your toes this entire day, because a number of exciting things could happen. Anyone of them could be a golden opportunity—possibly even for a new romance. You may also get some information you've needed in order to form a complete opinion. Now you know. The lucky number is 5.

Thursday, November 21 (Moon Pisces to Aries 8:00 p.m.) Someone is very generous with you today. Accept whatever he/she gives you gracefully, even if it is not to your personal taste. You Leos can be rather showy, and not everyone has the same view of things. Someone extends a hand and says let's shake on it. You should.

Friday, November 22 (Moon in Aries) Your urge to escape the everyday routine could be very strong today—and you could even take a fantastic voyage of the mind. Sometimes that's a good way to enlarge your viewpoint and your outlook on the world. When you come back to earth, resolve never to get involved in trivia again. Life is too short. A Pisces could be a wonderful person to listen to.

Saturday, November 23 (Moon in Aries) Today you may be thinking in terms of travel—and in terms of traveling with someone special. It's a good way to see if you both share the same view of the future. You are enjoying greater prestige now, and it shows in your life which is much more stable. Keep up the good work. The lucky number is 8.

Sunday, November 24 (Moon Aries to Taurus 8:37 a.m.) Now you are ready to break altogether with your small thinking of the past. Your viewpoint is much larger now, and you refuse to be drawn into arguments about slight differences. As you think big, don't forget to think about education. You do love to learn.

Monday, November 25 (Moon in Taurus) You start off the workweek with a good burst of energy. You've got some big ideas and the power to put them across now. Don't waste your time dealing with people who don't count; go right to the top. Good things can happen in your love life too.

Tuesday, November 26 (Moon Taurus to Gemini 9:02 p.m.) The pace slows down a bit, and the results may be less dramatic. However, you enjoy the quiet time, and should spend it thinking about future plans. It is important to avoid emotional extremes now. You feel passionate about something, but you should not force the issue. Listen to someone older who's been there before. The lucky number is 2.

Wednesday, November 27 (Moon in Gemini) As you keep your mind open to new ideas, you may learn more than you bargained for, you may feel that you are on a roller coaster of activity. Enjoy the popularity, but try to keep your wits about you. You are traveling with some fast types.

Thursday, November 28 (Moon in Gemini) Today you reap the rewards of some smart thinking you did lately. There's still a lot standing between you and success however; you've got to be willing to stick with things and see them through. You can play some other day. The lucky number today is 4.

Friday, November 29 (Moon Gemini to Cancer 8:59 a.m.) That fast pace is here again, but you are more up to it. Emotional fulfillment is on the agenda, as is a wish that comes true. Enjoy a face-off with a very verbal person—possibly a Gemini or a Virgo—and don't worry if you don't win. The lucky number is 5.

Saturday, November 30 (Moon in Cancer) The sweet things of life in every sense are very much on the menu today. You could literally find yourself dining in gourmet style, and enjoying it immensely. Don't forget your obligations to others in your personal search for pleasure—just try to keep things in balance.

DECEMBER 1985

Sunday, December 1 (Moon Cancer to Leo 8:04 p.m.)
Carefully guard a secret that is revealed to you. Sharing it with anyone could get you in serious trouble.

In another matter, things take an unexpected turn—and you must be ready to revise your thinking. Don't be afraid of variety, however, and let go of your fears and doubts. The lucky number is 5.

Monday, December 2 (Moon in Leo) You stand to gain a lot today with the moon in your very own sign. Don't undervalue your ability to bring sunshine into the life of others—particularly when you are at your Leo best. Today you should get personal satisfaction out of expressing yourself in some artistic manner. A Libra or a Taurus would be very compatible with you.

Tuesday, December 3 (Moon in Leo) Even though you are the friendliest of types, sometimes you appear aloof. You know it is just shyness, but others do not. Try to be more approachable and realize you have an aura of mystery about you. A very sensitive person may need some reassuring.

Wednesday, December 4 (Moon Leo to Virgo 4:38 a.m.) You are a great one for buying the best and the most expensive. This time, why not try to get it wholesale. There are people who can pull strings for you. Meanwhile, establish a greater rapport with someone who can further your business interests. It could be a Capricorn.

Thursday, December 5 (Moon in Virgo) Someone may be getting overly dependent on you and you should be aware of it. Though you want very much to help, realize you could overdo it. The best thing to do is not to be a crutch, but encourage the person to go it alone. The lucky number today is 9.

Friday, December 6 (Moon Virgo to Libra 9:44 a.m.) Someone may tell you you are a bit much today; realize that you can occasionally be overbearing. It's okay to express yourself, but give others a chance too. A shopping trip could pay off very well. Just don't go overboard and break the bank.

Saturday, December 7 (Moon in Libra) Don't be a procrastinating Leo; concentrate on your Christmas correspondence and gift sending now. There are a lot of friends and relatives who could be disappointed if they did not hear from you. For those nearer by, make some drop-in trips—you are always welcomed. A Cancer or a Capricorn may be around today and give you a rather rough time. Don't growl.

Sunday, December 8 (Moon Libra to Scorpio 1:05 p.m.) If you keep too many irons in the fire, you are likely to get burned. Sort things out for yourself and take people up on some very interesting invitations. You may be a bit distracted today, so make sure you don't lose something valuable. The lucky number is 3.

Monday, December 9 (Moon in Scorpio) Though it may be a bore, you are going to have to pay attention to some details today and get some basic tasks done. You feel rather hemmed in, but don't fret; tomorrow is another day. If you are practical now, you can afford to be a little frivolous later.

Tuesday, December 10 (Moon Scorpio to Sagittarius 1:11 p.m.) You are really getting in the holiday spirit. You've got lots of creative ideas, but not much time to put them all into practice. Sit down and decide which of them you are going to follow through on to turn things into a "winter wonderland." Use some of your own artistic talents and you will be able to make some very inspired gifts. With a lot of love in them. And those are the best kind.

Wednesday, December 11 (Moon in Sagittarius) You may be feeling rather sentimental today and it should add to your enjoyment. Don't let your mellow mood add to your waistline however; you will have to watch your sweet tooth during this holiday period. Have fun with children and luck with number 6.

Thursday, December 12 (Moon Sagittarius to Capricorn 1:03 p.m.) You can well afford to play the waiting game now—particularly in romance. The opportunity is not going to go away—and you should give yourself time to look at the situation more clearly. Insist on the facts and figures in every area right now; it is not the time to speculate wildly.

Friday, December 13 (Moon in Capricorn) Get a definite commitment from someone before you count on his/her backing. It's easy to say yes, and easy to forget it later on. No one would deliberately trick you, but enthusiasm can make for some rather unstable conditions. You've got new prestige in your own circle. Enjoy it, and try your luck with number 8.

Saturday, December 14 (Moon Capricorn to Aquarius 1:39 p.m) Be sure to get some nitty gritty details out of the way today, because you want to have a clear deck for action tomorrow. If you use some streamlined methods, you will be able to cut through things fast. Don't neglect someone who depends on you—possibly even a pet. The lucky number is 9.

Sunday, December 15 (Moon in Aquarius) You will be very much in the limelight today, so be sure you are projecting yourself the way you want to. If you see yourself as a trend setter, wear something rather bold and daring. Remember, however, that it is possible to be original without being aggressive. Let other people come to you. Another Leo may be around.

Monday, December 16 (Moon Aquarius to Pisces 6:21 p.m.) This is a time when it is best to watch and wait. Be willing to see the other person's point of view and able to hold your tongue when you are annoyed. Diplomacy will get you more than anything else. Partnerships are very much in the spotlight now, and you may be forced to remember you are not alone. The lucky number is 2.

Tuesday, December 17 (Moon in Pisces) Any money that you spend to increase your knowledge is not wasted. However, you should always draw the line at pointless extravagance. In this case, that means don't take on more than you can handle in the way of educational projects. You can do things one at a time.

Wednesday, December 18 (Moon in Pisces) As much as you love to do it, don't try to impress others with your showmanship. A practical gift is usually more appreciated than something flamboyant given for the sake of drama. Even you can find some bargains. Take a rather logical Aquarian with you when you go shopping.

Thursday, December 19 (Moon Pisces to Aries 2:55 a.m.) Some holiday plans may come apart today; don't let it spoil your Christmas mood. Be flexible and do some quick thinking that will accommodate everyone. You may have to travel farther than you intended to. The lucky number today is 5.

Friday, December 20 (Moon in Aries) This is a sharing day with the emphasis on harmony in every sense. Even if someone is out of sorts and rather stubborn, you can bring him/her around to be part of a group. You feel like embracing everyone today in a very spiritual sense.

Saturday, December 21 (Moon Aries to Taurus 3:09 p.m.) It's hard to concentrate on practical things now; your urge to get away from it all could be rather powerful. Instead of getting holiday jitters, take time out to reflect on what you really have. If you look at the long-range picture you will be very aware of the blessings there are for you. Talk things over with a sympathetic person—possibly a Pisces. The lucky number is 7.

Sunday, December 22 (Moon in Taurus) You may be surprised when you are suddenly rewarded for something you did a while back—and forgot. Other people did not, and they let you know it now. Be willing to make a deeper commitment to a close relationship; someone else is reminding you that you can't take a halfway approach.

Monday, December 23 (Moon in Taurus) Finish up something that needs doing and take some time to look at what your long-range career goals are—starting with the coming year. You should have an excellent perspective right now and a sense of your own potential. You should listen to someone who has some rather aggressive ideas; they could be very profitable for you!

Tuesday, December 24 (Moon Taurus to Gemini 3:46 a.m.) You are feeling very expansive on this holiday eve. If you could, you would take the whole world into your arms. As it is, it may be a special someone you do that with. You are feeling much more able to go your own way now in the sense of not following in a crowd. Good for you.

Wednesday, December 25 (Moon in Gemini) Today you should relax and let down your guard. After all, you are with those closest to you. You experience a warm glow today as people express affection toward you that shows the depth of their feelings. It feels good to be just who you are. Enjoy the day, but remember not to overdo it in the pleasure department. The lucky number is 2.

Thursday, December 26 (Moon Gemini to Cancer 3:41 p.m.) You will be much sought after today, but don't let it go to your head. Maintain your sense of humor and keep things in perspective. A light touch should be the order for the day, with the accent on lots of movement. Someone with a very broad view of things— possibly a Sagittarian—plays a major role in the day's events.

Friday, December 27 (Moon in Cancer) Your object today should be to focus on the practical, and to catch up on details. You will probably be working behind the scenes where you will not be very appreciated. Recognize the limitations of the day, and use self-discipline to carry yourself through. You have had a lot of fun lately. The lucky number is 4.

Saturday, December 28 (Moon in Cancer) Something you didn't know about now comes to light, and you realize why someone has been acting the way he/she has. This new understanding makes you much more willing to change plans to accommodate others. Let your feelings of compassion extend to someone who is confined in some way. That person would love to hear from you.

Sunday, December 29 (Moon Cancer to Leo 1:51 a.m.) A late gift comes in and you are delighted! It caters right to your love of luxurious and beautiful things. The timing is exactly right, because you feel like making a "personal appearance" today. You would stand out in any crowd now.

Monday, December 30 (Moon in Leo) Your holiday mood does not prevent you from puzzling over something. You do not like the feeling being at sea about it. If you do a little digging, you can get at the truth—and realize that someone is trying to sweep some details under the carpet. You are the one who must give things an airing. The lucky number today is 7.

Tuesday, December 31 (Moon Leo to Virgo 10:06 a.m.) What a way to wind up the year! A leadership role is thrust upon you, and you enjoy every minute of it. As you circulate, you will make some very valuable contacts. Jot them down in your memory book for use in the future. Among your resolutions should be a vow to take more responsibility in your most important relationship; that is the key to making it work better.

JANUARY 1986

Wednesday, January 1 (Moon in Virgo) You should be starting out the New Year on a very upbeat note. Things are looking good, and so are you. Spend some time today getting some insider's information—possibly about a financial matter. An Aquarian or a Scorpio would make an excellent opposite number now. The lucky number is 4.

Thursday, January 2 (Moon Virgo to Libra 3:45 p.m.) Good things start coming to you right away. In fact, some will have an old debt they had almost forgotten repaid now. Someone "stokes your fires" and lets you know he/she is totally loyal; you love the feeling of security it gives you. Others may see a new opening and try successfully for it. Good show!

Friday, January 3 (Moon in Libra) You probably are in a mood to test out some of your ideas today, and you've got some interesting and interested people to try them on. There's a lot of visiting back and forth indicated and fresh contacts as well. Some may even find romance along the way. A gentle but strong person—possibly connected with the arts—will add a grace note to your day.

Saturday, January 4 (Moon Libra to Scorpio 7:44 p.m.) You wake up today with a pretty clear sense of where you want to go—and not just today, either. A plan that's been hatching now takes more shape, and you find it gives you even more vitality than usual. When people ask, "Why the good mood?" you may decide to keep your thoughts secret. Let things get beyond the planning stage before you reveal anything.

Sunday, January 5 (Moon in Scorpio) This is a lot quieter day, although there is a major change in plan that is a bit unsettling at first. You quickly find out that you can use the time to good advantage, however. One thing you concentrate on is a special relationship that can use some special attention. The number 8 could be lucky today.

Monday, January 6 (Moon Scorpio to Sagittarius 9:47 p.m.) Choose your words very carefully today, because what you say in jest could be more true than you know. And you could hurt someone by it. Those future plans are shaping up quite nicely, and some kind of special permission comes through. A lot of you Leos are getting a nice big audience—and you like it. You are really going places!

Tuesday, January 7 (Moon in Sagittarius) Get ready for a new start in a new direction. The position of the moon highlights romance, change, and variety. You'll get a special chance to show your own style today, and no one is likely to step on your toes when you dance to your own tune. Some should prepare themselves for a very direct talk with a member of the opposite sex. There will be a confession involved.

Wednesday, January 8 (Moon Sagittarius to Capricorn 10:42 p.m.) Trust your first impressions today, because they are most likely correct. Your intuition is good, and your timing should be right as well. Utilize the element of surprise today, because it could work for you quite nicely. Women Leos especially will be quite popular now—although the men will not do badly either. For best results, mix with a Cancer or a Capricorn now.

Thursday, January 9 (Moon in Capricorn) You've got to step back and see the whole picture, and leave the details for another time. It is important that you get a broad view before you focus in on the nitty-gritties. Some will be bogged down with a lot of responsibility today, and it may seem as if everyone is depending on you. Your forces may be a bit scattered and you could be dealing with some restless people. Stay cool! For best results, listen to a Sagittarian.

Friday, January 10 (Moon in Capricorn) Don't just yawn and say you're bored when the time comes to revise something you've already done. Recognize the fact that you did it in a rather slapdash manner, and be willing to fix things up. Once again, many Leos will have people relying on them—and on their judgment. Be careful how you counsel someone. He/she will take it seriously. Someone who shares your ideals makes you feel rather good.

Saturday, January 11 (Moon Capricorn to Aquarius 12:01 a.m.) Cooperative efforts of all sorts are emphasized today—that includes marriage. It's a time to go slow and let other people take the lead. Hang back and take in all the information and impressions you can. Realize that time is on your side and you can afford to play a waiting game. The lucky number today is 5.

Sunday, January 12 (Moon in Aquarius) You may find yourself on a collision course with someone very close to you—possibly even your mate or live-in partner. Try to head it off by simply keeping your mouth shut. For some, the day will turn out surprisingly well, and they will be unexpectedly entertained. In a few cases, there could be a new love by this evening.

Monday, January 13 (Moon Aquarius to Pisces 3:39 a.m.) Look for someone to intrigue you, fascinate you, and challenge you today. If you react like the "typical" Leo, you are likely to blow the whole deal. Try to keep a cool head in the situation. For many, what appears to be a closed situation is open again and it looks quite positive. It could be a legal matter. The lucky number is 7.

Tuesday, January 14 (Moon in Pisces) Whatever balance you may have lost yesterday you completely recover today. In fact, some may recover something they thought was lost forever. In a few cases, that will be a romantic interest. All should dig deep now because there is really paydirt there. Play private eye, and do your own investigating.

Wednesday, January 15 (Moon Pisces to Aries 11:03 a.m.) What once seemed very far away is now close at hand—are you ready for it? Do not fear to deal with the situation, because you will have a lot of help and support from others. Some will have a major roadblock to progress removed now. The lucky number today is 9.

Thursday, January 16 (Moon in Aries) The emphasis now is on new starts—of every kind. Some will be positively inspired by a member of the opposite sex, and plunge into a new mad affair. For others, the scenario will be less dramatic, but you should feel as if you are on a new road and traveling at quite a good speed. An Aries or a Libra could figure prominently today.

Friday, January 17 (Moon Aries to Taurus 10:14 p.m.) It is a time to show how pioneering and enthusiastic you can be, even if you do not feel as confident as others think you are. It is important to display leadership characteristics now and a willingness to take a chance on your own abilities. Some will be attracting admirers—possibly by a display of talents or even wares. Sell up a storm!

Saturday, January 18 (Moon in Taurus) Your best friends today could be your sense of humor, and your willingness to be flexible. Some plans are going to change rather suddenly and could cause you a moment of anxiety. For some, prestige is on the rise, and they learn that someone they thought was an enemy is actually on their side. An excellent social atmosphere prevails.

Sunday, January 19 (Moon in Taurus) You are going to have to speak quite frankly today about a rather delicate situation. Frankly, however, there are concessions that must be made on both sides—including yours. Some people—a little tough for you—may give you a hard time today. One could be a Taurus or another Leo. Refuse to be intimidated. You are going in the right direction despite detours.

Monday, January 20 (Moon Taurus to Gemini 11:12 a.m.) Many will be delighted to find out that one of their pet ideas is being seriously considered. Others will be much less restricted than in the recent past. The road to romance may be rocky, but those who are on it should be feeling a little more emotionally secure. Don't neglect your standing in your career area or your community environment. There are eyes on you.

Tuesday, January 21 (Moon in Gemini) Someone in your immediate circle helps to make one of your wishes come true. Don't just think about doing something nice for this person—do it! Today a lot of things come to you, possibly even a gift. All will feel they are among friends and should have a hopeful attitude toward the future. The lucky number is 6.

Wednesday, January 22 (Moon Gemini to Cancer 11:14 p.m.) You should be feeling a lot more optimistic now—particularly since you've been able to eliminate one big problem. It's also encouraging that you are getting positive feedback from people you try your ideas out on. Today you speak to some particularly receptive "characters" who have views similar to your own. Somebody makes a "big production" of something rather minor and it could annoy you.

Thursday, January 23 (Moon in Cancer) Today you feel a bit more confined than you have been, but oddly enough you find it rather pleasant. You haven't had much time alone to think for a while now. In your ruminating remember to pick up the telephone and call someone who is waiting to hear from you. He or she counts on your support.

Friday, January 24 (Moon in Cancer) Refuse to quit, no matter how much someone tries to intimidate you today. It is important to finish what you start. Realize that your cycle is moving up, and that you will make a major breakthrough before long. Someone who recently asks your advice and counsel may reappear and praise you for your extraordinary perception. Good for you. The lucky number is 9.

Saturday, January 25 (Moon Cancer to Leo 8:47 a.m.) A brand new door opens up for you as the moon moves into your sign; now you can gain access to people and things which have been taboo for you until now. Many get a large boost to their egos when someone says, "You were right." Refuse to give in to the temptation to gloat over this.

Sunday, January 26 (Moon in Leo) This full moon period is particularly critical for Leo. All your emotions and instincts are likely to be particularly strong now. Though you should give vent to your feelings and to your desire to do something new and creative, it is essential that you keep a sense of proportion. You may yearn for travel but realize that plans must be put off for a while. In love, you are delighted when a member of the opposite sex makes an intelligent concession. An Aquarian could be particularly important to you today.

Monday, January 27 (Moon Leo to Virgo 3:51 p.m.) A rebuilding process starts today, and you are vigorous about attacking things. Know that your judgment is good right now, but take care not to burn yourself out. You can state your views with conviction and come off as superdynamic, so there isn't much more you have to do. The lucky number today is 3.

Tuesday, January 28 (Moon in Virgo) The bits and pieces are falling into place now, and you soon will have the complete story. In fact, you will have it before anyone else, and you should take advantage of this foreknowledge. Pay some attention to your financial situation, because you should find ways to do more with what you have.

Wednesday, January 29 (Moon Virgo to Libra 9:00 p.m.) Don't be too proud to ask someone if he or she could help you out of a temporary money bind. After all, you would do the same. If you are absolutely frank and make it clear that the funds will be put to good use, you will get a positive response. Don't play games, because the person will see right through you.

Thursday, January 30 (Moon in Libra) Someone who is generally rather shy and retiring speaks up now, and may give you some advice. Take it with good grace and realize that he/she is on the right track. Your budget has been taking a bit of a beating lately, but you should be enjoying the results of your overspending.

Friday, January 31 (Moon in Libra) Don't try to be everywhere at once today, or you will get nowhere at all. Your forces could easily be scattered, and your nerves could get a bit strung out. In one situation today, you are going to have to be openminded—without being gullible. Take what you hear with a grain of salt, but enjoy the exchange with the person on the opposite end. Stay away from someone who tries to lead you astray. The lucky number is 7.

FEBRUARY 1986

Saturday, February 1 (Moon Libra to Scorpio 1:19 a.m.) Something that got dropped the other day now is picked up again and begins moving forward. Make every effort to wrap things up today so you won't have it hanging over your head. Some associates are very helpful by pointing out to you the real value of something you have. You tend to underestimate what you own at times. The lucky number today is 5.

Sunday, February 2 (Moon in Scorpio) You've been neglecting an important relationship, and today someone calls you on it. Spend the time discussing things that so that you get to the heart of the problem. You two may find that it leads to a new start for everyone concerned, and that is what has been badly needed. Some will receive an especially meaningful token of love.

Monday, February 3 (Moon Scorpio to Sagittarius 4:31 a.m.) You start out the week on a rather busy note. You are very much wanted in several places, and as you make the rounds you will pick up some fascinating information. For some, it will concern a travel plan that's been in the back of your minds. It turns out to be an even better deal than you thought. Take care that you are not seeing one special person in an idealistic light. Get rid of the pedestal! The lucky number is 7.

Tuesday, February 4 (Moon in Sagittarius) Now you've got a much more balanced view of the situation, and see that you must take more responsibility. Some will find themselves making a long-range commitment—possibly involving a special person or children. When you run into one of your favorite people, you pick right up as if it were old times. He or she may be a Capricorn.

Wednesday, February 5 (Moon Sagittarius to Capricorn 7:02 a.m.) Even if you try to hide today, it would be difficult. People seek you out—in fact, they seek you out for some kind of honor. Others will breathe a sigh of relief when a burden is removed. Many will have a reason to celebrate tonight; however, you may not think that what you did was so unusual or outstanding. You should be most gratified.

Thursday, February 6 (Moon in Capricorn) A long-standing problem has new light shed on it today, and there is hope that you can solve it soon. It could be one of your dependents—or your own health—that is involved. Many will feel a return of vitality, and the reason could be that you get back in communication with someone you've been a bit on the outs with recently. It's nice to know you really do share the same concern.

Friday, February 7 (Moon Capricorn to Aquarius 7:35 a.m.) Your intuition is a quite reliable guy today; if you think you know what to do, you are right. However, you are going to have to spend some time delving into the psychology of another person who rather baffles you. Many will have their sense of direction restored after a rather unsettling time, and will receive reassurance from someone very important.

Saturday, February 8 (Moon in Aquarius) Things can't always go your way—particularly with the people who share the roof over your head. Today you may find it necessary to give in a little more than you would like, but the concession is a reasonable one. Someone just as stubborn as you must win out once in a while. Take it slow today, and realize that your confusion about a certain matter is only temporary. The lucky number today is 3.

Sunday, February 9 (Moon Aquarius to Pisces 11:32 a.m.) It may take all the patience you can muster today not to get riled. In a clash of ideas, someone is going to call you on what you consider a minor point. Be ready to prove it. On the positive side, you are able to present your views in a rather graphic manner.

Monday, February 10 (Moon in Pisces) You may have to exercise some charity today when you get a request for a favor that really puts you out in some way or another. Make your decision on the basis of the fact you would want someone to do the same for you. It really doesn't take that much time out of your day—or money out of your pocket. Some should be careful to take nothing for granted now—dig deep, or you may get fooled. The lucky number is 5.

Tuesday, February 11 (Moon Pisces to Aries 6:21 p.m.) It is highly possible that some are considering a move at this time; it is also possible that others are not in agreement on a plan. An open discussion could help a great deal. The moon emphasis now is on things hidden and a bit obscure. You could very easily recover some information that has escaped you up to now. And feel a lot more secure as a result.

Wednesday, February 12 (Moon in Aries) You may get a brainstorm today, but you should hold off revealing it. Be patient and let your thought mature; if you spring it too early you may get blank stares. It's an excellent day for some to attack a rather difficult problem; your powers of concentration should be quite good. Those involved in creative work should find it goes well now.

Thursday, February 13 (Moon in Aries) Today you feel as if some of your goals are in sight. You get an inspiration about how to make one of them a reality faster, and it may involve joining a class or some special training. Once again, use your mental clarity to get to the root of some difficult matters. Some may be thinking about submitting something to a publication. Nothing ventured, nothing gained.

Friday, February 14 (Moon Aries to Taurus 5:38 a.m.) Some of you are going to get a hardy pat on the back today when someone says, "You're doing more than okay!" Things should be going your way in the romantic area as well; this is one Valentine's day you'll have no doubt that at least somebody loves you. As people reach out to you now, you should respond in kind. The lucky number today is 9.

Saturday, February 15 (Moon in Taurus) You have every chance of expanding your sphere of influence now; however, before you can really wield your power, you must be willing to finish off a major effort. This large-scale task may seem quite formidable, but you are up to it. Don't let negative thinking hold you down. Someone important asks you for advice and counsel—you should feel honored!

Sunday, February 16 (Moon Taurus to Gemini 5:17 p.m.) You may go head to head with a very stubborn person today—possibly a Taurus. It is important to recognize that this person has your best interest at heart. Try not to let your pride and vanity make you totally deaf to what the person has to say. Some will be busy doing busy work, but should take the opportunity to play teacher to someone else. You get involved. The lucky number is 2.

Monday, February 17 (Moon in Gemini) You should be starting out the week quite fired up and ready for anything. Just about anything could come along—even a romantic proposal. Your personal magnetism is high now, and your vitality is strong. Use it to further a personal cause—and enlist the aid of a rather dramatic personality who has expressed an interest. Take special care with your appearance today, as it will be very important.

Tuesday, February 18 (Moon in Gemini) The accent is on quieter things now—such as home, family, and togetherness. What you seek is security rather than excitement, and you should be able to find it. A Gemini or a Scorpio may play an outstanding role, and you will learn where you stand with this individual. It should be heartwarming. Many of you will be feeling less restricted and able to move about more freely than in the recent past.

Wednesday, February 19 (Moon Gemini to Cancer 7:39 a.m.) Positive playback to a recent request is the order of the day for many Leos. Now that you've got the go-ahead, don't let anything hold you back. Even if there are some strings attached. This is an excellent day to get your ideas on paper, and to realize that when you put things in writing, people realize you are serious. A Virgo or a Sagittarian could play a key role.

Thursday, February 20 (Moon in Cancer) Check yourself when you feel inclined to accuse someone today; examine your own guilt in this matter. Try to keep the atmosphere harmonious, even if it means temporarily going into a little shell. Some will be learning a new secret—possibly involving a family member—and should realize that it is to be taken seriously. Show someone that you have good intentions.

Friday, February 21 (Moon Cancer to Leo 3:25 p.m.) You are better off seeking seclusion rather than the spotlight now. You should have a chance to renew your "spiritual fires." An old attachment may resurface now and you may realize what a major role this person has played in your life. It may make you reevaluate things. Contact someone who needs you—possibly someone who is in the hospital.

Saturday, February 22 (Moon in Leo) This should be an excellent weekend, with the moon in your sign. If you are not involved in an intense relationship, one could begin now. All should be experiencing good vibes from their opposite numbers. You should have no trouble dealing with anyone or anything now. Realize, however, that some practical matters need your personal attention. Don't leave attention to anyone else.

Sunday, February 23 (Moon Leo to Virgo 11:58 p.m.) Your power of personality is very strong today; use that extra charisma to get an idea across or make a special appeal for something you want. Now's the time to take the initiative, but you may have to get rid of something in the process. It will only make your way to success wider and easier to navigate.

Monday, February 24 (Moon in Virgo) This full moon throws its light on the area of your chart having to do with money. Some will be completing a major financial transaction—others should take some time to tie down loose ends in the area of bill paying and catching up and obligations. It's an excellent time to do that special search for something you have mislaid; you could easily find it now. Don't waste words in a possibly troubling discussion with a member of the opposite sex. Just say what you have to say and get out.

Tuesday, February 25 (Moon in Virgo) A minor breach of yesterday is healed today, and there will be some kind of reuniting. Pay special attention to all kinds of directions and instructions today, so that you will get them straight. For some, there is an indication that important new contacts can be made today. No matter how unusual a person appears to you, realize that he/she could be extremely important in the future. The lucky number is 2.

Wednesday, February 26 (Moon Virgo to Libra 4:07 a.m.) Shake off those little feelings of gloom! Now's the time to plunge into life with both feet—particularly into social activity. For some, there is a short trip indicated; for others, your traveling may be done by phone. If there is a matter hanging that you want to varify once and for all, now's the day to do it.

Thursday, February 27 (Moon in Libra) Your forces tend to be a little scattered today, and you should make an attempt to get it all together. Try not to take on more than you can handle, even though there is much to be done. Don't let some important details rattle you—or escape you. You are going to need them in order to build your case. Someone is going to help you turn an obstacle into a stepping stone to progress; he/she could be a Scorpio or a Taurus. The lucky number is 4.

Friday, February 28 (Moon Libra to Scorpio 7:06 a.m.) The accent is on change and variety now. Give in to that urge to investigate something new. Some will find themselves more in touch with those around them than in the recent past. This should be a good feeling. Sexual attraction is in the air, and it's highly likely to influence a number of you. The lucky number is 5.

MARCH 1986

Saturday, March 1 (Moon in Scorpio) The emphasis today is on home, property, and security. You will want to pay some attention to these things. You may find you have to rip something up and throw it away in order to start all over again. Don't get discouraged. Someone is going to say "I'm sorry" and it will make you feel very good. The lucky number is 6.

Sunday, March 2 (Moon Scorpio to Sagittarius 9:51 a.m.) Something may come out of the blue and disrupt some plans that you have made. Don't get rattled, learn to turn on a dime. Also be willing to be generous with someone who is a bit of a nuisance today. Even in this experience there is something to be learned. Someone will open a door that's been previously shut, and it will help you immensely.

Monday, March 3 (Moon in Sagittarius) This should be a bright and beautiful day for you. For many, there are some changes that give new freedom and a great sense of exhilaration. For others, the accent is on more responsibility, but there are a lot of good things attached, including financial rewards. Some may be "in love with love" at this time. All should be feeling quite romantic, with matters of love and romance on their minds. Others could well participate!

Tuesday, March 4 (Moon Sagittarius to Capricorn 12:56 p.m.) Let other people know that you mean business today; that may mean finishing what you start and letting others know that you are no lightweight. Some will be absolutely charmed when someone indicates that he/she has faith in you—and really shows it. Children and young people may be high on the list of important people in your life today. The lucky number is 9.

Wednesday, March 5 (Moon in Capricorn) Your self-esteem should be on the rise, and you can give it another boost by showing how independent you can be. In some cases, it may be a shock because it is so unexpected. There are a lot of nitty-gritty things that must be dealt with today. Some have to do with your own health. It may be an excellent time to get serious about diet and exercise.

Thursday, March 6 (Moon Capricorn to Aquarius 4:42 p.m.) Keep your attention focused on your goal and your purpose today, because it would be all too easy for you to get bogged down in details. Other people around you may be doing the same thing, and you will be asked to compare notes. Make sure you have something interesting to say. On the personal front, there are some obligations to be fulfilled. If the whole thing seems very familiar, it is true that you've probably been through this before. So, just go through it once more. The lucky number is 2.

Friday, March 7 (Moon in Aquarius) Try to step back and look at things in the large today. Again, you run the risk of not being able to see the forest for the trees. Let others take the lead, while you stay in the background. Your best role today is that of keen observer who is fact-gathering with the intention of using the data later on. Hasty action could be disastrous now.

Saturday, March 8 (Moon Aquarius to Pisces 7:48 p.m.) Your "significant other"—i.e., mate, partner, roommate—is asking for some new ground rules. Be willing to discuss them and remember that neither of you is perfect. Someone will practically take you by the hand to show you where it's at; it could be a Scorpio, and he/she is worthy of being listened to. The lucky number today is 4.

Sunday, March 9 (Moon in Pisces) Once again, someone is there at your side to help you analyze a problem. For some, it could relate to money, possibly in the form of an inheritance. For others, it will be simply a rather complex financial situation involving other people. Whatever the scenario for you, it is wise to take notes and keep track of what everyone says. A Gemini or a Virgo could be involved.

Monday, March 10 (Moon in Pisces) Now you are beginning to see what it's all about, and where other people are really coming from. For some, it may be a bit of a disappointment. The emphasis today is very much on your life-style—and that of your partner. Both may be thinking of making some purchases that could make everybody's life a little bit more comfortable and beautiful. A Taurus or a Libra could have some excellent tips.

Tuesday, March 11 (Moon Pisces to Aries 5:03 a.m.) More things begin to take shape today, and you are glad to have something solid to hold onto. You like knowing where you are and what's going on. For some, people at a distance—possibly those who speak another language—play a prominent role today. For others, there is a very interesting interlude with a member of the opposite sex, and you could share an excellent meal together. The lucky number is 7.

Wednesday, March 12 (Moon in Aries) Today's a day to make big plans—with a very special person. You should be able to think in long-range terms and to make an important decision or commitment. Some will have the commitment made to them. Your sights should be set high, and you are wise to think in terms of the ideal. Talk over your hopes and aspirations with someone sensitive, possibly a Cancer. The lucky number is 8.

Thursday, March 13 (Moon Aries to Taurus 3:04 p.m.) Some of you can expect a minor miracle to occur today; however, it will be by your own doing. All should be able to reach out and grab what seems impossible to achieve before. Someone you meet today will be a very beneficial element in your life; in some ways this person is a natural healer. He/she will help you overcome numerous barriers.

Friday, March 14 (Moon in Taurus) You are moving with the right people now and your standing in the community has gone up. Fortunately you are generally able to take an objective point of view about this sort of thing; you are not a snob. Be ready to accept some challenges. For some, an opportunity might fall right in your lap today.

Saturday, March 15 (Moon in Taurus) Praise comes from someone very important, and the reason for it is a decision you have made. It's an excellent day to inspire others; why not have them rally around and help you complete a large project. A Cancer, a Capricorn, or an Aquarian could be easily tapped for such a job. The lucky number today is 2.

Sunday, March 16 (Moon Taurus to Gemini 3:23 a.m.) Your social life is heating up, and you may be even more popular than you would like. For some, that may mean some visitors drop in unannounced. Be gracious! Someone brings you excellent news—or some very valuable information. Be prepared to put it to good use shortly. The lucky number today is 3.

Monday, March 17 (Moon in Gemini) You could make money and love today—possibly even both. The pleasure principle is strong now, and you may find yourself tempted to enjoy yourself more than is safe. With your self-confidence so high, you should be able to keep your desires under control. For some, the red tape will vanish and a dilemma will be resolved. The lucky number today is 4.

Tuesday, March 18 (Moon Gemini to Cancer 4:04 p.m.) You are going to have additional demands on your time, and you may not thoroughly like it. It could be a member of the opposite sex who wants your attention, and keeps insisting on it. Do as much as you can, but be clear about what the limits are. Others may find themselves making a few changes in their lives—for some, that means the beginning of a "torrid romance."

Wednesday, March 19 (Moon in Cancer) Some of you will be feeling unsettled today, and inordinately suspicious of others' actions. Realize that a lot is happening only in your own mind. It is possible that you will uncover some information you would rather not have; if it disturbs you, realize that it is an inevitable result of recent happenings. Things will look up soon. Commiserate with a Taurus or a Scorpio.

Thursday, March 20 (Moon in Cancer) Your uneasy feelings are wearing off, but you should still realize that you are a bit depressed, and that factor magnifies certain issues. Get yourself some precious privacy and you will find out that being alone is not the same as being lonely. Some will have to insist on not playing second fiddle to someone else.

Friday, March 21 (Moon Cancer to Leo 2:38 a.m.) This is your day! With the moon in your sign you are very much in the limelight. The day should be filled with lots of pleasant activity in which you are running the show for the most part. Something happens that makes you realize one person in your circle has been wasting your time; resolve to cut him/her out. It is not a cruel thing to do.

Saturday, March 22 (Moon in Leo) With your lunar cycle so high, you are very likely to attract a lot of attention. Make sure your physical outlook is as pleasant as your mental one. You may want to make some dramatic changes in your appearance in order to show your greater individuality. Some will breath sighs of relief at unloading a nagging problem to someone else.

Sunday, March 23 (Moon Leo to Virgo 9:39 a.m.) You are in the market for something today and you may be looking for it particularly avidly. Let your intuition be your guide, and you may come across a true bargain. Some recent restrictions are removed and you feel much less limited. Another Leo may be in the picture, and the two of you could enjoy an excellent time together. Expect to be in the right place at the right time. And try your luck with number 1.

Monday, March 24 (Moon in Virgo) A conservative course is the best one to take now. You will realize that it is in your own best interest not to "take a flier." Count on the fact that you are able to make a decision that is the correct one. If you have some doubt, talk it over with a Cancer or an Aquarian. The lucky number is 2.

Tuesday, March 25 (Moon Virgo to Libra 1:22 p.m.) This is a day many can expect a lucky break. It may come from an unexpected direction. You can feel proud that someone actually wants to know your opinion and seeks your counsel about how to proceed. You can derive a lot of vicarious pleasure from this situation.

Wednesday, March 26 (Moon in Libra) You may be working hard during this full moon, but you will also be making a lot of progress. Realize that the more time you put into something, the more everyone will get out of it. Though it may be a bit of a drag, you are going to have to fulfill an obligation—possibly to a relative. On the homefront, a frank discussion will help clear the air. The lucky number is 4.

Thursday, March 27 (Moon Libra to Scorpio 3:05 p.m.) You could combine business and pleasure today on a short trip. Just be sure to keep alert and to take nothing for granted. Something may not be as it appears. It is wise to get your observations on paper; by taking careful notes now, you could help prove your point in the near future. The lucky number is 5.

Friday, March 28 (Moon in Scorpio) A lot of recent fears and insecurities should vanish now and you should feel at home with yourself. You should even have the guts to make a break with a past living pattern that has held you back. It is a time to concentrate on the future and to start "imaging" much better things for yourself. One of those things could be a change of residence—or marital status.

Saturday, March 29 (Moon Scorpio to Sagittarius 4:20 p.m.) The focus continues on matters of home and property—possibly even in the sense of real estate. You've got much more of a growing concern than you may realize and should not sell yourself short. However, you've got to be rather canny in looking behind the obvious to see hidden motives. A Cancer or a Pisces could help you very much in this regard.

Sunday, March 30 (Moon in Sagittarius) The atmosphere lightens up considerably today. For some, it will come as a result of being back in touch with a delightful person you have not seen in a while. For others, it will come in the form of someone who says,

"Okay, you were right." Take advantage of this "green light day" by being creative. The lucky number is 8.

Monday, March 31 (Moon Sagittarius to Capricorn 6:25 p.m.) Have the courage of your convictions today, and realize that a lot of people are listening. It should be easy for you to put your own personal imprint on something that makes you look very good. The choice is yours now, to go for the brass ring or stick with the status quo. It all depends on how much energy you have. The lucky number is 9.

APRIL 1986

Tuesday, April 1 (Moon in Capricorn) Keep your guard up today, because someone may pull an April Fool that is really not so amusing. Don't get upset if you see some malicious intent behind it. The person is really not worth your time. Instead, concentrate on doing what needs to be done for those who rely upon you. You will gets lots of love in return. The lucky number today is 7.

Wednesday, April 2 (Moon Capricorn to Aquarius 10:11 p.m.) Be prepared for someone to pull strings on your behalf; the recommendation will do you a lot of good—if not immediately, then in the near future. For some, a relationship is growing a lot stronger, and you may be considering taking on more responsibility in connection with it. Others should be able to spot some half-hidden opportunities for extra bucks.

Thursday, April 3 (Moon in Aquarius) Someone who has seemed a bit distant recently now comes a lot closer and lets his/her interest in you and your situation be known. You can trust. For some, legal matters will require some attention. For others, it may be necessary to say good-bye to an old way of doing things or a person who is no longer relevent to your life. Don't be afraid to do it.

Friday, April 4 (Moon in Aquarius) The focus is squarely on partnerships today—of every variety, including marriage. You may have to stress your need for independence, and to have a separate identity. You can get to the heart of things without upsetting the applecart. Talk it over with another Leo or an Aquarian who turns up and makes it clear that you are on the right track. The lucky number today is 1.

Saturday, April 5 (Moon Aquarius to Pisces 4:03 a.m.) Some news comes through today which has an up side—more money—but a down side as well, your need to share it with someone else. Realize that fair is fair. Some should follow through on a hunch they have because it is uncannily accurate. Others will find themselves much more involved in a love relationship than they had anticipated. This time, it's a Scorpio who could give you some good advice.

Sunday, April 6 (Moon in Pisces) It's an excellent day to gather everyone around you and possibly mend some fences. With someone who has been not all you would like him or her to be, be generous with your feelings. Though it is difficult for you, do more listening than talking today. Two excellent people to listen to would be Gemini and Sagittarius. The lucky number today is 3.

Monday, April 7 (Moon Pisces to Aries 12:12 p.m.)
Don't get depressed when the first thing that hits you today is something you have to do over; no one gets *everything* right the first time. Some of you may feel that the better way is to go elsewhere; someone in your circle has excellent contacts, and you should call on him/her for help. Others should realize that an important person—possibly a Taurus—has a lot of respect for you, and really does want to see you succeed. Stick with it!

Tuesday, April 8 (Moon in Aries) Your thinking

takes you in an interesting new direction today, and you focus in on what you really value. It helps you decide upon a plan—possibly for further education or a career move—that has been brewing in your mind recently. You also resolve to improve communications with someone you love. Do a lot of productive things today, and try your luck with number 5.

Wednesday, April 9 (Moon Aries to Taurus 10:36 p.m.) You will be able to bridge some rather large distances today—even if they are not literally physical distances. Someone and you have not been seeing eye to eye, but you can change all that with a simple phone call. You should also indulge yourself by letting your mind roam free to those faraway places; someday you will get there.

Thursday, April 10 (Moon in Taurus) Something you were promised a while back now is given to you. However, there are a few strings attached, and it does not come on the proverbial silver platter. Don't worry—you will make it fit into your scheme of things. Some have hit upon a new way of doing things, and may have a "tiger by the tail." Don't let it go!

Friday, April 11 (Moon in Taurus) This could be a big day in your life. With the moon in a power position at the top of your chart, you should be able to ask for what you want—and get it. Just remember that you'll have to give something in return. If it is love, you have plenty of that to give. A Cancer or a Capricorn could play a paramount role today. The lucky number is 8.

Saturday, April 12 (Moon Taurus to Gemini 10:51 a.m.) Those who are trying to hold you back are in for a surprise now; you have more strength than they do. One thing your strength makes you do is break with the past, and say, "I won't do it anymore" to a job that is rightly not yours to do. Most will be getting wider recognition now, and see more places they can break through. Good going! The lucky number is 9.

Sunday, April 13 (Moon in Gemini) Many will get a lovely compliment from someone today—possibly a member of the opposite sex. No matter what the subject, it should give your morale a much needed boost. There is an indication that many will receive "something extra" today. Check your mailbox for good news! It's an excellent time to spend the day with people who have similar ideas, hopes, and wishes. Maybe together you can figure out how to make them come true.

Monday, April 14 (Moon Gemini to Cancer 11:42 p.m.) Trust those feelings you get early in the day about how to handle a certain situation. You've got the answer! All should realize that they are powerful persuaders now, and should attempt to sell anything they want to sell—including themselves. Another Leo or an Aquarian could be extremely important in the scheme of things today. The lucky number is 2.

Tuesday, April 15 (Moon in Cancer) Many will get a rare opportunity to ask questions of someone who really does have a lot of answers. Some will be introduced to a fascinating new subject—and get a backstage view. You'll feel like you've entered the "inner sanctum." Some Leos will suddenly understand the meaning of a recent dream or experience. It is significant.

Wednesday, April 16 (Moon in Cancer) If your feelings have bottomed-out, it is only logical. However, it is also means that your cycle is beginning to move up. Meanwhile, work quietly and get all your facts together. Before you know it, you will be asked to present your case. And you want to make it as air-tight as possible. It is important to read the small print today. Let a Taurus help you interpret it.

Thursday, April 17 (Moon Cancer to Leo 11:10 a.m.) Things are looking up, but there are still matters to be untangled. Get it out of the way early in the days so you will be ready when the moon moves into your sign. A member of the opposite sex could be a really good buddy today and help you move things forward. He/she could be a Gemini, a Virgo, or a Sagittarian. The lucky number is 5.

Friday, April 18 (Moon in Leo) Now's the time to get out there and strut your stuff. You can get what you go after, because your judgment is excellent now. However, remember that nothing happens unless you make it happen. That means, take the initiative. Some will receive a gift which goes straight to the heart and gladdens it.

Saturday, April 19 (Moon Leo to Virgo 7:24 p.m.) You may have to spell it out for someone else today. Don't be afraid to define your terms and demand things on your terms. In another area, it is an excellent time to clear the decks for action. That means to throw out the old in order to make room for the new. In every sense of the word. You could have a lovely time entertaining at home this evening with some interesting people. Possibly a Pisces or a Virgo could be involved.

Sunday, April 20 (Moon in Virgo) Focus on what you own, what you have borrowed, what you have and what you have to pay. It is possible that some have let their financial house fall into a state of disarray. This is an excellent time to get a second emotional wind. For some, a relationship may be going through a testing period; it will not be found wanting. Today someone proves that he/she is on your side, and it's a good feeling.

Monday, April 21 (Moon Virgo to Libra 11:50 p.m.) Your financial picture should be looking a bit better—especially if you did something about it yesterday. Have no fear that what seems lost will be recovered. Some should be willing to dump a losing proposition now in favor of a much more exciting scenario. Check it out with an Aries or a Libra. The lucky number is 9.

Tuesday, April 22 (Moon in Libra) Your enthusiasm could be at a very high pitch today—so high that you may have to bring yourself down to the ground. It's great to be optimistic, but not to be unrealistic. Some may be planning a trip and should take care not to overload the schedule. Another Leo could be an excellent opposite number today.

Wednesday, April 23 (Moon in Libra) You may come down off of that cloud with a bit of a bump today. Let someone who loves you help restore your sense of direction and purpose. It could be a relative you do not normally consider a confidante. Follow your instincts about making something safer and more secure. A member of the opposite sex could get a bit more serious than you are comfortable with. The lucky number is 2.

Thursday, April 24 (Moon Libra to Scorpio 1:15 a.m.) During this full moon it is essential to remain flexible and to keep your options open. Be willing to review all your plans and to go along with others who may differ with you. Don't waste time arguing with someone who's not worth your time. Be sure to read the fine print. The lucky number is 3 today.

Friday, April 25 (Moon in Scorpio) Now you should be feeling a bit better and the puzzle pieces should be falling into place. You should know what must be done, and be able to do it. Many will have a lot of help and support from their peer group. Others will find that a road block to progress has been removed, and that it's smoother sailing now. All should look for encouragement from a loved one.

Saturday, April 26 (Moon Scorpio to Sagittarius 1:16 a.m.) You are going to have to read between the lines now in order to protect your interests. Someone isn't exactly trying to fool you, but it does come close. For some, a serious flirtation is a real possibility—and an invigorating experience. For all, it is a day to experience pleasure in various forms—including the company of children. Enjoy!

Sunday, April 27 (Moon in Sagittarius) Be diplomatic as you know how today, especially with family members. Extra cooperation may be necessary in order to avoid an unpleasant scene. If you are feeling a bit edgy yourself, go out and play. A Taurus or a Libra could be an excellent playmate. The lucky number is 6.

Monday, April 28 (Moon Sagittarius to Capricorn 1:41 a.m.) Your heart may go out to someone today, but keep your hands in your pockets. If you are overly generous, you run the risk of being a patsy. Don't mistake sympathy for love. Some will be in the process of evaluating what they own, and of trimming down their possessions in some way or another. Just don't throw out what you may need in the future.

Tuesday, April 29 (Moon in Capricorn) Sooner or later it was bound to happen. Something you neglected to do before must be done now. Just get it over with. It may be necessary to put pride aside and seek help and counsel from someone who knows the ropes better than they do. For others, it is belt-tightening time—remember those resolutions about diet and exercise.

Wednesday, April 30 (Moon Capricorn to Aquarius 4:06 a.m.) Go slow, lie low, and let the other person take the initiative. If you are not careful, a clash of ideas could result in a rift that will take a while to close. It is a period that you gain most by playing a waiting game. For you, Leo, that means stepping out of the spotlight—it is only temporary. The lucky number is 9.

MAY 1986

Thursday, May 1 (Moon in Aquarius) What appears to be a setback will eventually work out in your favor. Don't let it throw you. In another area, an agreement will be reached and now these papers can finally be signed. You may end up with a lot more responsibility. Others are going to find themselves with more money or more love now. A Cancer or a Capricorn could be heavily involved in this rather unusual day. The lucky number is 8.

Friday, May 2 (Moon Aquarius to Pisces 9:30 a.m.) Someone may ask you for help today, but what is asked is a bit much. You sense that the person is operating out of a confused state of mind. Do some creative stalling to put the issue off to another day. You will both be glad you did. Some might find themselves actually flirting with with fame.

Saturday, May 3 (Moon in Pisces) You are going to get involved, whether you like it or not. The situation may be confusing and a bit unpleasant, but you can help a great deal by going straight to the heart of things—at which you are so good. A solution will be found to a mystery that's been bugging some Leos of late. An Aquarian will figure prominently. The lucky number is 1.

Sunday, May 4 (Moon Pisces to Aries 8:01 p.m.) Face the fact that you can sometime be gullible. Look for the story behind the story someone is trying to give you; not everyone is as honest as you are. If you dig a little deeper, you will discover the key to future actions. Try not to get disillusioned. For some, a boost to the morale comes when someone says, "I know you can do it."

Monday, May 5 (Moon in Aries) It is important to

keep a sense of your priorities today. Do the thing that makes you look best to those who count. It doesn't hurt to use some privileged information to get what you want. It's an excellent time to diversify your interests and get around a lot. Accept any social invitation that comes your way. The lucky number is 3.

Tuesday, May 6 (Moon in Aries) Today you should be feeling on a lot more solid ground, and your long-range plans should be coming into focus. Someone is going to ask you to step up to a different level now, and a new way of doing things. You are up to it! Some may find they have idealized someone a bit much, and that he/she is quite not as "romantic" as you thought.

Wednesday, May 7 (Moon Aries to Taurus 4:59 a.m.) Be prepared for all kinds of revisions today. Nothing may go as you thought it would. For some, a rather unsettling notice comes in in connection with your living space or career space. Don't let it rattle you. A Gemini or a Virgo could be exceptionally helpful today by getting you to look at things clearly.

Thursday, May 8 (Moon in Taurus) Many will feel the pull between home and business today. There is a definite conflict of interest indicated. The key is to be as diplomatic as possible, and to remain calm. You may have to assure someone that you are aware of his/her needs and will take care of them when you are able.

Friday, May 9 (Moon Taurus to Gemini 5:26 p.m.) Don't fall into the trap of thinking that someone in authority is infallible. He/she may be sincere, but is possibly misguided. Use your own wits and have alternatives at hand. You could come out the winner. Some will find that a jealous individual makes a scathing remark; realize that person is rather mediocre and that you've really got what it takes. The lucky number is 7 today.

Saturday, May 10 (Moon in Gemini) The moon position highlights friends and associates today. What that means for most is that you will have a lot of support at hand. For some, the arena could be a power struggle, but you will win. Once again it may be necessary to be a bit idealistic about someone who looks perfect but really isn't. A Cancer or a Capricorn figure in a rather busy day. The lucky number is 8.

Sunday, May 11 (Moon in Gemini) Finally you hit upon the "missing link" and are able to make that last connection. Now you should feel a lot more secure and certain that you are on the right track. Some Leos will receive a call that makes them feel happier than they have in the recent past. Others may find an ingenious way to cut corners and bring expenses down. This is a happy time, and you should have reason to celebrate.

Monday, May 12 (Moon Gemini to Cancer 7:18 a.m.) You may find yourself laughing at your own foolishness today; something you've been dreading turns out to be "a piece of cake." Let others in on the joke and demonstrate how often we let our fears run away with us. Some may have to work hard to gain greater independence now; someone could be trying to hold back. Refuse to be held back.

Tuesday, May 13 (Moon in Cancer) Try to remember yesterday's scenario; it will help you realize that what appears to be threatening on the surface is really nothing to fear at all. Try to separate out your thoughts from your feelings, which are not a reliable guide now. Many will find themselves dealing with people in groups today—particularly women. Though you may not feel at your best, you can be your best. The lucky number is 2.

Wednesday, May 14 (Moon Cancer to Leo 6:15 p.m.) You are gradually coming out of the doldrums, and you receive some news which lightens your burden.

If an invitation comes along early in the day, grab it, because this should be a wonderful evening. Be receptive to everything, but don't forget your determination about losing weight and shaping up. The lucky number today is 3.

Thursday, May 15 (Moon in Leo) Now your moon cycle peaks, and you can successfully take the initiative. No longer is it difficult to show how independent and individualistic you can be. However, for best results, you may want to tear something down in order to rebuild it to your own specifications. Another Leo or a Scorpio could be tremendously helpful today. Especially with paperwork.

Friday, May 16 (Moon in Leo) Now you've really got a green light to go ahead for change and variety. Many will feel their creative juices flowing and should put them to good use. An interesting and productive dialogue with an attractive member of the opposite sex spices up this day. Many should have their confidence restored when a promise comes in writing.

Saturday, May 17 (Moon Leo to Virgo 3:45 a.m.) Money seems to fall from the sky for that vacation you've been dreaming about. Someone close to you may provide the extra funds in order to bolster your spirits. Be properly respective and thankful. Others may find something they thought was lost, or stumble upon an opportunity for successful investment. All in all, this should be a reasonably decent weekend.

Sunday, May 18 (Moon in Virgo) Once again, some can look for a surprise source of extra money. Others will have a wish come true in another form. All should realize that their position is strong and that they have no lack of supporters. A Pisces or a Virgo could be especially supportive now. The lucky number is 7.

Monday, May 19 (Moon Virgo to Libra 9:41 a.m.) You make a remarkable recovery today when something that seems to be getting away from you reverses its position and boomerangs in your favor. Lucky you! Many will feel a relationship intensifying and want to take it to the limit. Others will feel a definite sense of being in charge of their own destiny. Thank someone who never lost faith in you.

Tuesday, May 20 (Moon in Libra) Don't let a bright idea you get today get away; it can be turned into something very viable and even valuable. Your new strength should help you make a break with the past that is indicated. It is a favorable one. An Aries, a Libra, or another Leo are among the best buddies you can find today. The lucky number is 9.

Wednesday, May 21 (Moon Libra to Scorpio 12:02 p.m.) A rather stimulating and dynamic individual bursts on the scene today and gives you a run for your money. Instead of being competitive, be cooperative—you have a lot to learn from this person. Many are going places, and can prove it today. Othes may find that a rather quite individual is madly in love with them. Surprise, surprise!

Thursday, May 22 (Moon in Scorpio) For some, security is at stake and you may have to fight for your "territorial rights." You will be the winner if you are absolutely forthright and display the courage of your convictions. Know you are in no real danger, it is necessary to take a stand in order to regain your sense of direction. Follow through on your intuition today. The lucky number is 2.

Friday, May 23 (Moon Scorpio to Sagittarius 11:57 a.m.) This full moon could find you feeling full of energy and more than willing to cut out and try something new. It's an excellent time to give yourself more room and to realize you have a right to experiment. Do not let anyone hold you back. Someone who does may simply have to go—and you should realize it. A Gemini will be very prominent in the day.

Saturday, May 24 (Moon in Sagittarius) Some of your preconceived notions are totally smashed today. And you love it. You will be attracted by someone very attractive, and could easily fall prey to his/her flattery. Keep a cool head! Travel, physical attraction, and your own personal charisma are important elements in the day. Some may even win a contest!

Sunday, May 25 (Moon Sagittarius to Capricorn 11:15 a.m.) No matter what your personal situation, you should be feeling positively bathed in affection now. Take time out to write that letter or make that phone call that will assure someone else of your affection. Though it is a fairly lazy day, you will get an opportunity to show off in your own inimitable style. Just realize that there are others in the room. Some will receive tangible evidence that they are on the right track.

Monday, May 26 (Moon in Capricorn) Moderation is the key word for the day. That means, don't go overboard in anything. Except possibly work. This is a marvelous day to pull yourself up by the bootstraps and tighten your belt. Both in the area of spending and indulging. By evening you should be feeling very virtuous. Someone wants to help you redecorate; don't turn him/her down unless you want to create an enemy.

Tuesday, May 27 (Moon Capricorn to Aquarius 12:00 noon) You could possibly get caught in the crossfire of conflicting ideas and opinions. You can keep it light if you keep everybody's sense of humor working. Family relationships—particularly the marital kind—are high on the list of what's important today. Tread lightly. Somebody who relies on your judgement will get in touch today and you will have to spend some time worrying about someone else's problem. The lucky number today is 7.

Wednesday, May 28 (Moon in Aquarius) Don't sign anything until you get someone else's opinion about it—possibly a legal opinion. Illusion is the order of the day, and it works two ways. You could transform one of your fantasies into reality; on the other hand, you could be totally taken in by someone who gives you a good line. Once again, all kinds of cooperative efforts, including marriage, are emphasized.

Thursday, May 29 (Moon Aquarius to Pisces 3:54 p.m.) Someone will test you today, and if you pass the test, you will find yourself a bit further up the ladder. Realize that you do have something of value to offer, and refuse to be intimidated by someone who is merely envious of you. A Libra or an Aries could be particularly important today.

Friday, May 30 (Moon in Pisces) Face the fact that you can sometimes be gullible. Look for the story behind the story someone is giving you; remember you have lots of bargaining power. If you keep alert to possible trip-ups, you will come out smelling like a rose. Someone has something that really belongs to you; in order to get it back, you may have to play private eye.

Saturday, May 31 (Moon Pisces to Aries 11:43 p.m.) Feelings are running both high and deep today. A romantic partner may be feeling even more romantic; it's a good time to cement those ties. The feeling of security and self esteem that comes from a good relationship will be yours today. Some will receive a rather unusual offer.

JUNE 1986

Sunday, June 1 (Moon in Aries) A lot of people would like to get in touch with you today. In more ways than one. Your popularity enables you to get enough help to complete a project and assign another of your jobs to someone else. Enjoy being in the spotlight, and try your luck with number 9.

Monday, June 2 (Moon in Aries) Today's a good day to look ahead and ask some questions about a travel plan that may be on your mind—or possibly an educational interest that you have. Someone who's helped you out before suddenly pops up; don't let past pride get in the way of things now. Show your willingness to pioneer a project, and you could end up a leader.

Tuesday, June 3 (Moon Aries to Taurus 10:45 a.m.) A long-range project comes into sharp clear focus now. You will know exactly what to do, and how to move it forward. Sometimes you tend to be a bit too idealistic, but this is one time you are proven right about someone. Don't lose the faith. The lucky number is 2.

Wednesday, June 4 (Moon in Taurus) You are able to focus your energies right on what needs to be done today without scattering your efforts. Take advantage of this particular strength while you have it. Some will have a lot of demands made on their time, but most will be enjoyable. Others will concentrate on their outward appearance—and possibly indulge in a shopping spree.

Thursday, June 5 (Moon Taurus to Gemini 11:26 p.m.) Don't let some small-minded people bring you down; stand up tall for your principles. Though you may feel you are under attack, you really are building on a very stable base. For some, a Scorpio could come along and teach you some valuable things about how to get maximum rewards for your efforts.

Friday, June 6 (Moon in Gemini) Get set for some very enjoyable changes. Variety is definitely the space of this day. For some, it's a like a dream come true when they are able to persuade someone to go along with their way of thinking. Others stand to gain for the written word. Do something about it! The lucky number is 5.

Saturday, June 7 (Moon in Gemini) A rather shy person may approach you for advice; be receptive but don't pry too much. There may be something here that is too painful to reveal, but you can offer good support without knowing the whole story. As for your own life, realize that one of your ideas is potentially very profitable. Enjoy the support of someone who is all for you and willing to go all out for you as well. The lucky number is 6.

Sunday, June 8 (Moon Gemini to Cancer 12:16 p.m.) Don't be disillusioned with someone who makes promises but is unable to carry them through. He/she is sincere but really rather ineffectual. It's up to you to gather your own forces and tend to your own needs. In another area, a Pisces may be part of a rather tricky situation and can help you take a peek behind the scenes.

Monday, June 9 (Moon in Cancer) You've got the inside track now, and you should be more confident. This can be a very powerful day for you in terms of scoring points with a boss or a loved one. Something that has seemed just out of reach now becomes available.

Tuesday, June 10 (Moon in Cancer) Refuse to be discouraged by somebody who claims to figure out something you don't know. Not only is that incorrect, you are the one who really has your finger on the situation. Just get on with things and finish what you started. For some of you, there will be an occasion to show off just how sharp your timing is and to dazzle others with your superior abilities at quick repartee. Your opposite number could be an Aries or a Libra.

Wednesday, June 11 (Moon Caner to Leo 12:11 a.m.) All your doubts about yourself should vanish as the moon moves into your sign. Now you should be at your "Leo best" able to take total control of a situation. Today's a day to try some rather unorthodox methods—even if they shock others a bit. Some will have a pleasant family reunion or be invited to a gourmet dinner. An Aquarian could be very important.

Thursday, June 12 (Moon Leo to Virgo 10:18 a.m.) This is a superexcellent day for you, Leo. The status quo gets a real shaking up and you come out the winner. No matter what else happens today, you will have a number of occasions to laugh and feel all's right with the world. Don't miss an opportunity to expand your personal horizons by going off the beaten track. The lucky number is 3.

Friday, June 13 (Moon in Virgo) Someone may be out to put the arm on you so to speak. Don't give away anything you'd rather not part with. It is important to protect your assets in every area of life, including the romantic. Is someone else moving in on your territory? It's also time for you to call in some old debts that are owed you.

Saturday, June 14 (Moon Virgo to Libra 5:38 p.m.) A call or message could open the door to adventure —or at least an exciting new experience. Some will find themselves in a competitive situation now where timing is critical; don't speak before it is time to speak. Take time out to see just what the other person's motives are. The lucky number today is 5.

Sunday, June 15 (Moon in Libra) Your radar is working very well today and you seem to know exactly what to do and when to do it. One intuition you have involves a trip to see someone who means a lot to you. Some bright ideas you have are beginning to take some real shape. Don't drop the ball, Leo; carry it all the way and you'll score. The lucky number is 6.

Monday, June 16 (Moon Libra to Scorpio 9:36 p.m.)
A rather unusual dream or vision has a lot to say; take the trouble to analyze it. Some will receive a call that verifies their view, especially about a member of the opposite sex. Isn't it nice to know you were not wrong? Others will get an excellent chance to play reporter and should make the most of it.

Tuesday, June 17 (Moon in Scorpio) You're going to have to defend your territory today; one way to do that is by being absolutely definite about where the lines are drawn. On the positive side, some will find out that what they own is worth more than they originally thought. Others will be able to get in touch with the right people or the right authorities to move a personal cause forward. A Capricorn could be critical in this or another scenario.

Wednesday, June 18 (Moon Scorpio to Sagittarius 10:36 p.m.) Some of your friends may get the impression you are a mind-reader because you have such an excellent picture of what is going to happen in advance. The real truth is that your sense of perception is heightened now. That means you will get some solid impressions and should take them quite seriously. Some will be feeling more secure, either financially or emotionally. Take some time out for private meditation and try your luck with number 9.

Thursday, June 19 (Moon in Sagittarius) Today you should be ready to gamble on your insights of yesterday. It's okay, but proceed with caution and look before you leap. You are really in the mood for change, but you can't change things over night. As you get rolling on your new project, don't forget a recent decision to stay within the bounds of a sensible diet. Physical attraction is an important part of the scenario.

Friday, June 20 (Moon Sagittarius to Capricorn 10:00 p.m.) Today most should get a nice warm feeling that they have loving support from friends and family members. For some, that warm feeling could be almost sizzling—in the romantic area. It is one of those days to expect the unexpected; there is little that indicates that status quo will stay intact. Sudden travel is even possible. Listen to a sensitive Cancer who has some advice about how to deal with children or young people.

Saturday, June 21 (Moon in Capricorn) Last night's full moon fell in the area of your chart that deals with basic security—and gainful employment. For some, it means the pressure will really be on today—but there are meaningful results. Some will receive an encouraging sign from someone who has been silent or about a situation which has been dormant. It is an excellent day to satisfy your curiosity about someone who puzzles you.

Sunday, June 22 (Moon Capricorn to Aquarius 9:50 p.m.) Refuse to compromise your principles now and others who are as idealistic as you are will come to your support. You don't have to feel foolish about being noble. For some, some sort of minor health problem will require care. For others, it is a good time to remember to make an appointment with the dentist. A stimulating evening is a good possibility for all.

Monday, June 23 (Moon in Aquarius) Some can expect a face-off today with a clash of ideas; however, the exchange attracts the attention of someone important. And could mean something important for you. There appears to be a great deal of activity in the relationship area, which could mean your most important partnership needs a bit of attention. Maybe you should put it in writing.

Tuesday, June 24 (Moon in Aquarius) Today you may be called upon to make a tough decision, but you are able to do it. You are also able to be diplomatic in the process. Some may see room at the top that they would like to occupy; start working toward it. Others will find their financial picture is not as bleak as they thought. The lucky number is 6.

Friday, June 25 (Moon Aquarius to Pisces 12:12 a.m.) Go ahead and be nosey today, because it's important that you know what's going on. Someone may be actually trying to cut you out of what is rightfully yours. Don't lose heart now, because you are on the brink of something big. Try to analyze your feelings today, and you will see how you can become more emotionally stable—and therefore more secure. The lucky number today is 7.

Saturday, June 26 (Moon in Pisces) For some, excellent news comes through—possibly in connection with an inheritance. For others, the "big win" comes through the ability to stretch current resources. It is one of those periods during which a rather casual relationship can turn into something quite different. The stronger feelings may be on the other side, but you should be aware of them.

Sunday, June 27 (Moon Pisces to Aries 6:35 a.m.) It is important to learn the rules before you begin to test them; sometimes you are a bit too impatient. In another area, you get off to a good start and stand to make some solid gains. For some, a rather unusual social invitation could turn out to be the most interesting thing that's happened in weeks! Try your luck with number 9 today.

Monday, June 28 (Moon in Aries) Don't wait for things to come to you today—you will get recognition when you reach out. Those who wait for fate to take a hand rarely win the day. Your ideas are reaching a wider audience, and your prestige is growing. Your philosophical nature should help you let things roll off your back. Someone shares your ideals and lets you know it.

Tuesday, June 29 (Moon Aries to Taurus 4:54 p.m.) Take a chance on love today—or something else you have an instinctive feeling about. Your hunches are liable to be good. It is obvious that others are envious of you, and you should make it obvious that you do not care. It isn't like you to be petty. Resolve to be serious when a family member talks about putting financial things on a much more stable basis. You can be a bit too open-handed at times.

Wednesday, June 30 (Moon Aries to Taurus 4:54 p.m.) You should find yourself starting out the work week full of determination to make a good showing. Having a good supply of energy, you should find yourself willing to put in some fairly long hours. Just remember: You asked for it. If no one happens to give you that pat on the back you want, don't go away mad. If it's glory you're looking for, make sure you make it very clear to the right people just how dedicated you are.

JULY 1986

Tuesday, July 1 (Moon in Taurus) This could be a real breakthrough day—particularly in your job or career life. Keep alert to all opportunities. Understanding someone else and why he/she acts that way can lead to greater self-understanding for you. And you can use it. Talk it over with another Leo who can offer insight.

Wednesday, July 2 (Moon in Taurus) If you learned something yesterday, you can put it to practical use today, in terms of moderating your own behavior. Don't hesitate to congratulate yourself on your new sense of direction by doing something slightly self indulgent. However, you should not go overboard because your digestion could be a bit delicate. Your lucky number is 2.

Thursday, July 3 (Moon Taurus to Gemini 1:32 a.m.) Dress your best and you will give the best impression today. You may want to appear to be someone of substance; you can do it. You will be elated when a wish is granted, and you should be extremely grateful. Why not say "Thanks" in some tangible way?

Friday, July 4 (Moon in Gemini) Don't let someone discourage you from this pleasant holiday day. Even if some restrictions are placed on you, you should be able to overcome the opposition and win. Don't get involved in an argument when you come into contact with a rather stubborn person; if you really talk to each other, you will find that you have mutual admiration.

Saturday, July 5 (Moon Gemini to Cancer 6:19 p.m.) Today it is your turn to show someone how much you love him/her. Whether you give a gift or simply say something complementary, you will find it has a marvelous effect. As a matter of fact, it should prove to you how creative you can be. Some will get a chance to show off how versatile they are; enjoy being on-stage.

Sunday, July 6 (Moon in Cancer) You may be feeling guilty about a promise you haven't kept; today is the day to keep it—even if it means going out of your way. In return, give yourself a chance to do your own thing, which may be something you haven't tried before. Walk on eggs with someone who is a bit testy; it could be a Taurus or a Libra.

Monday, July 7 (Moon in Cancer) You've been hearing a little voice whispering inside of you. That voice may get a bit louder today. Let it guide you in making some changes both internally and externally. You will find you have a lot of enthusiasm and support behind you from people who really care about you. Appreciate it. Some will have a romantic encounter and should be aware that it may not be all it seems.

Tuesday, July 8 (Moon Cancer to Leo 5:56 a.m.) Today you bounce back with a vengeance, as the moon moves into your sign. You can be exceptionally productive, productive enough to warrant a promotion. Your rewards could come in the form of loving words from someone you love. Don't waste a minute today; if the pressure is not on, put it on yourself. You'll be at the right place at the crucial moment.

Wednesday, July 9 (Moon in Leo) Somebody places the power in your hands today when you least expect it. Be prepared to make a prompt decision—and to grab the reins. For some, credit comes in that is long overdue and it should give you a sense of satisfaction. Others will have the energy to finally finish off something that's been a real drag to complete.

Thursday, July 10 (Moon Leo to Virgo 3:50 p.m.) A verbal battle you get into today could be extremely constructive; controversy often results in fresh new ideas. And, on top of it, you make an excellent new friend. He/she could point out an attractive opportunity. Consider it, but follow your own counsel. Some will find themselves very much in the spotlight—has anyone asked for your autograph before? The lucky number is 1.

Friday, July 11 (Moon in Virgo) Today you defy all odds as the elements of timing and luck ride with you. No matter how much opposition you get, you are able to oppose it. Your ties with those you love—particularly family members—improve and things become a lot more harmonious. Pay some attention to your health today, and do something constructive about it.

Saturday, July 12 (Moon Virgo to Libra 11:40 p.m.) You are going to have to be very selective today, and that means choosing quality over mere quantity. A lot of opportunities and a lot of interests are likely to present themselves—but they are not all equal. Prove to a special person your willingness to go more than halfway; sometimes you talk a good gain, but do not follow through on it. Now's the time to do so. The lucky number is 3.

Sunday, July 13 (Moon in Libra) A recent contact you made could now be a key to a brand-new ball game. However, you are going to have to demonstrate your ability to deal with details and all those other minor matters you ordinarily like to avoid. A short trip may be on the agenda, and you may find yourself in contact with someone who believes you have all the answers. Be honest about your limitations. The lucky number is 4.

Monday, July 14 (Moon in Libra) Someone knows you better than you think, and you are wise to listen. His/her assessment of you has a ring of truth to it. Something comes along and breaks some bonds that have been restricting you; utilize the opportunity to move onward and upward. Put on your "reporter's cap" today, and take notes about everything you see and hear. It could prove valuable later on.

Tuesday, July 15 (Moon Libra to Scorpio 4:58 a.m.) Whatever you do, don't force any issues today. Particularly with those you live with. If you stick to the basic rules and regulations, you will avoid a lot of unpleasantness. Flexibility is important in everything today, as is a light touch and making others feel loved and wanted. Your time will come. The lucky number is 6.

Wednesday, July 16 (Moon in Scorpio) Know when to be on and when to be off today; if you are not sensitive to all the nuances, you will really ruffle someone's feelings. Some will be able to find a genuine bargain today and negotiate for it quite candidly. Cooperate with someone who claims to have psychic knowledge; it could be a Pisces, and he/she could be more right than you think.

Thursday, July 17 (Moon Scorpio to Sagittarius 7:34 a.m.) Someone around you is a bit bored, and may be asking for a lot of attention. Maybe you have not been as attentive as you should have been recently. Why not plan a little diversion? Physical attraction is very important to you at all times—and particularly today. Indulge yourself, but stay within the rules and regulations.

Friday, July 18 (Moon in Sagittarius) Now you are coming out of the woods, and a mission is being completed. For some, a burden is removed, and the whole world seems lighter and brighter. For others, love is becoming more and more important—with a particular person. Try your luck with number 9 today.

Saturday, July 19 (Moon Sagittarius to Capricorn 8:10 a.m.) You should be particularly inventive today, and able to show how creative you can be. Don't hesitate to stamp your own individual style on everything you do today. It is not like Leo to be modest, but sometimes you do tend to hide your light under a bushel. Some will be delighted when they get a very heartfelt compliment from someone whose opinion counts. You can trust the fact that it is sincere. An Aquarian or another Leo may play a key role today.

Sunday, July 20 (Moon in Capricorn) Although this is theoretically a day of rest, there's a lot for you to do. However, there should be people around to share the load and help you figure out how to polish things off quickly. In some cases, you are going to feel a bit overburdened. Promise yourself something nice in the day—even an excellent meal that you share with someone close. Just remember your diet resolutions.

Monday, July 21 (Moon Capricorn to Aquarius 8:17 a.m.) It is possible to be open-minded without being gullible. This full moon places an emphasis on your tendency to like people who place you on a pedestal. Just be aware when you are being used. Expect people who depend on you to make a lot of demands today. If you can't handle everything, at least be available for consultation. The lucky number today is 3.

Tuesday, July 22 (Moon in Aquarius) You may have to change your mind, but you should not change your principles. Be flexible, and see where you can compromise. For some, the change that comes about makes it necessary to read between the lines and ask "Why?" Partnerships and cooperative efforts are under the moon's influence today; be willing to give as well as take. The lucky number is 4.

Wednesday, July 23 (Moon Aquarius to Pisces 9:59 a.m.) Someone special makes some suggestions, and you should listen to them—but analytically. You are under no obligation to use any of them. Some will get an excellent opportunity to have things on their terms; be confident; but don't be overly demanding. It's an excellent time to explore new avenues of expression, Leo.

Thursday, July 24 (Moon in Pisces) Some may find themselves smack in the middle of a rather sticky situation involving someone else's resources. It may be that someone has overestimated what he/she can contribute. Don't let it throw you. In other matters as well, what you see on the surface may not be a true indication of what lies underneath. Don't be afraid to dig deep. There could be a jackpot!

Friday, July 25 (Moon Pisces to Aries 3:02 p.m.) Now things begin clearing up, and you see them for what they really are. In some cases you end up with a big advantage. Make the most of it! Other Leos will be dabbling in a fascinating new subject—possibly connected with the occult. The people you learn from are as important as what you learned. The lucky number today is 7.

Saturday, July 26 (Moon in Aries) Some will be mixing pleasure with business today, quite successfully. In some cases, travel is involved. The pleasure principle of this day leads in other cases to a quite lovely romantic interlude; it could be "romantic" in the good old-fashioned sense, which generally appeals to Leo. The lucky number is 8.

Sunday, July 27 (Moon in Aries) This is a day for reaching agreements and opening up the lines of communication with people who have been rather "closed." For some, an agreement that seems temporary will turn out to be quite long-range. And you will like it. For other Leos, someone holds out a hand and says, "I'll help"; don't let false pride turn him/her down. The lucky number is 9.

Monday, July 28 (Moon Aries to Taurus 12:11 a.m.) Try a new approach today, because it could be a very successful maneuver. Many of you will be feeling particularly creative, but should remember that there are some boundaries to where you can go. Concentrate on improving your standing where you stand before you expand into many different directions. A fixed Aquarian or Taurus could be most helpful.

Tuesday, July 29 (Moon in Taurus) Don't get involved in a dispute with someone who talks in a rather threatening manner; realize that he/she is really saying very little. One piece of information you pick up, however, is the clue to the whole situation. Use it wisely. Your intuition should tell you you are going places. The lucky number is 2.

Wednesday, July 30 (Moon Taurus to Gemini 12:19 p.m.) You could be feeling rather frivolous today. And it could lead to a shopping spree. Be practical, but do give into that feeling to change your image. You are right on target. Someone stimulates your intellectual curiosity, and you should follow through on what you learn. For some of you good news comes in in connection with travel—or love.

Thursday, July 31 (Moon in Gemini) A lot of red tape is getting untangled, and it's a big relief. Now you will be much freer to accept an invitation that comes along. For some, it could include a trip. Some Leos are at the top of the heap right now and have gained a certain degree of fame. Keep your options open and realize that fame could be fleeting. Let a Gemini tell you all about it.

AUGUST 1986

Friday, August 1 (Moon in Gemini) Someone says what he/she means; you should realize that he/she also means what they say. If you underestimate the seriousness of the situation, you will be in trouble. Set your sights on some new goals, and count on your own abilities to make wishes come true. Remember, the more solid the people you choose to associate with, the better off you will be. The lucky number is 2.

Saturday, August 2 (Moon Gemini to Cancer 1:04 a.m.) Your soft side is showing today. It might mean that you would like to indulge your love for the beautiful—in art, music, or whatever. For some, you will be able to work out this urge by entertaining at home in some beautiful way. A lot of things should come easily to you now—and you should have more room.

Sunday, August 3 (Moon in Cancer) A very cozy relationship could be developing. Don't get overeager and blow it out of proportion. Some Leos should follow up on resolutions to keep in touch with someone who has a problem—and is possibly temporarily confined. Be the good Samaritan.

Monday, August 4 (Moon Cancer to Leo 12:26 p.m.) Once again, you should be generous with your time. You have lots of it—and it's all quality time. With your cycle moving up, your opinion may be sought out in connection with something fairly important. Give a reasoned answer. Try a Gemini or a Sagittarian for good company today.

Tuesday, August 5 (Moon in Leo) Some good things may appear to drop out of the blue today. And some of you may wonder "What did I do that was so special?" Maybe nothing, but enjoy it anyway. All of you have a fresh start now and should be able to put your individual stamp on anything you do. It's a rather off-beat but exciting day. The lucky number is 6.

Wednesday, August 6 (Moon Leo to Virgo 9:44 p.m.) A mysterious person may come upon the scene today and play a key role. Since you are still in a very good part of your moon cycle, realize that your position is quite strong. And that you can see beyond the surface indications. Use your judgment—and some help—to unsnarl a rather sticky problem. Get rid of what you don't need!

Thursday, August 7 (Moon in Virgo) This should be an excellent and quite productive day. As a matter of fact, some may receive a promotion or a raise. All will find that they are able to score a lot of points. If there's something you can't locate, try looking for it today. You could possibly turn it up in the least expected place. The lucky number is 8.

Friday, August 8 (Moon Virgo to Libra 5:05 a.m.) Don't get distracted by some rather tender feelings that someone evokes in you today. It is important to finish what you start. A dynamic person is the one you should get really involved with today, because he/she knows where the action is. Spend some time catching up on money matters; it's possible that some of you have let them slip.

Saturday, August 9 (Moon in Libra) In order to avoid confusion, compare notes with someone you have made plans with. It's possible that he/she has something slightly different in mind. It's important to take nothing for granted where any kind of directions or instructions are concerned. Do accept an invitation to what may be a new kind of circle for you; there's a lot to be learned, a lot of interesting people to be met.

Sunday, August 10 (Moon in Libra) Someone around you is feeling very sensitive today, and is easily bruised emotionally. You should know it and act accordingly. Once more, you may be checking with people at a distance about future plans. Keep them air-tight.

Monday, August 11 (Moon Libra to Scorpio 10:36 a.m.) Don't try to do too many things at once today. It's important to concentrate on a major project that has a major role in your life. Think about things in the long-term, not the short. Some will be a little discouraged, but should be aware that what looks a bit doubtful now will eventually go in your favor. Let a Gemini or a Sagittarian cheer you up.

Tuesday, August 12 (Moon in Scorpio) Some of you will be feeling a bit tied down, but should know that you will be set free before long. Someone who is a bit boring is also quite right. Listen to him/her about suggestions for taking something apart and putting it back together again. It's worth the trouble.

Wednesday, August 13 (Moon Scorpio to Sagittarius 2:17 p.m.) There are ways to improve things without spending a lot of money. Some are taking a look at their living quarters and realizing that something's got to get done. Someone in your circle knows a lot about such things, and you should not hesitate to ask. Some will be surprised by an unusual gift from an unusual source. Realize that if you accept it, you will be saying, "Yes, I'm serious too."

Thursday, August 14 (Moon in Sagittarius) Yes, you are right. What you think is going to happen is quite accurate. Use your advanced knowledge to your own advantage. Some are facing a rather big adjustment in their life-style; it needn't be unsettling. A philosophical type—possibly a Sagittarian—can help you over this rough spot. The lucky number is 6.

Friday, August 15 (Moon Sagittarius to Capricorn 4:22 p.m.) Many will be particularly moody today, and someone may point out that you're in a world of your own. Let him/her know that your condition is temporary, and that you'll come back down to earth very soon. On the positive side, you could be positively psychic today. Keep your sensors out.

Saturday, August 16 (Moon in Capricorn) Today you may come back down to earth, and find it not the most enjoyable place to be. The day's scenario indicates a lot of pressure and responsibility. However, there is also a lot of love indicated, and some will learn where they stand as far as a long-term relationship goes. You will like it.

Sunday, August 17 (Moon Capricorn to Aquarius 5:44 p.m.) You could play the role of efficiency expert and show others how to get the job done faster for less money. Some of you will be gratified when someone comes across and says, "Okay, you win." Just don't gloat too much. Have fun with an Aries or a Libra and try your luck with number 9.

Monday, August 18 (Moon in Aquarius) You should have little difficulty getting others to cooperate today;

in fact, you will find people extraordinarily receptive to your requests. In a partnership arrangement—possibly your most important partner—you could take unfair advantage. Clarify your intentions. Some Leos are in for a big win—it could be a contest where you come out number one.

Tuesday, August 19 (Moon Aquarius to Pisces 7:52 p.m.) This full moon hits Leo square in that part of the chart having to do with marriage and partnerships—actually, all one-on-one relationships. If you handle things right, you can convert an enemy into a friend. You will recognize your opportunity today when you have a clash of ideas. In another area, bits and pieces of information are very frustrating; soon you will have the complete story.

Wednesday, August 20 (Moon in Pisces) Now you will get a lot of answers to those questions that have been bugging you. Don't hesitate to ask more. Many will find themselves quite popular now and will be very aware of their physical appearance. It's an excellent time for a complete "makeover."

Thursday, August 21 (Moon in Pisces) Take time out to check up on your budget and your checkbook. You may have to revise some spending plans. Somebody who's been boasting about his/her ability to manage money may really have some good tips; inquire. A Scorpio could play a very important role today. The lucky number is 4.

Friday, August 22 (Moon Pisces to Aries 12:27 a.m.) If you realize you are going through a learning process, you will be less impatient with current conditions. True maturity is possible now. Many will be absolutely fascinated by something they read or see now—share it with a friend. Others may be feeling the urge to write; you should try it. The lucky number is 5.

Saturday, August 23 (Moon in Aries)   This is an excellent weekend to do something new and daring. For some, it means committing to a rather ambitious travel plan. For others, it could simply be investigating a new subject or form of communication. Some of you are going to give in where others are concerned. But you'll like the results.

Sunday, August 24 (Moon Aries to Taurus 8:36 a.m.) You could easily be fooled now by the surface look of something or someone. Be aware that wishing can't make it so. There is a dangerous tendency now to act first and think later. Be aware of it. Don't give up something of value for nothing.

Monday, August 25 (Moon in Taurus)   It is very possible you make some kind of step forward now, and the most likely place to do it is where you work. Many will have extra responsibility handed to them, and may feel rather pressured. Do what you can, but remember that you are being observed by higher-ups. A Cancer or a Capricorn could help you see how to do more more easily.

Tuesday, August 26 (Moon Taurus to Gemini 8:00 p.m.)   There is a definite feeling of relief today as a burden gets lighter. Someone you think a lot of indicates that he/she feels the same way; you may be asked to consult on a subject of importance to this person. Many are beginning to feel they can see light at the end of the tunnel. The lucky number today is 9.

Wednesday, August 27 (Moon in Gemini)   There is a much lighter tone to this day, and many will find a reason to play. For some, a very vivacious person proves to be an excellent playmate—and a possible romantic partner. Also on the up side, you see positive results from recent efforts. The lucky number is 1.

Thursday, August 28 (Moon in Gemini) Many will find it amazingly easy to swing someone over to their side now. He/she turns out to be a lot less reluctant than you thought, and you've not got a terrific team member. He/she is possibly a Cancer or a Capricorn. You are still in a cycle of change and variety. Take advantage of every opportunity.

Friday, August 29 (Moon Gemini to Cancer 8:40 a.m.) You may be tempted to overindulge today—in food and drink or something equally pleasurable. Make sure you moderate your pleasure. There is a light-hearted tone to this day, and a definite indication that something important will go your way.

Saturday, August 30 (Moon in Cancer) Whatever you do, do not reveal a secret someone confides in you. Even if you are just bursting to tell it. It is not wise to gain at the expense of another; you've got enough coming to you now to feel satisfied. The lucky number is 4.

Sunday, August 31 (Moon Cancer to Leo 8:08 p.m.) It might be a good idea to retire from "the madding crowd" today and get some time by yourself. Some recent experiences need to be thought over and assimilated. Some may feel like indulging a rather unusual interest—possibly in psychic phenomena. It looks like a quiet easy day.

SEPTEMBER 1986

Monday, September 1 (Moon in Leo) The pace abruptly changes and gets quite a bit faster. With the moon in your sign, you should be full of energy—and charisma. Expect a lot of good things to happen today if you mingle with the right people. One of them could be a Gemini. The lucky number is 3.

Tuesday, September 2 (Moon in Leo) It's possible

to take someone by surprise today and thereby gain an advantage. It could make up for something you dropped the ball on not too long ago. Know that you can trust your instincts to time yourself properly now. An Aquarian could easily fall in step with you.

Wednesday, September 3 (Moon Leo to Virgo 5:06 a.m.) Someone may tell you exactly where you stand today, but it should not be unsettling. You are ready for this kind of frankness. Some may get a small shock with regard to their financial status; it is important to keep accurate records.

Thursday, September 4 (Moon in Virgo) Someone is rather restless today, and it could be you. You are in the mood for a change, and you should investigate the possibilities of making one. Many will receive a lovely token of affection.

Friday, September 5 (Moon Virgo to Libra 11:33 a.m.) It's clean-up time, and you should be willing to get rid of what you no longer need. On the job that may mean being willing to do something in a new way. Don't be stubborn! This is an excellent time to make some kind of investment. Talk it over with a Pisces or a Virgo.

Saturday, September 6 (Moon in Libra) It's all too easy for you to be led astray today; know your limits. It's possible to have fun without breaking the bank. In another matter, demand something in return for something that is asked for you. You do not have to be overgenerous.

Sunday, September 7 (Moon Libra to Scorpio 4:12 p.m.) There is a nice warm feeling about this day, and many can expect an old emotional wound to be healed. The occasion may be some kind of reunion with someone you have not seen in a while. For others, someone will finally say, "Thank you." You should be very constructive today and able to help others with their problems. One who may come to you could be an Aries or a Libra.

Monday, September 8 (Moon in Scorpio) Many Leos could feel a bit hemmed in and tied down today. Don't let it bum you out; this period will pass. You can score some points today by pointing out how to break new ground without breaking the rules. Another Leo could be an excellent teammate.

Tuesday, September 9 (Moon Scorpio to Sagittarius 7:40 p.m.) It's very easy for you to have your suggestions acted on today. People accept them because you are obviously on familiar ground. Another comfortable area should be what you find out by reading the small print; you are a lot more secure than you thought.

Wednesday, September 10 (Moon in Sagittarius) Be prepared for a midweek "pleasure break." You should have lots of freedom, and you should use it wisely. For some, that means focusing on looks and body image. You could do some very good "overhauling." A Sagittarian may be very prominent today.

Thursday, September 11 (Moon Sagittarius to Capricorn 10:28 a.m.) Be prepared for a sudden switch of plans today and do not let it throw you off balance. In fact, for most it will result in a particularly pleasureable day. Even those who must stick to their task at hand will get a lift from a very meaningful compliment made by someone who counts. Spend some time with or on children today.

Friday, September 12 (Moon in Capricorn) It is important not to "fall off the wagon" now in the sense of backsliding about your resolutions to do with general health—and work. You may feel like goofing off, but you are best off sticking with what must be done.

You will have lots of help and support. Particularly from a Gemini or a Virgo. The lucky number is 5.

Saturday, September 13 (Moon in Capricorn) There is no doubt that you have a lot of friends, but sometimes you overcommit. That means some people may be rather annoyed with you today when you don't show up at the right time and the right place. How could you? You were somewhere else. Try to get your act together. Many will find out that a gift is on the way, and should be prepared to reciprocate.

Sunday, September 14 (Moon Capricorn to Aquarius 1:07 a.m.) You may have to tiptoe around someone else's feelings today—someone you share a roof with. Refuse to be drawn into an argument, or into making a hasty decision. In another area, someone will hand you a story that you should be a bit skeptical of. You can be open-minded without being gullible. The lucky number is 7.

Monday, September 15 (Moon in Aquarius) In one way or another, the law is on your side today. You could literally be involved in a legal matter, or be trying to straighten out rights and permissions with another individual. Many should realize that a delay does not mean a defeat. Try to stay out of somebody else's quarrel.

Tuesday, September 16 (Moon Aquarius to Pisces 4:27 a.m.) For many, an emotional involvement is getting much more involved; the game-playing could be over and this could be for keeps. Others should not accept superficial answers now; insist on the real information. For others, a goal is in sight.

Wednesday, September 17 (Moon in Pisces) For many Leos, love once again plays a major role. Others will find themselves in love with a new idea, and a new start. All should be feeling highly "creative" now. Today it's possible for you to know without knowing, because your instincts are quite accurate. The lucky number is 1.

Thursday, September 18 (Moon Pisces to Aries 9:33 a.m.) This full moon could make you overly emotional; keep a tight rein on your temper. On the other hand, this day could find some Leos winning a major battle, possibly a legal one. In other cases, it is a very basic commitment that is made. The lucky number is 2.

Friday, September 19 (Moon in Aries) Today you should be able to overcome all kinds of barriers. Communication is much easier than in the recent past, and you may even find yourself understanding someone you considered rather strange. Some will get an intriguing invitation from someone more than interesting. Could love be involved?

Saturday, September 20 (Moon Aries to Taurus 5:25 p.m.) Your tendency to act on impulse is very strong today; if you do, at least protect your personal interests. Physical attraction and sensations of all kinds are very much in the air. Some will find this an excellent time to review recent events—and possibly revise some opinions.

Sunday, September 21 (Moon in Taurus) In one way or another, many Leos will find themselves in the spotlight today and regarded as people of prestige. Take full advantage of the situation, and realize what there is to gain. For some, a member of the opposite sex makes a move. Realize that he/she does care and is trying to prove it.

Monday, September 22 (Moon in Taurus) You may start off the week a little on the dissatisfied side, and will try to make up for it by overindulging in sweets or other equally pleasurable things. It's okay to tell yourself it's okay. For now. Something nice happens when someone says Yes to your suggestion. The lucky number is 6.

Tuesday, September 23 (Moon Taurus to Gemini 4:13 a.m.) Some of you will find yourselves in a "secret meeting." Enjoy the spice, but just don't do anyone else in in the process. It is an excellent day to "take the bull by the horns" and try to swing someone over to your side; you should be able to do it with ease. For some, rewards are due. The lucky number is 7.

Wednesday, September 24 (Moon in Gemini) Some Leos are in for a shock when they realize that something somebody said just recently is much more serious than you thought. Can you deal with it? The best investment you could make right now is in your own talents and abilities; don't sell yourself short. The lucky number is 8.

Thursday, September 25 (Moon Gemini to Cancer 4:44 p.m.) There's no point in beating a dead horse. Get rid of a losing proposition now! Once you are unburdened, you will be able to reach beyond your current expectations—and expect to win. Try mingling with another Leo, an Aries or a Libra for best results today.

Friday, September 26 (Moon in Cancer) Stand your ground today when someone tries to sway you from one of your favorite opinions; you are not always right, but you are an individual. Stay that way. Some will get a backstage view and learn a secret that is to their advantage. The lucky number today is 1.

Saturday, September 27 (Moon in Cancer) If yesterday's experience left you feeling a little rocky, today someone close will help you feel you are on steady ground again. Some should try to get some peace and quiet and to retire from the scene as much as possible. Others should do something nice for someone who needs it. The lucky number is 2.

Sunday, September 28 (Moon Cancer to Leo 5:39 a.m.) Now you are really coming into your own as the moon comes into your sign. Your forces may be a little scattered, but there is little you can do to go wrong today. Many will get excellent news about something that has been accepted. Others will be surrounded with adoring friends. It's a wonderful day!

Monday, September 29 (Moon in Leo) It's great to start out the workweek with the moon in your sign. There is every possibility that you will get a second chance to correct something you goofed before. With your beacon of personality on so high, there is no way you will not be noticed. And admired. The lucky number is 4.

Tuesday, September 30 (Moon Leo to Virgo 1:57 p.m.) Again, it's a good day, and you should find a lot of constructive, profitable outlets for your talents and energy. Almost without meaning to do so, you take the spotlight—at just the right time. And it pays off. Have fun with a Virgo or a Sagittarian. The lucky number is 4.

OCTOBER 1986

Wednesday, October 1 (Moon in Virgo) This is one of those days you should make every attempt to balance the book—in every sense of the word. Delays are indicated, as are demands from demanding people. One could be a potential love who is testing you in advance. Decide whether you like to be tested.

Thursday, October 2 (Moon Virgo to Libra 8:03 p.m.) Count your change today, because somebody wants something for nothing—and you could be the prime target. Don't overlook something someone gives you to read today; it contains a lot of pure gold information for you. Somebody will confess to you, and you should be gracious.

Friday, October 3 (Moon in Libra) Things make an abrupt about-face today, and you are going to have to make a major adjustment in your way of doing things. The staging area is likely to be your own home ground. You will not get anything you want by insisting or challenging; it is important to be as diplomatic as possible.

Saturday, October 4 (Moon Libra to Scorpio 11:35 p.m.) At all costs, make your meaning very clear today. It is the only way to keep things in balance. Many of you will be in touch with people just passing through who may want to sell you something. Check for defects. It is important to be self-protective now.

Sunday, October 5 (Moon in Scorpio) Get down to business right away, and leave the frills for another time. Though you theoretically are off today, you are definitely on in your own home environment. Now is the time you must teach others how to be practical. You can do it. Somebody is waiting for a proper signal from you and then he/she will not appear indifferent.

Monday, October 6 (Moon in Scorpio) Don't overstay your welcome today; know when it's time to get out. For some, that will mean letting go of something comfortable from the past, and taking a bold step into the future. Someone of an equally fiery nature cares about you, and will help you make the big move.

Tuesday, October 7 (Moon Scorpio to Sagittarius 1:48 a.m.) Your timing should be excellent now, and it comes in handy where romance is concerned. You are easily able to ignite a spark. Some may have to really talk turkey with a member of the opposite sex, but the relationship improves all the way around. The lucky number is 1.

Wednesday, October 8 (Moon in Sagittarius) You may feel like doing something a bit kooky, and you can rest assured it will have the desired result. Some will have an excellent opportunity to learn by teaching today; there may be actual involvement with children. For some, a family reunion is indicated.

Thursday, October 9 (Moon Sagittarius to Capricorn 3:52 a.m.) Once again you feel like doing things any way but the usual way; it is an excellent day to display your versatility. For some who have been feeling a bit off-key, your health improves and your appetite comes back. Perhaps with a vengeance. Don't overdo. Some plans you made recently will be clarified. The lucky number is 3.

Friday, October 10 (Moon in Capricorn) Today you are far more restricted than in the recent past, but you may not mind it at all. Most likely you are feeling like business as usual. Beware of someone who claims to like you, but really wants to see you fail. Do not let him/her trip you up. A Scorpio could be the key.

Saturday, October 11 (Moon Capricorn to Aquarius 7:45 a.m.) You may be a victim of circumstances today, but only in the sense that you may be forced to go along with the plans of others. Show just how sweet and tractable you can be by agreeing with a smile. There really isn't any other way. Some should get their ideas on paper, because there is an indication of gain through the written word.

Sunday, October 12 (Moon in Aquarius) As the saying goes, beware of Greeks bearing gifts. Someone may just be trying to get you on his/her side. It's okay to be shrewd and to be gracious at the same time. Some of you will have a definite change of scene. The lucky number is 6.

Monday, October 13 (Moon Aquarius to Pisces 11:03 a.m.) Realize that time is definitely on your side, and that you can play a waiting game and win! Some will be frustrated when certain people change their mind and throw a monkey wrench into the machinery. However, you are far better off not making any long-range commitments now.

Tuesday, October 14 (Moon in Pisces) Today you will find people more and more cooperative than yesterday. In fact, someone at your job will absolutely astonish you by making a concession to what you want. Some of you may be engrossed in a new subject—and it could provide enlightenment. The lucky number is 8.

Wednesday, October 15 (Moon Pisces to Aries 5:13 p.m.) It is wise not to have any preconceived notions now. The best thing is to start out on a whole new footing and to reject anything that smacks of the superficial. Someone comes on very strong and aggressive, but really wants to be a good pal and ally. Be receptive. The lucky number is 9.

Thursday, October 16 (Moon in Aries) You may be feeling a little delicate today and you should not overdo. Either physically or emotionally. Spend your time with someone very supportive who helps you regain your independence and pride. You really are at the beginning of a new adventure.

Friday, October 17 (Moon in Aries) Many will be faced with a major decision now concerning the family, residence, or future security. Do not be afraid of it. Once again, some may have to deal with a minor health problem. Have you been taking care of yourself? The lucky number is 2.

Saturday, October 18 (Moon Aries to Taurus 1:35 a.m.) A sudden side trip may be necessary; regard it as a "special mission." If anything that's happened recently has you a bit on edge, get in touch with someone who is capable of pulling strings in your favor. It could possibly be a Taurus.

Sunday, October 19 (Moon in Taurus) You can make definite progress toward your goal today. One key for some is to let yourself be seen and known in the wider community. There is definite indication that an obstacle can be overcome quite simply.

Monday, October 20 (Moon Taurus to Gemini 12:15 p.m.) The air is definitely clearing now, and you have a much better fix on what to expect in the very near future. For some, the key is to get into change and welcome variety. It need not be threatening. The lucky number today is 5.

Tuesday, October 21 (Moon in Gemini) A sudden change of pace puts romance, dreams, and wishes right at the top of your mind. Something wonderful could come from a surprise source. As for doing it yourself, your sales ability is excellent now. You can do a lot on your own behalf. The lucky number is 6.

Wednesday, October 22 (Moon in Gemini) Clear the decks! It's time to dump old ways of doing things and turn the corner. For many, love and romance are still uppermost—and could definitely flavor the day. A Pisces or a Virgo will help many Leos to make valuable contacts. You've got some excellent new friends!

Thursday, October 23 (Moon Gemini to Cancer 12:37 a.m.) Someone reveals a secret, and you gain "secret power" as a result. Use it wisely. Some kind of mystery that has been nagging at you now can be resolved. Some should take care not to be taken in by illusion or what appears "glamorous" but really is rather dangerous.

Friday, October 24 (Moon in Cancer) Someone who's been simply impossible to reach now becomes available, and could prove the focal point of the day. Many will have to be exceptionally self-reliant now, but you should have great confidence in your own abilities to handle things. A special person means well, but is probably simply making an error in judgement. Don't get fooled.

Saturday, October 25 (Moon Cancer to Leo 1:02 p.m.) A wonderful thing happens for many Leos when someone who has hurt you in the past comes back and tries to rectify that. Get to the root of the problem with this person, and you will come out much happier as a result. Some Leos are going to be asked to take the lead in a project, and should.

Sunday, October 26 (Moon in Leo) Today's the day, and many of you know it! With the moon in your sign, your intuition is extremely sharp. This is one time it would be very difficult to fool you, Leo. Many will breathe a sigh of relief when they get the full story on something that's been rather shadowy. The lucky number is 2 today.

Monday, October 27 (Moon Leo to Virgo 11:20 p.m.) Everyone wants to be with you today, and you can expect a number of invitations. With such a busy day facing you, you should try to plan your time carefully. There may even be some kind of surprise, and you wouldn't want to be taken off-balance. The lucky number is 3.

Tuesday, October 28 (Moon in Virgo) Check, check, and double-check today. You could easily slip up on something. Some will be paying their dues but it is definitely worth the price. Others will be dealing with a very canny individual—possibly a Scorpio—who may be sympathetic, but definitely means business.

Wednesday, October 29 (Moon in Virgo) You may have to put your beliefs on the line today in order to take advantage of an opportunity. In other words, you may have to put your money where your mouth is. You can do so with a fair degree of confidence. For some, a relationship is getting a lot more serious. Maybe you should too.

Thursday, October 30 *(Moon Virgo to Libra 6:04 a.m.)* You should be at your smiling Leo best today and capable of dealing with a minor crisis in your domestic sphere. Listen carefully when someone talks about how much goes out versus how much goes in; you may have to do a little belt-tightening. However, you can afford a little gift for someone special.

Friday, October 31 *(Moon in Libra)* No matter what happens today, you can take it in your stride—even a prank that isn't really funny. It would be an excellent evening to get together with neighbors or siblings. Your family ties should feel very strong.

NOVEMBER 1986

Saturday, November 1 *(Moon Libra to Scorpio 9:19 a.m.)* A message is on the way, and it could relate to travel. Some of you are very puzzled about a recent occurrence, and should make some efforts to figure out what really was going on. It's important that you do. Someone may help you find something you thought you lost.

Sunday, November 2 *(Moon in Scorpio)* This is your day to play the role of peacemaker and to smooth over a family dispute. On a pleasanter side, the focus is on things of beauty—and possibly people to match. You may find a Taurus or a Libra particularly attractive. On the practical side of life, you could have a brainstorm about how to increase your income.

Monday, November 3 *(Moon Scorpio to Sagittarius 10:19 a.m.)* It's important not to fool yourself about anybody or anything now; be sure to see others in a realistic light. For some Leos, a member of the opposite sex is trying to tell you something. Listen hard. All should speak quite clearly now and define their terms.

Tuesday, November 4 (Moon in Sagittarius) Some Leos will be getting more responsibility now, and some of the things that go along with it—like money. You may have to make a commitment, and you should be sure it is sincere. Some will find themselves fascinated by someone or something of great physical beauty; it can be yours if you want it. The lucky number is 8.

Wednesday, November 5 (Moon Sagittarius to Capricorn 10:49 a.m.) Don't be afraid to stretch yourself and to reach beyond what you currently can grasp. It is an excellent time to see how far you can go—even if only in your thinking at the present moment. Some will be able to get out of an annoying commitment, and others will be thinking about travel with a very delightful travel companion.

Thursday, November 6 (Moon in Capricorn) Be independent today, no matter how others try to make you go along with the crowd. Your health should be a bit better now, and you should be working in much more congenial surroundings than in the recent past. Some should be prepared to render a very special service. The lucky number is 1.

Friday, November 7 (Moon Capricorn to Aquarius 12:29 p.m.) Listen when someone older or more experienced tries to give you some advice about how to do something rather basic. There's always a new way to do something old. Many will see their role in life much more clearly defined now, and will be moving forward with a greater sense of purpose. Follow through on a hunch, and try your luck with number 2.

Saturday, November 8 (Moon in Aquarius) Look at the big picture today, and fill in the details at another time. It would be much too easy to get lost in a morass of small things. You should be able to win over some new friends from what formerly was the opposition. Keep on thinking positive, but check out some legal matters that might cause a snag.

Sunday, November 9 (Moon Aquarius to Pisces 4:30 p.m.) No matter how you try to get away from them, there are some obligations you must fulfill now. In fact, some may now have to fulfill on a promise that they made a while ago. For a number of Leos, the question of marital status will arise. Stand up for your principles, and try your luck with number 4.

Monday, November 10 (Moon in Pisces) Many will be thinking big thoughts today for which there are no immediate answers. It's a good time to indulge that interest in something beyond the usual. You have a good mind for it. A rather restless person will cause you a bit of confusion today; takes notes on his/her performance and you will understand it later on.

Tuesday, November 11 (Moon Pisces to Aries 11:14 p.m.) Be prepared for some kind of surprise today—and it could take tangible form. If it is a gift, give your thanks in a way that will satisfy this particular giver. He/she is not easy to please. For some, a recent storm clears and everyone is a lot more cooperative.

Wednesday, November 12 (Moon in Aries) This is a good day to advertise yourself. It's easy for you to appear rather glamorous and rather interesting today—play it up! For some, spiritual values are coming into focus, and you are taking greater charge of your own destiny. The lucky number today is 7.

Thursday, November 13 (Moon in Aries) A decision goes in your favor, and you should have reason to celebrate. Some will even be able to grab power they didn't have before. Someone who has been hard to get now becomes very available, and an interesting relationship begins to develop. The lucky number is 8.

Friday, November 14 (Moon Aries to Taurus 8:24 a.m.) Don't be afraid to strike out on your own now; you really don't need any support. Others should prepare themselves to get a rather unusual assignment, one that will involve meeting interesting people—and possibly going interesting new places. For many, a project is completed, and an Aries or a Libra will be a person to say, "Thank you" to.

Saturday, November 15 (Moon in Taurus) You are full of energy and ideas today and will be the leader of the pack, no matter what you do or where you are. For some, there is a definite boost in prestige indicated. You might be elected to an office in a community or a charity group. No matter what the day's scenario, you will end up knowing you have loyal allies and that your efforts are appreciated.

Sunday, November 16 (Moon Taurus to Gemini 7:26 p.m.) This full moon throws its light on that area of your chart having to do with your Leo destiny or purpose in life. That means something in that area will culminate soon. Keep this in mind as you follow through on a hunch. Many will be able to pull off a surprise and delight someone who deserves being delighted.

Monday, November 17 (Moon in Gemini) Today may see you make definite progress on the job. At least you will have a lot more confidence than you have in the recent past, and you will be able to put a pet plan into action. There is a lot to gain from taking chances now. In both business and social life. The lucky number is 3.

Tuesday, November 18 (Moon in Gemini) Don't be discouraged when you've got to rectify a past mistake. The moon position continues to indicate fulfillment of your desires. That means, no matter what else happens today, you can be sure you are making progress. A minor glitch can occur if you ignore the small print.

Wednesday, November 19 (Moon Gemini to Cancer 7:46 a.m.) Your sense of showmanship is at a high today, and you could pull a dramatic scene. Hopefully it will be a positive one. Don't overplay your hand, however, because there are other rather dynamic individuals involved. The lucky number is 5.

Thursday, November 20 (Moon in Cancer) You're forced to make an adjustment today, but it's nothing to worry about. In fact, you will probably be more comfortable as a result too. Diplomacy is your best course in everything today, including how you react to a rather shocking secret someone tells you. Stay cool! A money dilemma will be resolved. The lucky number is 6.

Friday, November 21 (Moon Cancer to Leo 8:25 p.m.) After a slight delay early in the day, you will start moving toward a peak. Spend your time clearing the decks and mapping out the territory you want to conquer. A Pisces or a Cancer will be sensitive to your vibes today; you should do likewise.

Saturday, November 22 (Moon in Leo) With the moon in your sign, this is a day to really score points. All cycles point to a lot of achievement and a lot of love. For some of you, a relationship will become quite intense, and you may have to deal with a new set of circumstances. The lucky number is 8.

Sunday, November 23 (Moon in Leo) Get ready to take some bows and to hear some applause. You will be able to show off your rather unique talents to a very appreciative audience. Without your planning, you end up in the right place at the right time. Romance is not bad at all either.

Monday, November 24 (Moon Leo to Virgo 7:46 a.m.) You are at your most attractive Leo best now. However, you should be aware of the costs of some changes you are thinking about making in your living environment. You can't do everything! You may be delighted to find that a member of the opposite sex shares your values and your dreams.

Tuesday, November 25 (Moon in Virgo) Don't let anyone fast talk you today; insist on a definition of terms. Make it clear that you have neither money nor energy to burn. There may be some papers to sign, and you must be absolutely certain about what you are agreeing to. Someone wants to make a situation permanent.

Wednesday, November 26 (Moon Virgo to Libra 3:59 p.m.) Timing and luck are both on your side today. You will be very conscious of your personal image as others turn their heads to look at you. You may decide the time has come to do something about your recent weight gain. You should have the willpower to see it through.

Thursday, November 27 (Moon in Libra) This should be a particularly pleasant holiday for you, even though you are trying to exercise control in the area of food intake. One of the things you are most thankful for—or should be—is the greater degree of freedom that you have now, both of thought and of action. A Taurus will figure prominently in the day's events.

Friday, November 28 (Moon Libra to Scorpio 8:13 p.m.) This is a time for action and for taking chances. You may even find yourself blowing your own horn, which is a wise thing to do now. Love and romance can be found very, very close to home. Keep your options open, and do read between the lines.

Saturday, November 29 (Moon in Scorpio) The emphasis today is on home and family matters. You may even be thinking about a possible change in residence, and want to look into some promising opportunities. Someone will be very helpful, a source of warmth and affection. Realize how lucky you are. The lucky number is 6.

Sunday, November 30 (Moon Scorpio to Sagittarius 9:08 p.m.) It may be necessary to make some minor sacrifices today in order to achieve major gains. Realize that where you scrimp and save now is where you can spend later. Get rid of some safety hazards around your home base, as well as some unnecessary expenses. An answer comes in an intuitive flash.

DECEMBER 1986

Monday, December 1 (Moon in Sagittarius) Today you should be ready for anything, and one thing may be a travel plan that someone suggests. At any rate, you'll be thinking in rather long-range terms and planning for the future. Someone around you is very open-handed and makes a gesture to restore harmony. Extend your hand as well. The lucky number is 6.

Tuesday, December 2 (Moon Sagittarius to Capricorn 8:26 p.m.) Try to get away by yourself today, if at all possible. You need some time alone to gather your wits back together and to meditate. Some may be sharing their solitude with a very loving person—possibly a Pisces or a Virgo. No matter what you do, you will be anything but lonely.

Wednesday, December 3 (Moon in Capricorn) You may find yourself smack in the middle of a rather confusing situation which could get even more confused if you interfere. Sit back and let others handle it. Meanwhile, stick to the job at hand, and try to figure out a better way of doing it. Things go well in your work environment.

Thursday, December 4 (Moon Capricorn to Aquarius 8:23 p.m.) A new opportunity may present itself today, but you should realize it requires a lot of discretion at this initial stage. If you talk about it too much, you will lose your edge. Don't spend so much time thinking about it, however, that you do not finish what you start. You'll be dealing with some sharp rather fiery people.

Friday, December 5 (Moon in Aquarius) It will become obvious in the day that a new approach is necessary—particularly with regard to the person you share living quarters with. If you get competitive, so will the opposite side. Don't fight over unimportant things. Some Leos could take advantage of "winning vibes" and come out victorious in another situation.

Saturday, December 6 (Moon Aquarius to Pisces 10:48 p.m.) Help comes from a very unexpected quarter today; for some Leos, it could be someone who suddenly turns up and reminds that he/she "owes you one." It's a pleasant surprise. Show how diligent and dedicated you can be today, and you will find that a lot of people are in your corner. Many should follow through on a hunch they have, even if it seems off the wall. The lucky number is 2.

Sunday, December 7 (Moon in Pisces) You should be in excellent humor today and ready to try your hand at a couple of new and different things. Use your leisure time to satisfy some intellectual curiosity you have developed about a special subject. Some Leos will get excellent news regarding money—it may have something to do with an inheritance. The lucky number is 3.

Monday, December 8 (Moon in Pisces) The week starts out on a rather quiet note, and you may enjoy being able to hide. You are not feeling particularly Leo today. Use this down time to build a more secure base—right where you are. A Scorpio, a Taurus, or another Leo might prove very important today.

Tuesday, December 9 (Moon Pisces to Aries 4:49 a.m.) There's a lot to be gained today by making yourself visible with the right people. Though you can talk a good game now, you are better off getting your ideas on paper. Some may have the opportunity to publish a pet idea. For some, sex rears its lovely head today and provides a delightful interlude. A Gemini, a Virgo, or a Sagittarian could be involved.

Wednesday, December 10 (Moon in Aries) An area of some Leos' lives that has been in turmoil now settles down and harmony returns. You should be feeling a lot more optimistic than in the recent past. Some will receive a call that puts everything in focus; others will get a favorable report on their financial situation.

Thursday, December 11 (Moon Aries to Taurus 2:10 p.m.) Keep your mind on faraway places today, because a travel plan could take definite form now. However, some Leos will find out that they have simply been fooling themselves about someone who has said he/she is ready to go. Be as clear as possible in defining your terms today. For some, there will be an aura of intrigue, possibly involving someone glamorous. The lucky number today is 7.

Friday, December 12 (Moon in Taurus) If you're in tune with the moon, your attention will be focused on your financial life today. In some cases, the job offers a potentially rewarding opportunity to show what you can do. For others, this day brings the comfortable feeling that the backing you need is there. A Cancer or Capricorn may be a person who gives you the news. The lucky number is 8.

Saturday, December 13 (Moon in Taurus) Some of you will be feeling particularly charitable today—with both your money and your time. When you lend a hand, you get a lot of recognition, too, so in a way you have done something for yourself as well. A Taurus becomes surprisingly supportive of your point of view and gives you the benefit of his/her experience. Some Leos will find themselves unexpectedly "in the news."

Sunday, December 14 (Moon Taurus to Gemini 1:41 a.m.) There is a definite indication of a new start in a new direction. And it should make you feel very positive. If you want to get something out of someone, try it today—you should be very persuasive. For some, a member of the opposite sex shows that he/she finds you particularly attractive—and wants to do something about it. Another Leo may be involved.

Monday, December 15 (Moon in Gemini) Many will have the uncomfortable feeling of being pulled in two directions now. Fortunately, a good friend will help you make the right decision. Someone very different and exotic may walk onto the scene and startle you; he/she could be very important in the future. The lucky number is 2.

Tuesday, December 16 (Moon Gemini to Cancer 2:09 p.m.) This could be a very confusing full moon for many Leos. For some, it is vital to check and recheck all arrangements you have made. You could easily miss someone. Others will find they are overloaded in the social area and may feel the effects of having too much all at one time. Don't act on impulse!

Wednesday, December 17 (Moon in Cancer) You may breathe a sigh of relief today when someone who is more familiar with certain procedures agrees to do the paperwork. You are not a great one for handling red tape. A powerful person—possibly a Scorpio—can provide excellent guidance now. He/she knows how to make the most of what is available.

Thursday, December 18 (Moon in Cancer) You could be feeling particularly sentimental today, and that leads you to play right into someone's hands. It may be a member of the opposite sex who is simply waiting for you to express your deep concern and affection. Just take care not to go overboard. Your cycle is moving up, and you should be ready for change.

Friday, December 19 (Moon Cancer to Leo 2:44 a.m.) With the moon in your sign, you are able to get that fresh start feeling and get more in a holiday mood. Some Leos will have the opportunity to show how original they can be and act as the standout attraction at a social event. Appreciation is easy to get now, as is an adjustment in your home life. Don't take advantage of others!

Saturday, December 20 (Moon in Leo) Some kind of promise is fulfilled today, and it makes all the difference in your mood. Some Leos will find that terms are being defined now, and the territory lines are being drawn. Most will come out better off than they were before. A Pisces may make you feel like crying—with happiness.

Sunday, December 21 (Moon Leo to Virgo 2:30 p.m.) Things are still on the upswing, and some of you will have a great satisfaction of finding out you were right all along. It's a good thing to have your views vindicated. It is essential to watch your timing now, because it is critical. This is one period of time when haste could easily mean waste—literally.

Monday, December 22 (Moon in Virgo) You are feeling particularly efficient and are able to tie up a lot of loose ends. You feel even better when you discover that something you hoped would happen is happening now. Those who have been out of touch now make contact with you, and it gives you a warm feeling. The lucky number is 9.

Tuesday, December 23 (Moon in Virgo) Even though the holidays are upon you, it is essential to deal with a matter concerning who owes what to whom. Be generous, but protect your interests. A message you get may be a bit garbled, and you should be aware of it. At all costs be discriminating now, particularly with another Leo who could easily foul things up.

Wednesday, December 24 (Moon Virgo to Libra 12:05 a.m.) For many Leos, this will be the busiest pre-holiday day in years. There is an incredible amount of coming and going, and a lot of generosity in the air. Fortunately, that extends to generosity of spirit—and someone will inspire you to become a better person in all ways. In many cases, it means an easing of conscience as a result of confidential information received.

Thursday, December 25 (Moon in Libra) This is an up day all the way around. However, some Leos may find themselves fairly worn out by the end of it. Though you are "highly charged," make it a point to slow down and enjoy some quiet moments. Really, you will not miss anything. The lucky number today is 3.

Friday, December 26 (Moon Libra to Scorpio 7:06 a.m.) There's a lot of cleaning up to do today, in every way. For some, a slight confusion will cause a bit of anxiety. But the moment will pass. All should try to be practical about practical matters now, and go back to reading the fine print. A Scorpio or a Taurus could help you sort out some problems. The lucky number is 4.

Saturday, December 27 (Moon in Scorpio) This could be a very significant day in many a Leo's life. An important question is answered, and an equally important issue resolved. A permanent partnership could be the subject. For others, a less momentous day is indicated, but you too will get the message and feel more secure as a result. Give free reign to your creative thinking.

Sunday, December 28 (Moon Scorpio to Sagittarius 8:20 a.m.) Not everyone still has the holiday spirit, and you are going to have to exercise your diplomacy today. By all means, be patient and understanding—and more mature than those around you. On the light side, you will be surprised by an extra gift that comes along by surprise. A Libran could provide excellent solace now.

Monday, December 29 (Moon in Sagittarius) Many Leos can expect VIP treatment today. Your charisma is glowing very brightly, and the lunar position indicates a lot of excitement. For some, the thrill comes when you get a view behind the scenes. Others will find themselves getting congratulated on a job well done.

Tuesday, December 30 (Moon Sagittarius to Capricorn 7:54 a.m.) There is no way you can play games now. If you do, you will hurt someone else very much—he/she is serious and expects you to fulfill your promise. Some Leos will feel a lot lighter and freer to move around. Some will do a lot of moving around, possibly making plans for a big celebration. Children could be very important in today's scenario.

Wednesday, December 31 (Moon in Capricorn) Many Leos will wind up the year realizing that their burden is lighter, and that they are looking toward a year of much greater fulfillment. Have fun, but don't get carried away by people who want you to celebrate more than is prudent. It should be no problem, however, because your sense of caution is operating on high today. The lucky number is 9.

About This Series

This is one of a series of
Twelve Day-by-Day Astrological Guides
for the signs in 1986
by Sydney Omarr

About the Author

Born on August 5, 1926, in Philadelphia, Omarr was the only astrologer ever given full-time duty in the U.S. Army as an astrologer. He also is regarded as the most erudite astrologer of our time and the best-known, through his syndicated column (300 newspapers), and his radio and television programs (he is Merv Griffin's "resident astrologer"). Omarr has been called the most "knowledgeable astrologer since Evangeline Adams." His forecasts of Nixon's downfall, the end of World War II in mid-August of 1945, the assassination of John F. Kennedy, Roosevelt's election to a fourth term and his death in office ... these and many others ... are on record and quoted enough to be considered "legendary."

SIGNET Books of Special Interest

(0451)

- [ ] **WRITE YOUR OWN HOROSCOPE by Joseph F. Goodavage.** A leading astrologer tells how you can chart your individual horoscope with the accuracy of a trained professional. This ancient science is explained with explicit details and rare clarity that will unlock the secrets of your character—and your future—as no other book can. (130936—$3.50)*

- [ ] **YOU CAN ANALYZE HANDWRITING by Robert Holder.** Here is the fascinating book that explains, stroke by stroke, the significance of every type of handwriting including that of famous public figures like Richard Nixon, Helen Gurley Brown and Walter Cronkite. A practical tool for self-knowledge and personal power. (115422—$2.95)

- [ ] **FORTUNE IN YOUR HAND by Elizabeth Daniels Squire.** Let this world-famous authority guide you into the realm of fascinating perceptions about the past and future, about yourself and others through the science of palmistry. (080610—$1.75)

- [ ] **1001 WAYS TO REVEAL YOUR PERSONALITY by Elyane J. Kahn, Ph.D. and David Rudnitsky.** This authoritative book by a prominent psychologist lets you use all your actions, preferences, and habits to tell you more than a mirror about yourself and those around you. (120124—$3.50)

- [ ] **YOUR MYSTERIOUS POWERS OF ESP by Harold Sherman.** Explore the whole new world of your mind—and unlock the secrets of your own amazing psychic sensitivity! One of the world's great sensitives, writers, and lecturers on psychic phenomena explains why and how mind-to-mind communication is possible, exploring: telepathy, extrasensory healing, communicating with the dead, and out-of-body travel. With documented testimonies and case histories. (093151—$1.95)*

*Prices slightly higher in Canada

Buy them at your local bookstore or use coupon on last page for ordering.

Titles of Related Interest from SIGNET

(0451)

- [ ] **THE POWER OF ALPHA THINKING: Miracle of the Mind by Jess Stearn.** Through his own experiences and the documented accounts of others, Jess Stearn describes the technique used to control alpha brain waves. Introduction by Dr. John Balos, Medical Director, Mental Health Unit, Glendale Adventist Hospital. (133099—$3.50)*

- [ ] **SELF-MASTERY THROUGH SELF-HYPNOSIS by Dr. Roger Bernhardt and David Martin.** A practicing psychoanalyst and hypnotherapist clears up many misconceptions about hypnosis (it is not a form of sleep, but actually is a state of heightened awareness), and shows how to put it to use as a therapeutic tool in everyday life. (126963—$2.50)*

- [ ] **SELF HYPNOTISM: The Technique and Its Use in Daily Living by Leslie M. LeCron.** Using simple, scientifically proven methods, this guidebook provides step-by-step solutions to such problems as fears and phobias, overcoming bad habits, pain and common ailments, and difficulty with dieting—all through the use of self-suggestion therapy.

    (127471—$2.95)*

- [ ] **TRANSCENDENTAL MEDITATION by Maharishi Mahesh Yogi.** The new prophet of worldwide peace, who believes that "the natural state of man is joy," describes his simple technique of deep meditation.

    (121848—$3.95)

- [ ] **DAVID ST. CLAIR'S LESSONS IN INSTANT ESP by David St. Clair.** Through astoundingly simple techniques, discovered and perfected by a recognized authority on ESP, you can learn how incredibly gifted you are—and put your gifts to practical and permanent use to enrich and expand your life. (127382—$2.75)*

*Prices slightly higher in Canada

Buy them at your local bookstore or use this convenient coupon for ordering.

NEW AMERICAN LIBRARY,

P.O. Box 999, Bergenfield, New Jersey 07621

Please send me the books I have checked above. I am enclosing $_____ (please add $1.00 to this order to cover postage and handling). Send check or money order—no cash or C.O.D.'s. Prices and numbers are subject to change without notice.

Name _____

Address _____

City _____ State _____ Zip Code _____

Allow 4-6 weeks for delivery.
This offer is subject to withdrawal without notice.

COUPON

PROF. LALLEMEND
Dept SO-8 • POB 252
BROOKLYN, N.Y. 11204

516 Fifth Ave., N.Y., N.Y. 10036

Dear Reader,

You do not have to 'merely believe' Professor Lallemend, the renowned astrologer, because he will **PROVE** to you how he can help you make your life better!

Just fill out this form and mail it. Professor Lallemend will prepare **YOUR HOROSCOPE** and predict—without charge **TWO ESSENTIAL EVENTS IN YOUR LIFE**. You will be thoroughly convinced by the precision of the forecast and will also learn how you can gain success and inner contentment, as well as avoiding everything which can be an obstacle in the path of your happiness. You will receive his advice absolutely free of charge. All you have to do is, answer the questions below, and mail the coupon TODAY.

Please send me free of charge and without any obligation on my part my horoscope and two predictions in an unmarked envelope.

My Birthdate ....
Time .... Place ....

Please let me know as well, my lucky numbers. I enclose here a number between 0 and 9 which suddenly comes to my mind:

_____

NAME.....................
ADD. ....
....
CITY ....
STATE .... ZIP ....

How well do you know yourself?

This horoscope gives you answers to these questions based on your exact time and place of birth…

How do others see you?
What is your greatest strength?
What are your life purposes?
What drives motivate you?
How do you think?
Are you a loving person?
How competitive are you?
What are your ideals?
How religious are you?
Can you take responsibility?
How creative are you?
How do you handle money?
How do you express yourself?
What career is best for you?
How will you be remembered?
Who are your real friends?
What are you hiding?

Many people are out of touch with their real selves. Some can't get ahead professionally because they are doing the wrong kind of work. Others lack self-confidence because they're trying to be someone they're not. Others are unsuccessful in love because they use the wrong approach with the wrong people. Astrology has helped hundreds of people with problems like these by showing them their real selves.

You are a unique individual. Since the world began, there has never been anyone exactly like you. Sun-sign astrology, the kind you see in newspapers and magazines, is all right as far as it goes. But it treats you as if you were just the same as millions of others who have the same Sun sign because their birthdays are close to yours. A true astrological reading of your character and personality has to be one of a kind, unlike any other. It has to be based on exact date, time, longitude and latitude of your birth. Only a big IBM computer like the one that Para Research uses can handle the trillions of possibilities.

A Unique Document Your Astral Portrait includes your complete chart with planetary positions and house cusps calculated to the nearest minute of arc, all planetary aspects with orbs and intensities, plus text explaining the meaning of:
★ Your particular combination of Sun and Moon signs.
★ Your Ascendant sign and the house position of its ruling planet. (Many computer horoscopes omit this because it requires exact birth data.)
★ The planets influencing all twelve houses in your chart.
★ Your planetary aspects.

Others Tell Us "I found the Astral Portrait to be the best horoscope I've ever read." —E.D., Los Angeles, CA
"I could not put it down until I'd read every word. It is like you've been looking over my shoulder since I arrived in this world!" —B.N.L., Redding, CA
"I recommend the Astral Portrait. It even surpasses many of the readings done by professional astrologers. —J.B., Bristol, CT

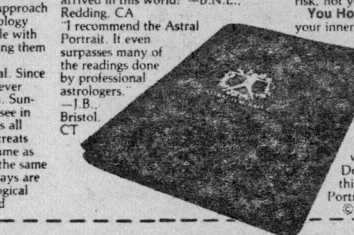

Low Price There is no substitute for a personal conference with an astrologer, but a good astrologer charges $50 and up for a complete chart reading. Some who have rich clients get $200 and more. Your Astral Portrait is an analysis of your character written by some of the world's foremost astrologers, and you can have it not for $200 or $50 but for only $22. This is possible because the text of your Astral Portrait is already written. You pay only for the cost of putting your birth information into the computer, compiling one copy, checking it and sending it to you within two weeks.

Permanence Ordinarily, you leave as astrologer's office with only a memory. Your Astral Portrait is a thirty-five-page, fifteen-thousand-word, permanently bound book that you can read again and again for years.

Money-Back Guarantee Our guarantee is unconditional. That means you can return your Astral Portrait at any time for any reason and get a full refund of the purchase price. That means we take all the risk, not you!

You Hold the Key The secrets of your inner character and personality, your real self, are locked in the memory of the computer. You alone hold the key: your time and place of birth. Fill in the coupon below and send it to the address shown with $22. Don't put it off. Do it now while you're thinking of it. Your Astral Portrait is waiting for you.

© 1977 Para Research, Inc.

Para Research, Dept. BT, P.O. Box 61, Gloucester, Massachusetts 01930 I want to read about my real self. Please send me my Astral Portrait. I understand that if I am not completely satisfied, I can return it for a full refund. ☐ I enclose $22 plus 1.50 for shipping and handling. ☐ Charge $23.50 to my Master Card account. ☐ Charge $23.50 to my VISA account.

Card number		Good through Mo.	Day	Yr.
Mr/Ms		Birthdate Mo.	Day	Yr.
Address		Birthtime (within an hour)		AM/PM
City		Birthplace City		
State	Zip	State	County	

Know in advance the changes in your life

Wouldn't it be useful to know when important events in your life are going to happen? How would you respond? What will you experience emotionally, intellectually and psychologically? And how will these experiences affect your life.

Your transits can provide valuable clues to various trends or stages of personal growth. This is especially true for the slower moving outer planets—Jupiter through Pluto. The transits for these planets are long lasting and profound in their psychological consequences. Many occur only once in a lifetime. The Astral Forecast is all about the outer planets.

This horoscope provides a reliable tool for astrological forecasting. The Astral Forecast will show you how the outer transits affect your sense of timing, that is, the times that are appropriate for you to take certain kinds of actions and inappropriate for others. This horoscope includes every significant transit to your outer planets that occurs in a twelve-month period. You can use your Astral Forecast to better understand how the outer planets affect such important life issues as career, child rearing, love, marriage and more.

For example, when Jupiter is in the first house, this transit represents a major growth cycle in your life. This is the best time for you to explore who you really are as an individual. Under this transit, you will feel more secure about yourself and the impression you make on others. Therefore, understanding yourself and your influence on others can make this transit an especially powerful and important time in your life. This is also a time for learning and gaining new experience. All this is part of your present need for personal growth, which affects not only yourself, but also the way you deal with the world as a whole. This is one time when persons and resources are likely to be drawn to you, and you should take constructive advantage of them.

You can find out in advance what your transits are going to be. But if you do it on your own, you will have to consult several astronomical tables to find the positions of each of the transiting planets every day and then compare them mathematically to the positions of the planets at the time of your birth.

There's an easier way to learn of your transits. Our IBM System/36 computer will handle all the calculations and provide you with information on all your outer transits based on your exact time and place of birth. With the Astral Forecast you not only receive the most accurate calculation of your personal transits for the next twelve months, you will also receive an extensive printout interpreting the character and significance of your individual transits.

Your Astral Forecast is the most accurate and authoritative guide to the outer transits that you can receive. It is based on the work of Robert Hand, one of America's most famous astrologers, and the author of several astrology books.

Like all Para Research horoscopes, the Astral Forecast is inexpensive. For just $16.00 you can have the same kind of advice that would otherwise cost you hundreds of dollars. This low price is possible because the astrological data is stored in our computer, and can be easily formatted and printed. Also, the mathematical calculations can be done in a matter of minutes. Your only cost is the cost of putting your personal information into the computer, producing one copy and then mailing it.

When you order your Astral Forecast, you receive an unconditional money-back guarantee. This means you can return your Astral Forecast at any time and get a full refund of the purchase price. We take all the risk.

Order your Astral Forecast today. Discover how the transits can bring energy to each part of your personality, fulfill your potential and help you gain more control over your own life.
© 1983 Para Research, Inc.

Para Research, Dept. BT, P.O. Box 61, Gloucester, Massachusetts 01930 Please send me my Astral Forecast. I understand that if I am not completely satisfied, I can return it for a full refund. ☐ I enclose $16 plus $1.50 for shipping and handling. ☐ Charge $17.50 to my MasterCard account. ☐ Charge $17.50 to my VISA account.

Card number		Good through Mo.	Day	Yr.
Mr/Ms		Birthdate Mo.	Day	Yr.
Address		Birthtime (within an hour)		AM/PM
City		Birthplace City	State	
State	Zip	Start calendar with Mo.		Yr.

Don't Let A TERRIBLE THING HAPPEN TO YOU!

SECRET KNOWLEDGE REVEALED THAT HAS BEEN HANDED DOWN THROUGH HISTORY. TO HELP GIVE YOU A RICHER LOVE FILLED, HAPPIER LIFE.

Will The POWER Of The OCCULT DOLL Work For YOU?

- **OCCULT SUPPLIES**—For centuries it was and still is a tradition that in Secret Ancient Rituals and Magic of Haiti, Africa, and Latin America, dolls and spells were used to carry out every purpose desired. Used for Love, Luck, Riches to gain power. These ancient rituals were rare a constant source of comfort and hope to those who practice.

We have been making these OCCULT DOLLS and RITUALS for certain customers with Special Problems to see if they were able to help. We are happy to tell you that we feel they have been a great success. Each Doll is made of a certain color with Amulets, Charms, and Herbs sewn in. Believed to attract WHAT YOU WANT. Each Doll is handmade with Great Care by one who knows and believes. Comes with full instructions.

LOVE DOLL
We feel the Most Powerful Love Occult Ritual is done with Red, and special items sewn in. Used to bring a love back to you or get your relationship back to the love and excitement you once had we believe. Comes with special Red tipped pin, powerful instructions.
D300 . . . . 5.98

- **MONEY DRAWING DOLL**
Green Doll handmade with coins and herbs sewn inside. We believe that Green has the power of attracting money to one in need. Strong money directions included.
D500 . . . . 5.98

- **OCCULT RITUAL HANDBOOK**
Everything you always wanted to know about Occult Rituals and Magic—songs, chants, spells for every purpose. Use of Roots, Herbs, Oils plus ceremonial rites and more. The secrets are here.
Bk120 . . . . 4.98

Triple Win BINGO BAG

Did you ever wonder why some people always win at BINGO? Do they have a secret? Now you can have your own secret! Your own BINGO BAG to carry with you.

NOW YOU CAN WIN TOO!
When your numbers are called, you be the one to shout BINGO! You get Bingo Oil, Gemstone, Charm, Seal plus Green Bag and full instructions.
KK795 All 7 items 7.95

LOVE RUB

Rub on your hands or body — or on the body of the one you love. Get what you want and use it wisely.

K371-Red-Passionate Love
K372-Pink-Win love and conquer Evil
K373-Green-Money Drawing
K374-Light Blue-Power to Find a Job

3.98 Any 3 for 11.50

FOLLOW ME COLOGNE

Comes with "LUCKY FORTUNE" A Few Drops Does The Trick. To attract your love, wear this whenever you go out. Sprinkle in your draws also.

K297 Large 4 oz. size

4.98

SPIRITUAL OILS

Used by many thousands of satisfied people because the fragrance charms the senses. Try them today!

2.25   Save 77¢
Order any 3
Only 5.98

- K-4 — Attraction
- K-100 — Commanding
- K-2 — Compelling
- K-101 — Concentration
- K-102 — Crossing
- K-103 — Dragon Blood
- K-16 — Fast Luck
- K-104 — Finance
- K-105 — French Love
- K-106 — Good Luck
- K-107 — High Conquering
- K-109 — Holy Spiritual
- K-110 — Jinx Removing
- K-111 — King Solomon
- K-14 — Lady Luck
- K-11 — Lodestone
- K-112 — Lovers
- K-113 — Lucky Money
- K-114 — Lucky Hand
- K-8 — Money Drawing
- K-7 — Power
- K-117 — Protection
- K-121 — Spirit
- K-8 — Success
- K-122 — Uncrossing
- K-123 — Van Van

SPECIAL INCENSE

2.25   Save 77¢
Order any 3
Only 5.98

Burn incense to attract, to dispel wicked odors. Best incense available, attracting fragrances, satisfying results.

NUMBER IN EVERY BOX
People are used to buying incense with a number. And considering it lucky. We don't claim these numbers as such.

- K-77 — Commanding
- K-42 — Compelling
- K-78 — Concentration
- K-97 — Crossing
- K-80 — Dragon Blood
- K-41 — Fast Luck
- K-33 — Finance
- K-81 — French Love
- K-62 — Good Luck
- K-83 — High Conquering
- K-48 — Success
- K-34 — Jinx Removing
- K-84 — Lady Luck
- K-86 — Lovers
- K-87 — Lucky Hand
- K-88 — Lucky Money
- K-91 — Masters
- K-47 — Money Drawing
- K-39 — Power
- K-43 — Van Van
- K-35 — Uncrossing

Write to: ANN HOWARD DEPT.SY1 200 West Sunrise Highway, Freeport, N.Y. 11520

$5 Dollar Deposit on all C.O.D. Orders! Prepaid Orders Please Add $1.95 for Postage.
FREE- Latest Catalog-Candles, Oils, Incense, Spells, More. Just Write. No claims are made. These alleged powers are gathered from writings, books, folklore & occult sources. Sold as curios.

"Next to my mother, you have been the greatest inspiration of my life."

You'll be amazed!
When you read what Marguerite Carter has to say about your life in the year ahead you'll be amazed. She delves into the most important areas of your life: romance, money, goals, and significant changes. You'll find out all the wonderful ways you can live a better life when you have your Unitology Forecast prepared for you by Marguerite Carter.

She'll help you.
Marguerite Carter has counseled thousands of enthusiastic followers around the world for decades. She has been the guiding light and helping hand for people from all walks of life: business leaders, hollywood stars and just everyday folks. There is a good reason why they seek her services year after year. They get the help they need in the most important areas of their lives!

'. . . it was amazing.'
People write all the time telling about how Marguerite Carter has helped them.

MARGUERITE CARTER

". . . it was amazing. I just can't believe it." W.C., Canada

". . . could not put it down until I read it cover to cover." M.L., Illinois.

"Without a doubt, next to my mother, you have been the greatest inspiration of my life. Many others could probably say the same thing." M.A., PA

In letter after letter people comment on the realistic guidance they've received for getting what they want from life. They've found the help they need in times of decision or resolving personal problems. These are judgments by a caring counselor, not some impersonal computer.

Hidden Opportunities
The things you want most may not be out of reach. Marguerite Carter says, "Many people are completely unaware that the opportunities for money, love or advancement are passing them by almost daily . . ." Without knowledge of when the conditions are favorable or unfavorable, the chances for success and happiness are greatly diminished.

Get your Unitology Forecast with special notations by Marguerite Carter. It will be prepared to your specific birthdate information. Remember that you will receive a full year of guidance, regardless of when your request is received, and you'll know that your forecast has come from one of the world's most highly respected astrologer-counselors.

Marguerite Carter • P.O. Box 807 • Indianapolis, Indiana 46206   O-6

☐ Yes Miss Carter, Please send me my Unitology Forecast for the year ahead. Enclosed is my remittance of $9.95 plus $1.00 for postage and handling. (First Class $1.30) Make all checks payable in U.S. funds. Allow 4 weeks for delivery.

Name _____

Address _____

City _____ State _____ Zip Code _____

Birthplace _____

Month _____ Day _____ Year _____

Place _____ Hour _____

Astrology Questionnaire

Help us bring you even better astrology guides by filling out this survey and mailing it today.

A. Book Title (Sign): _____

B. Using the scale below how would you rate this astrological guide? (Place one rating from 0–10 in the space provided.)

Poor	Not So Good	O.K.	Good	Excellent
0 1	2 3	4 5 6	7 8	9 10

Rating

Overall Opinion of book

Essay On:
1. Defining Terms
2. Your House of The Sun
3. The Geometry of Relationships
4. Twelve Places at the Table
5. Moods of the Moon
6. Venus and Mars
7. Venus Sign Position Chart
8. Mars Sign Position Chart
9. The Planets as "Stars"
10. Astrotrivia
11. Sun Sign Changes
12. Your Sign: The Big Picture
13. Your Sign: Objectives and Obstacles
14. Pairing Off With Your Sign
15. Your Sign's Sex Role Dilemma
16. Your Sign: Female
17. Your Sign: Male
18. Your Sign: Help Wanted
19. How "Pure" a _____ are you?
20. Find Your Rising Sign
21. Your Sign: Astro-Outlook for '86
22. 15 Months of Day-By-Day Predictions

C. In total about how many astrology guides have you purchased for yourself in the past 12 months?
# of books _____

D. What topics would you be interested in having Sydney Omarr write about in the 1987 Astrology Guide?

_____

_____

E. What is your education?

1( ) High School   3( ) 4 yrs college
2( ) 2 yrs college 4( ) Postgraduate

F. What is your occupation? _____

G. What is your marital status?

1( ) Single   3( ) Divorced   5( ) Widowed
2( ) Married   4( ) Separated

H. Age: _____   **I.** Sex: 1( ) Male
                              2( ) Female

Please Print Name: _____

Address _____

City _____ **State** _____ **Zip** _____

Phone # ( ) _____

Thank you. Please send to New American Library, Research Dept., 1633 Broadway, New York, NY 10019